# Ptolemaic Empire

*An Enthralling Journey Through a Greek-Ruled Kingdom in Egypt, Royal Power Struggles, Court Plots, Cleopatra, and Rome's Rise*

# Free limited time bonus

Stop for a moment. We have a free bonus set up for you. The problem is this: we forget 90% of everything that we read after 7 days. Crazy fact, right? Here's the solution: we've created a printable, 1-page pdf summary for this book that you're reading now. All you have to do to get your free pdf summary is to go to the following website:

**https://livetolearn.lpages.co/enthrallinghistory/**

Or, Scan the QR code!

Once you do, it will be intuitive. Enjoy, and thank you!

# Table of Contents

# Part 1:
# The Ptolemaic Kingdom

*An Enthralling Guide to the Empire Where Ancient Egypt Met Greek Genius*

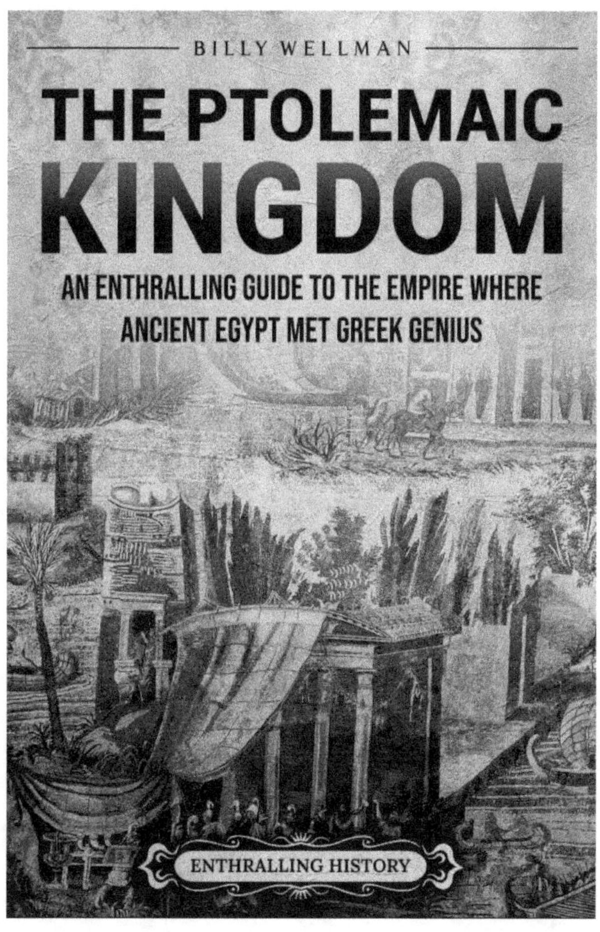

# Introduction

Roaring cheers rang out as Alexander the Great marched into Egypt in 332 BCE. The Egyptians pragmatically hailed him as their savior from the oppressive Persians. Undoubtedly, the Egyptians had been weighing their options as Alexander's army approached Egypt.

"Did you hear what Alexander did in Tyre because they resisted for six months? He crucified the men!"

Everyone shuddered. "He smashed Gaza's walls down! Wasn't that supposed to be impossible?"

"That coward, King Darius, ran off the battlefield when he met Alexander's army! He left his men behind. He even left the royal women behind!"

"It's weird that the Persians take their women to war. Now Alexander has the queen, her two daughters, and the queen mother!"

"They say he's treating them well."

The Egyptians nodded. "It's no use resisting. We're better off welcoming him. After all, we share a common enemy."

And thus, the Egyptians danced, sang, and threw flowers as Alexander arrived. His trusted general, Ptolemy, rode at his side. A decade later, Ptolemy became Egypt's first Macedonian pharaoh, the mastermind of an exciting fusion of Hellenistic and Egyptian culture. His dynasty lasted three centuries, ending when Egypt's pharaoh, Cleopatra VII, committed suicide.

What came in between? The Ptolemaic Kingdom brought spectacular strides in science, mathematics, art, architecture, and economics. The glistening city of Alexandria beckoned scholars and artists to its intellectual and creative hub. Yet, the Ptolemaic Kingdom also featured ruinous family feuds, unbridled ambition, horrendous wars, and epic rebellions.

This book dives into the stories of the Ptolemaic pharaohs and how this unique kingdom shaped history, bridging the legacies of two ancient civilizations. What unexpected event led to Ptolemy's takeover of Egypt? How did he and his successors merge Greek and Egyptian cultural elements like art, architecture, and religion? For instance, why did the Ptolemaic pharaohs marry their sisters? Was that an Egyptian or Macedonian thing?

Did the Alexandrian Library really have a half million scrolls? Which Ptolemaic pharaoh ordered the translation of the Jewish Torah into Greek, and why? Who figured out that the Earth travels around the sun each year and rotates on its axis once a day? What genius who studied at the Library of Alexandria discovered pi ($\pi$), the law of the lever, and the compound pully?

The Ptolemaic Kingdom had few dull moments. This book unlocks the empire-building, scientific breakthroughs, and royal family drama. Two rich cultures came together, yet each kept their distinctive identities. More than anything, it is a story of passionate people and power struggles. This book brings their trials and triumphs to life as the Ptolemaic dynasty's story unfolds.

What's the point of reading history? Aside from being fascinating and fun, knowing the past helps us understand our present. History helps us recognize the catalysts for change, both good and bad. We especially see the intrinsic role of leadership. Wise rulers lead their country into prosperity, progress, and peace. Inept leaders can drag their country into desperate straits. The Ptolemaic Kingdom had both. Let's unpack how it all played out.

# Chapter 1: Birth of a Dynasty: The Rise of the Ptolemies

"Ptolemy! Come quickly!"

In the dead of night, Ptolemy awakened to someone pounding on his door. It was Lysimachus. Like Ptolemy, he was an officer under Alexander and one of his seven bodyguards.

"It's Alexander! He's getting worse!"

Ptolemy frowned. Alexander had fallen ill a week earlier, shortly after a flock of ravens fell from the sky, dying at his feet. Alexander had fever, chills, excessive thirst, and abdominal pain.

"Is the doctor there? What's happening?"

"Yes, his doctor is there, and they've called in some specialists from Babylon. He can barely speak or sit up. When he does say something, it makes no sense. He's delirious!"

"Let's go!" Ptolemy threw on his cape and grabbed his sword. "He needs his friends there!"

They hurried to Alexander's quarters, where the doctors huddled. Alexander's first wife, Roxanne, sat at the bedside, her belly swollen with his only child. The doctors' best efforts were hopeless. Struggling to breathe, Alexander became increasingly weaker.[1] Four days later, he died

---

[1] J. S. Marr and C. H. Calisher, "Alexander the Great and West Nile Virus Encephalitis," *Emerging Infectious Diseases*, 9, no. 12 (December 2003): 599-603, https://doi: 10.3201/eid0912.030288. PMID: 14725285; PMCID: PMC3034319.

at age thirty-two, leaving a vast empire that spread over three continents.

"I'm burying him in Egypt!" Ptolemy declared. "That's where he wanted to be buried. I was with him when the priest at Memphis crowned him the new pharaoh. I heard the oracle at the Siwa Oasis declare him the son of Egypt's high god Amun! Alexander wanted to be buried in the land of his heavenly father."

What would happen to Alexander's empire? Who was Ptolemy I Soter, and what did he and his fellow officers do after Alexander died? What power plays in the Middle East, Egypt, Greece, and Macedonia led up to this point? To answer these questions, we have to go back.

Ancient Middle East map [1]

## How did two major Middle Eastern shakedowns affect everything?

In 612 BCE, Babylon joined a massive coalition force to destroy the Neo-Assyrian Empire. The Assyrians had terrorized the Middle East for three hundred years. The surviving Assyrian royals escaped to Syria, hoping to regroup and make a comeback. They desperately messaged Pharoah Necho of Egypt, their only remaining ally. Necho mustered his forces and marched north.

King Josiah of Judah barred Necho's way, refusing passage through his country. In Megiddo, Necho killed Josiah and defeated the Judean army. But the delay doomed the Assyrians and Egyptians. Eager to utterly destroy the Assyrians, the Babylonians had surrounded Carchemish. Necho found Nebuchadnezzar II, Babylon's crown prince, waiting for him.

In the brutal 605 BCE Battle of Carchemish, the Babylonians wiped out the Egyptian army and the Assyrian nobility. Assyria never recovered, and Egypt went into a tailspin. Up to this point, Egypt had controlled much of the coastland between Egypt and Syria. Necho lost it all to the Babylonians and never got it back, except for Gaza, the ancient Philistine city. Egypt lost control of its lucrative trade routes, especially with Phoenicia. Economically and militarily weakened, Egypt limped along for 130 years until it fell prey to Persia, as foretold by the Jewish prophet Ezekiel:

> "For so said the Lord God: The sword of the king of Babylon will come upon you. With the swords of the mighty, I shall cause your multitude to fall, all of them the strong of the nations, and they will plunder the pride of Egypt, and all its multitude will be destroyed."[2]

Nebuchadnezzar II swept Judah, the Sinai Peninsula, Syria, southern Turkey, and ancient Iraq into the Neo-Babylonian Empire. Yet, his descendants turned out to be inept rulers. Decades later, Cyrus the Great united the Medes and Persians (today's Iran), and their joint forces conquered Central Asia and the entire Babylonian Empire by 539 BCE.

# What was happening in Egypt before Alexander arrived?

Cyrus the Great planned to invade Egypt, but first, he wanted to subdue the troublesome nomadic tribes northeast of Persia. That proved a fatal move. Queen Tomyris of the Massagetae sliced off his head in 530 BCE. Five years later, Cyrus's son, Cambyses, attacked Egypt. The Egyptians fought fiercely to defend their land with archers, catapults, and chariots.

---

[2] *The Complete Tanakh: The Jewish Bible with a Modern English Translation and Rashi's Commentary.* https://www.chabad.org/library/bible_cdo/aid/63255/jewish/The-Bible-with-Rashi.htm, Nevi'im, Yechezkel (Ezekiel) 32:11-12.

Yet, Phanes of Halicarnassus, once a Greek mercenary for Egypt, defected to the Persians' side. He suggested an ingenious and unusual battle strategy: cats!

The Egyptian war goddess was Bastet, who featured a woman's body and a cat's head. The Egyptians considered cats sacred animals, and killing a cat brought the death penalty. Phanes instructed the Persians, "This is how you can unhinge the Egyptians—paint Bastet's portrait on your shields. Round up hundreds of cats and let them go on your frontlines. They won't want to shoot at you for fear of harming a cat or hitting Bastet's image."

As they gathered at the battlefield, the Egyptians stared in horror. What could they do? They didn't dare incur Bastet's wrath. Suddenly, the Egyptians turned and ran away.[3] Egypt unhappily became part of the Persian-Achaemenid Empire in 525 BCE. For the first time in history, foreigners ruled Egypt. The Egyptians spent the next two centuries trying to break free from Persia. The Persians cruelly repressed any rebellion as the Egyptians seethed.

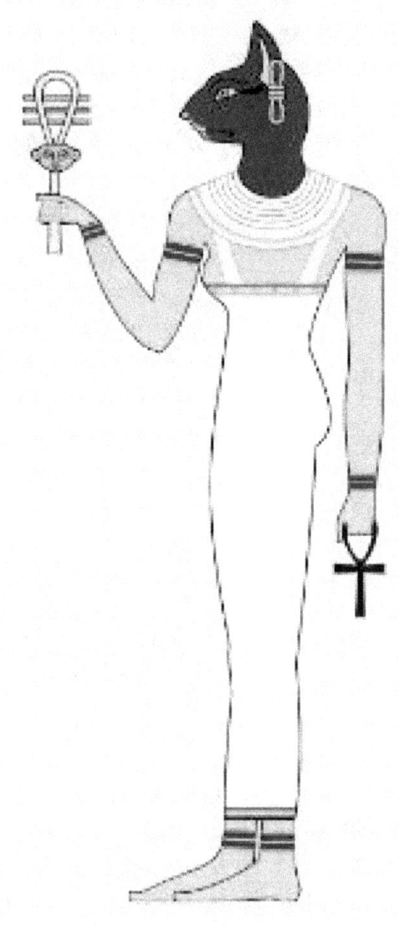

Bastet, Egyptian goddess of war[2]

---

[3] Polyaenus, *Stratagems: Book Seven*, trans. R. Shepherd, 1793, http://www.attalus.org/translate/polyaenus7.html.

Persia's Cambyses II captures Pharaoh Psamtik III.[3]

# What was the situation in Greece and Macedonia?

In ancient times, Greece was never a unified country. Instead, it had multiple city-states with independent governments. On rare occasions, they united to fight the Persians. However, most of the time, the Greek city-states fought each other. Macedonia was a large but poor Greek kingdom that covered modern-day North Macedonia, part of today's northern Greece, and bits of Albania, Serbia, Bulgaria, and Kosovo. It had never been a significant player in the ancient world and was in peril of being swallowed up by its neighbors. When Philip II became king, everything changed.

Philip spent his teen years as a hostage in the Greek city-state of Thebes, where he learned the Theban art of war. He returned to Macedonia with an extraordinarily ambitious goal. He would transform Macedonia into the world's premier fighting machine. Philip even developed his own weapon, a spear called a sarissa that was three times longer than a man.

Among his soldiers was a young man named Ptolemy. He was older than Philip's son Alexander, but the two of them had studied together under Aristotle. Philip had hired the renowned philosopher to tutor his son and the sons of other nobility. Ptolemy was officially the son of a nobleman named Lagos, yet rumors swirled that he was Philip's illegitimate son and Alexander's half-brother. That's doubtful because, unlike the other Greeks, the Macedonian kings could have more than one wife. Philip had four wives from foreign royal families. He also had three lesser wives or concubines and a series of male lovers, usually his bodyguards.

Macedonian army with sarissas[4]

With a well-trained army and his bristling sarissas, Philip set out to build his empire. He started with the lands surrounding Macedonia. Once he accomplished this, Philip left his sixteen-year-old son Alexander as regent of Macedonia while he marched south to conquer central Greece. A few years later, Philip and Alexander overpowered all southern Greece except Sparta. Macedonia and most of Greece formed the League of Corinth in 337 BCE, which was determined to bring Persia to its knees.

And then, it all came crashing down. Just before marching into Asia, Philip hosted a wedding for his daughter. Everyone was horrified when his bodyguard, a jilted lover, suddenly shoved a dagger into Philip's side. With Philip's blood pooling in the banquet hall, the Macedonian generals crowned Alexander their new king.

As soon as they heard, Athens and Thebes pulled out of the League of Corinth, followed swiftly by several other Greek cities. Alexander spent the next year thrashing the Greeks until they got back on board. Then, in 334 BCE, Alexander, Ptolemy, and 40,000 soldiers crossed the Dardanelles Strait into Asia.

# Alexander and Ptolemy in Asia

The Persian navy was superior to Alexander's, so he needed to change that. He successfully attacked Miletus and Halicarnassus, Persia's most important naval ports (in today's western Turkey). Without the ports, the Persian navy couldn't get supplies and reinforcements. Alexander left Ptolemy and three thousand troops to finish mopping up in Halicarnassus. When the unsuspecting Persian warships sailed into their homeport, Ptolemy's men pounced on them, commandeering the ships for the Greek navy.

Ptolemy caught up with Alexander just before the crucial Battle of Issus. They were marching down the Mediterranean coast, near the border of Anatolia (Turkey) and Syria, when suddenly they were ambushed. Persia's King Darius launched a surprise attack at their rear. He trapped Alexander's army between the sea and the mountains. However, Alexander's well-trained and highly disciplined army immediately fell into formation.

Ptolemy was on the left flank with General Parmenion and the cavalry from Thessalonia and Thrace. Alexander and his Macedonian cavalry were on the right flank with the Bulgarian javelin throwers. The infantry, with their eighteen-foot-long sarissas, held the middle. The swiftly flowing Pinarus River separated the Greeks from the Persians.

King Darius panicking on the battlefield[5]

The Persian cavalry galloped across the river, crashing into the Macedonian left side as Parmenion and Ptolemy desperately fended them off. Alexander raced his Macedonian cavalry over the river toward the Persian foot soldiers. Meanwhile, the Macedonian infantry tried to cross but floundered in the swiftly flowing river. Their shields and unwieldy sarissas weighed them down. The Persian archers shot volleys of arrows toward the helpless men in the river, darkening the sky.

When Alexander realized his infantry was in peril, he charged toward the Persians' middle section to draw off the archers. King Darius's chariot was in the center section. When he saw Alexander ferociously racing in his direction, Darius froze, petrified with fear. Then, he whipped his horses around and fled the battlefield, leaving his men behind. Eventually, the Persians realized their king had abandoned the battle. They looked at each other, shrugged, and ran after him.

The second time Alexander and Ptolemy faced off against Darius was in the pivotal Battle of Gaugamela in today's northern Iraq. This time, Darius was better prepared. His army was twice the size of Alexander's, and he had war elephants and two hundred chariots with razor-sharp scythes that could cut a man's leg in half protruding from their wheel hubs. The Macedonians and Greeks had not fought against elephants or scythed chariots before.

Once again, Alexander stationed his cavalry forces on each end, with his infantry in the middle. Ptolemy and Parmenion were on the left flank again. After several skirmishes, Alexander's infantry

Pompeii mosaic of Alexander at the Battle of Issus[6]

pretended to retreat. The Persian cavalry chased them, leaving a gap in the Persian lines. Instantly, Alexander charged through the gap, his horses mowing down the Persian infantry. Darius sent his scythed chariots out, but the Bulgarian javelin-throwers picked off the charioteers as the Greek foot soldiers nimbly dodged the scythes. Darius was so unnerved that he forgot to deploy his elephants. Instead, shaking in horror, he raced off the battlefield again.

Alexander suddenly realized that the Persian cavalry was mowing down his left flank. He rushed over to save Parmenion, Ptolemy, and their cavalry. It was a brutal fight in which sixty Macedonian horsemen died. Eventually, the Persians realized their king had fled the field and abandoned the battle, to the Greeks' relief. Alexander had scored two victories over the Persians. However, King Darius was still out there.

Darius fled east, hoping to regroup and assemble another army. But betrayal cut his plans short. Bessus, his satrap (governor) of Bactria, murdered him, announcing himself as Persia's new king. Alexander gave Darius a royal burial, then sent Ptolemy east to hunt Bessus down. The Bactrians did not want to fight Alexander, so they left Bessus at the side of the road, chained to a stake. Ptolemy placed an iron collar with a chain around Bessus's neck and dragged him naked back to Alexander. Darius's brother, Oxathres, cut off Bessus's nose and ears, then tied him to a cross where archers shot arrows at him until he died.[4]

Alexander marched on to Persepolis, the ceremonial capital of the Persian Empire. Ptolemy's mistress, Thais, who was from Athens, was in Persepolis at the time. The Athenians held a bitter grudge against the former Persian king Xerxes. A half-century earlier, he had burned their beautiful city and destroyed the ancient temples. In Persepolis, the Macedonians and Greeks enjoyed a grand banquet, and everyone was drunk. Suddenly, Thais jumped up and made a speech:

> "Sitting here at this luxurious dinner brings me immense pleasure after all the hardships of wandering around Asia. Do you know what would make it even sweeter? Let's set fire to Xerxes's palace! That disgraceful man burned Athens down! He committed sacrilege against our great temples. I'll throw the first torch myself! People should know that the women who follow Alexander have gotten revenge for the atrocities the Persians did to Greece."[5]

---

[4] Arrian, "Alexander the Great," in *The Anabasis and the Indica,* trans. Martin Hammond (Oxford University Press, 2013).

[5] Diodorus, Siculus, *Library of History, Volume VIII,* trans. C. Bradford Welles (Harvard University Press, 1963).

The Greeks leaped up, cheering loudly. Alexander arose from his couch. Holding up a torch, Alexander beckoned to the female musicians to follow him, playing their flutes and singing. With Thais leading the way, Alexander and all the officers traipsed outside to Xerxes's palace, where Thais hurled the first torch. Everyone else threw their torches, and flames consumed the palace.

Alexander was eager to march east to the Ganges River in India, the "end of the world." Yet, he and his men had been conquering Asia for four years, and his soldiers were tired and homesick. General Parmenion's son Philotas led a conspiracy to assassinate Alexander. When he discovered the plot, Alexander executed Philotas and then selected seven trusted friends as his bodyguards. Ptolemy was one of the seven.

They reached the Persian Empire's eastern boundary, the Jaxartes River, and crossed over. Alexander's weary men forged on, climbing the 3,500-foot Khyber Pass over the Hindu Kush mountains and descending into the Indian subcontinent. Ptolemy commanded one-third of Alexander's forces on this expedition. A poisoned arrow struck Ptolemy at the Indus River, and Alexander used herbs to draw out the poison.

But Alexander never made it to the Ganges. His men mutinied, refusing to go one step further east. Enough was enough! Alexander had no choice but to return with his men to Persia.

In 324 BCE, he threw a huge wedding celebration in Susa. Ninety Persian princesses married the Greek and Macedonian nobles. It was a fusion of East and West. Alexander married King Darius's daughter, Stateira, and Parysatis, the daughter of Artaxerxes III, an earlier king. He gave the Persian princess Artakama to be Ptolemy's bride. Alexander also reunited with his first wife, Roxana, the daughter of a Sogdian chieftain, who soon became pregnant.

# What happened when Alexander the Great unexpectedly died?

Alexander never saw Roxana's child. His sudden death, as we described earlier, cast everything into confusion. Who would replace Alexander? Roxana was due to give birth in three months. Alexander had a half-brother named Arrhidaeus, but he was cognitively challenged. Alexander's generals met to hash out a plan.

General Perdiccas held up Alexander's ring. "Alexander gave this to me on his deathbed. He meant for me to serve as regent for Arrhidaeus and Roxana's son. Arrhidaeus is Alexander's only living brother."

"We don't know if Roxana's baby is a boy or girl!" the other generals grumbled. "Even if it's a boy, he won't be able to rule on his own for years. And we all know Arrhidaeus isn't up to the task. If you're their regent, you're the de facto emperor."

"Why don't we wait to decide until Roxana gives birth?" one general suggested.

Ptolemy growled, "Look here! Roxana's child shouldn't even factor into our decision. She's not Macedonian or Greek. She's a Sogdian war captive. Do we want the conquered ruling the conquerors?"

"You have a point," General Meleager murmured. "Maybe we should give Arrhidaeus a chance."

"He hasn't the intellect! Does he even want to be the emperor?" the generals protested. However, a roar of approval from the soldiers filtering into the room drowned them out.

"Bring Arrhidaeus in!"

Meleager went out to get Arrhidaeus, but the overwhelmed young man took one look at the generals and fled. One of the soldiers gently persuaded him to return. The soldiers flung Alexander's royal cape over his trembling shoulders and handed him Alexander's crown.

Tears streaming down his face, Arrhidaeus protested. "I am not worthy. Someone more qualified should wear it!"

The next day, the generals met again. They agreed to have two kings: Roxana's child (if a boy) and Arrhidaeus. Perdiccas, Meleager, and Arrhidaeus would form a triumvirate, ruling together. However, Perdiccas's soldiers grumbled. "Alexander chose Perdiccas as his regent! Why is Meleager inserting himself?"

The soldiers murdered Meleager, sending everyone back to the drawing board.

Ptolemy cleared his throat. "I suggest doing away with the idea of one huge kingdom. We should divide the empire into loosely united states. Instead of a king over the empire, we'll have a council representing all the states."

Everyone looked blankly at Ptolemy. Yes, they were in unprecedented times, but Ptolemy's proposal was such a radical break from tradition that they couldn't wrap their heads around it. Finally, they agreed to the Partition of Babylon. Arrhidaeus would be king. They arranged for him to marry his niece, Eurydice. If Roxana's child were a boy, he would be a joint king. They would follow Alexander's wishes for Perdiccas to be regent, and he would also command the empire's army.

Third century BCE bust of Ptolemy I[7]

The generals followed Ptolemy's advice about dividing the empire among themselves. Technically, they answered to the dual kings, but each took a large swathe of land to rule. Macedon, Illyria, and Greece went to Antipater, who had already ruled them as Alexander's regent for the past decade. One-eyed Antigonus took the rest of the provinces in Anatolia (Turkey). Ptolemy took Egypt, Arabia, and Libya. Syria went to Laomedon, and Arcesilaus got Mesopotamia (ancient Iraq). The eastern provinces continued under the leadership of the Asian leaders already ruling them.

Perdiccas ordered Alexander's body be sent back to Macedonia for burial in his family necropolis. Nevertheless, Ptolemy was determined to bury Alexander in Egypt. The mourners put the body in a casket full of honey. As they passed through Damascus, Syria, on the way to Macedonia, Ptolemy stole Alexander's body! He hauled the casket to Egypt. At first, he placed Alexander in a tomb in Memphis. Later, he moved the casket to the new city of Alexandria. Three hundred years later, Octavian (Caesar Augustus) began the tradition of Roman emperors visiting Alexander's burial site to pay their respects.

Ptolemy insisted he was honoring Alexander's wishes, and he probably was, at least partially. (Alexander had said he wanted to be buried at the Siwa Oasis, not Memphis or Alexandria.) Nevertheless, the Macedonian custom was for the new king to bury the one who just died. His rivals were sure that Ptolemy was openly challenging Perdiccas for the empire's throne. Was he? Ptolemy's role in the Wars of the Diadochi sheds some light on that question. But first, let's look at his family situation.

## Ptolemy's First Wives

One of Ptolemy's first steps after Alexander's death was rearranging his private life. Athenaeus of Naucratis said that Ptolemy married his mistress, Thais, who had instigated the palace burning in Persepolis. There may have been some rivalry between Ptolemy and Alexander regarding the young woman. Athenaeus said that Alexander liked having Thais around. However, he might have meant that he found her amusing, not that they were sexually involved. Thais was known for being witty and fun.

At any rate, Ptolemy and Thais had three children together. Yet, his oldest son, Lagus, did not inherit his father's throne, and Ptolemy did not make Thais his queen. She had been a hetaira: an entertainer and conversationalist at the men's banquets who also provided sexual services. However, Ptolemy did arrange a wedding for their daughter Eirene to King Eunostos of the city-state of Soloi on the island of Cyprus.

As mentioned, Ptolemy had married the Persian princess Artakama in the mass wedding orchestrated by Alexander shortly before his death. Artakama was the great-granddaughter of Artaxerxes II, king of the Persian Empire. However, she disappeared from history after Alexander's death. Many Greek officers who married Persian princesses in the mass wedding at Susa divorced them when Alexander died. Artakama's lineage of Persian royalty would have been awkward for Ptolemy since he wanted people to see him as their savior from harsh Persian rule.

Ptolemy I, Egypt's first Greek pharaoh[8]

# Ptolemy and the Wars of the Diadochi

*Diadochi* means "successors," and these wars between Alexander's officers rocked his former empire for decades. The generals had divided the empire, but the one-time comrades-in-arms were now at each other's throats. Roxana gave birth to a son, Alexander IV, three months after Alexander died. To eliminate any competition, she poisoned Alexander's two Persian wives. General Perdiccas helped her dispose of the bodies in a well.[6]

---

<sup>6</sup> Plutarch, *The Life of Alexander the Great*, trans. John Dryden (Modern Library Paperback Edition, 2004).

The uneasy truce between Alexander's successors quickly crumbled. Perdiccas married Antipater's daughter Nicaea but then discovered that the husband of Alexander's sister Cleopatra had died. She was back on the marriage market. If he married her, he could be king of Macedonia. He messaged Cleopatra with a proposal, telling her he intended to divorce Nicaea. When Antipater found out, he was livid. Cleopatra rejected his offer, but the damage was done.

Ptolemy, Antipater, and Antigonus formed a rebel force. Meanwhile, Perdiccas vowed revenge against Ptolemy for stealing Alexander's body. In the First War of the Diadochi (322-321 BCE), Perdiccas invaded Egypt.

When he reached the easternmost branch of the Nile near Pelusium, he realized Ptolemy had a large garrison stationed there. He marched north along the Nile until he reached a shallow ford across from Avaris. Perdiccas tried to cross the Nile with his elite infantry and war elephants. However, the Ptolemaic forces stopped him. Perdiccas turned south and marched toward Memphis. The Nile's current here was strong, but his strategy was to line his elephants across the river, forming an elephant dam to slow the river's force. He also lined his cavalry across the Nile downstream to rescue any of his infantry that lost their footing while wading across. This plan worked initially, and part of his army crossed to an island in the middle of the Nile.

But then, disaster struck. The elephants' feet got stuck in the mud, and they couldn't withstand the Nile's strong current. The elephant dam began falling apart, and the river grew too swift for more soldiers to cross. Worse, the soldiers on the island couldn't get back to shore. Over two thousand men drowned or were devoured by crocodiles trying to get off the island.

It was all over for Perdiccas. He had lost the confidence of his army, what was left of it. That night, three of his officers murdered him, and his army defected to Ptolemy.

The officers wanted Ptolemy to be the next regent of the empire, but he refused. He thought it was safer to maintain control of his chunk of the empire than to take a gamble on ruling the whole thing.[7]

With Perdiccas dead, who would be regent? The generals made Antipater the new regent and co-ruler with Arrhidaeus. Antipater took King Arrhidaeus, Queen Eurydice, Roxana, and baby Alexander IV back

---

[7] Diodorus, *Library of History*, Volume IX.

to Macedonia for their safety. At this point, Ptolemy cemented his alliance with Antipater by marrying his daughter, Eurydice (not Arrhidaeus's wife). They had four or five children together. In 317 BCE, Ptolemy married Eurydice's lady-in-waiting and cousin, Berenice. Her oldest son with Ptolemy was Ptolemy II Philadelphus.

Antipater's death in 319 BCE caused a new crisis in the empire. Just before he died, he appointed another of Alexander's generals, Polyperchon, as his successor. Hardly anyone was pleased with this arrangement, especially Antipater's son Cassander, who had expected to be the next regent. In the Second War of the Diadochi (318-316 BCE), Ptolemy and Antigonus supported Cassander in ejecting Polyperchon and making Arrhidaeus the only king, with Queen Eurydice as his de facto regent.

Polyperchon scooped up Roxana and her four-year-old son Alexander IV and took them to Epirus. He allied with Alexander the Great's mother, Olympias, to fight Arrhidaeus and Eurydice. This proved successful because the Macedonian military refused to fight the mother of Alexander. Meanwhile, Cassander, Ptolemy, and Antigonus were too late to save Alexander's brother. Arrhidaeus and Eurydice died under Olympias's orders.

When Cassander arrived in Macedonia, he had no qualms about killing Olympias. He locked Roxana and her son Alexander in a tower in Macedonia, where they languished for years.

Ptolemy returned to Egypt to protect his kingdom, while Polyperchon fled to southern Greece, where he controlled Corinth and much of the Peloponnese Peninsula.

Antigonus ended up controlling virtually all western and central Asia—an enormous swathe of territory—but Ptolemy wanted Syria, Judea, and Cyprus. They would serve as buffer zones for Egypt and would bring lucrative trade. The Third War of the Diadochi (315-311 BCE) began when Ptolemy allied with another of Alexander's generals, Seleucus, to fight Antigonus.

Ptolemy invaded Syria; however, Antigonus took it back. Then, word arrived that Cassander had poisoned the boy-king, Alexander IV. Ptolemy was now fully Egypt's ruler, and it was no longer part of an empire.

# Chapter 2: Alexandria, the Jewel of the Mediterranean

In 332 BCE, following his conquest of Gaza, Alexander the Great crossed the Sinai Desert with his 40,000 troops. After endless miles of blistering sand and jagged mountains, the landscape gradually turned lush and green. They soon arrived in Pelusium on the eastern edge of the Nile Delta.

Alexander's navy had sailed north from Phoenicia and was waiting for him in Pelusium's harbor. The Persian governor Mazaces (or Mazaus) graciously welcomed Alexander. He knew Alexander's arrival meant a new era in Egypt. King Darius had disgracefully run away from the Battle of Issus, at which the previous governor of Egypt had died, and Mazaces had only been in charge for a few months. Alexander had conquered or accepted the willing surrender of the coastal cities of Syria and Phoenicia. Mazaces hoped being friendly to Alexander would bring him a prominent position in the new empire, and it did.

After leaving an army unit in Pelusium, Alexander led his troops along the Nile to Memphis, Egypt's capital. Meanwhile, his navy sailed up the Nile to meet him there. The Egyptians looked on approvingly as he offered sacrifices to the primary Egyptian gods. Everyone enjoyed the show when Alexander's Greek artists put on a music and gymnastics performance.

From Memphis, Alexander sailed north with his fleet, following the westernmost branch of the Nile back to the Mediterranean. This part of the seacoast had an isthmus with the sea on one side and a lake on the other. Alexander sailed around the lake, where Bedouins lived in their tents. The more Alexander saw of the area, the more excited he got.

**Alexandria and the Nile Delta**⁹

"Ptolemy! This isthmus would make a great area for a city! It's perfect for trade around the Mediterranean. We'll build a port where the Nile empties into the sea."

Ptolemy nodded. "It's not far from Greece. I can imagine a lot of trade back and forth."

"That's right! Egypt produces more than enough grain. We'll ship it to Greece from here." Alexander dipped his hand in the lake water. "This lake is freshwater! A large city would have this as its drinking water." (Over the past two millennia, Lake Mariout has become saline, but it was fresh in Alexander's day.)

"And, of course, the Nile is the conduit to Memphis and the rest of Egypt. I can't imagine why the Egyptians never built a major city here," Ptolemy mused.

"Well, I'm going to! I'll call it Alexandria. It will be the jewel of Egypt! I have great plans for Alexandria. It'll be the busiest and most prosperous port on the Mediterranean."

Alexander pointed to a small island less than a mile from the isthmus. "Wouldn't that be a fantastic location for a lighthouse? We could build a causeway from here to there."

Alexander jumped out of the boat to the shore and scouted the area. He excitedly walked in a large circle, pointing out the boundaries of his city. His men hurried behind him with stakes, marking the places he named.

"I'll build the agora here! People will assemble to hear speeches, worship the gods, and watch entertainment and athletic contests. We'll have stalls for the merchants and nearby workshops."

Ptolemy scribbled notes as the enthusiastic Alexander dashed around. "Here! We'll erect temples in this area. We'll build a temple to the Egyptian goddess Isis on that little island. We need to show our appreciation of the Egyptian culture. But, of course, we'll have our Greek gods."

Alexander rattled off a list of how many temples to build and which Greek god each temple would honor.

"And, of course, we'll need a wall. Not just one—we'll have two walls! We'll build one inside the other for better protection. First thing, though, we'd better consult the priests! I want to ensure the gods like these plans."

The diviners offered sacrifices on the site and examined the entrails of the sacrificial animals. "All is well," the priests nodded. "The omens are favorable. The gods will be happy with temples and a new city here."

One of the soothsayers, Aristander the Telmissian, assured Alexander, "This city will be prosperous in every way, but especially regarding the fruit of the earth. It will grow enough grain to feed Egypt and other lands."

Alexander clapped his hands in glee and dashed back to make more plans for his city. His men had run out of stakes, so they resorted to throwing barley on the ground to mark out the outer and inner walls.[8]

Alexander organized workers to lay the foundations of the city. Yet, after a couple of days, ever restless, Alexander was ready to press on. "I want to go to Libya! I hear that the temple of Amun in the Siwa Oasis

---

[8] Arrian, "Alexander the Great," chapters I and II.

gives exact information when you ask it a question. Did you know the hero Perseus consulted it?"

Ptolemy nodded. "And Heracles."

"Well, then, it's settled! Both are my ancestors, you know."

They sailed along the coast to Libya, then marched inland, getting lost in the desert. Ptolemy reported that two serpents hissed at them and led the way. Alexander was only in North Africa for a few months. Soon, he would lead his expedition to central Asia. Before leaving Egypt, he appointed Cleomenes as nomarch (governor) of northern Egypt and put him in charge of building Alexandria. Cleomenes was Greek and had grown up in the Greek colony of Naucratis, Egypt, up the Nile from Alexandria. Alexander appointed Dinocrates of Rhodes as the architect for the new city.

An artist's interpretation of how Alexandria may have looked[10]

# Alexandria's Early Days

Dinocrates laid out the new city with a "Hippodamian" grid plan in a rectangular shape. It had straight streets intersecting others at right angles and an open agora area in the center. The Canopic Way, Alexandria's man thoroughfare, ran east and west through the city's center. Crates of Olynthus, a hydraulic engineer, designed Alexandria's sewers. An efficient drainage system was especially critical as Alexandria sat on swampy land. Dinocrates also built a three-quarter mile causeway called the Heptastadion from the mainland to Pharos Island, the city's port.

Cleomenes decided that the new city needed people to live in it, so he wanted to move the population of Canopus, an ancient Egyptian town about sixteen miles east, to Alexandria. Homer said King Menelaus built Canopus during the Trojan War, and it served as the major trade center on Egypt's coast. However, it had suffered earthquakes and tsunamis, perhaps one reason the Egyptians hadn't built a major city in the region.

Rising sea levels threatened to submerge Canopus, yet its citizens were indignant when ordered to leave their ancient home. They bribed Cleomenes to let them stay in their hometown, and he initially agreed. Cleomenes was known for extorting people to build his personal wealth. For instance, a crocodile ate one of his sons, so he commanded the Egyptians to kill all the crocodiles. Yet, the Egyptian priests considered crocodiles sacred and refused. Instead, they gave Cleomenes a big pay-off to save the crocodiles, which Cleomenes accepted.

As Alexandria's construction continued, Cleomenes again demanded that the citizens of Canopus move to the new city or pay another hefty sum. They could not produce the money this time, so most of the population moved to Alexandria.

Meanwhile, Alexander was on his expedition to the Indian subcontinent. When he returned to Babylon in 323 BCE, he chastised Cleomenes for accepting bribes. Alexander's closest friend, Hephaestion, had suddenly died a few months earlier, and Alexander had asked the oracle at Siwa to grant divine status to his dear friend. He wrote Cleomenes with a command to build a magnificent monument to Hephaestion:

"Use Dinocrates as its architect. I'll overlook your unacceptable behavior if you zealously perform this to my satisfaction."

Alexander never saw his new city, the Jewel of the Mediterranean, as his untimely death cut off his plans to return to Egypt.

## How did Alexandria become Egypt's capital?

After hashing out the details of the Partition of Babylon, Ptolemy traveled to Egypt to claim his piece of the empire. Memphis had been Egypt's capital, on and off, over three millennia. It had a distinguished history. Yet, Memphis also had priests so powerful they had essentially run the country, or parts of it, for centuries.

Ptolemy felt that the best course of action was a fresh start. He planned to forge a new kingdom that blended the best of Egyptian culture with Hellenism, the Greek culture. Ptolemy had shared Alexander's enthusiasm for building Alexandria on the Mediterranean coast. The westernmost Canopic branch of the Nile (almost entirely silted up today) was the water highway to the rest of Egypt. The Mediterranean linked

Egypt to Greece, Phoenicia, Syria, Carthage, Sicily, and beyond. The trade would make Alexandria unimaginably rich. Yes! He would move Egypt's capital to Alexandria—a new city for a new era!

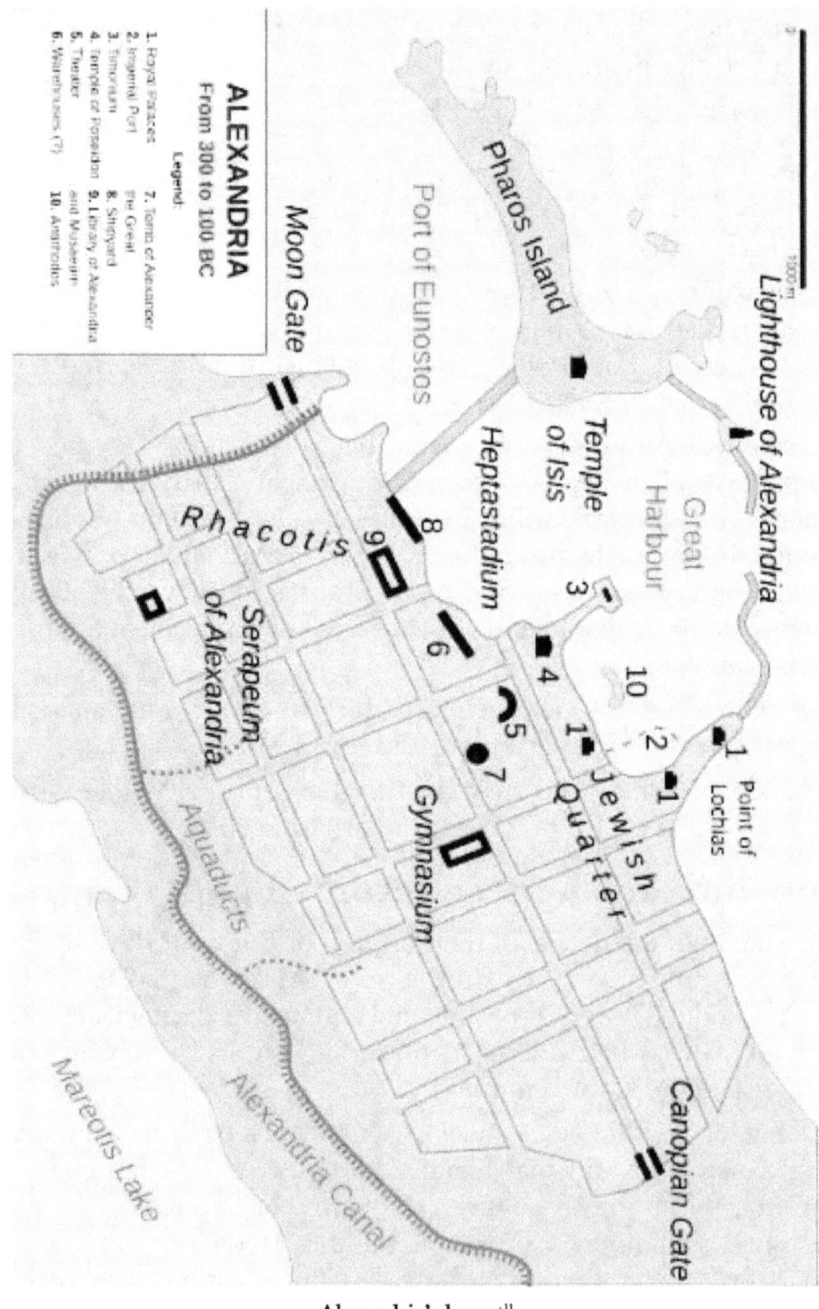


Alexandria's layout[11]

# What made Alexandria exceptional?

Ptolemy also envisioned Alexandria as a vibrant center of scholarly studies and artistic exchange. He immediately set about attracting scholars and artists from around the Mediterranean. He brought in scientists, mathematicians, philosophers, architects, and other brilliant thinkers, cementing Alexandria's status as one of the ancient world's most illustrious cities. Alexandria soon reigned as the ancient world's new artistic and scientific powerhouse. The stunning metropolis grew to a population of half a million with thriving commerce.

The Gate of the Sun welcomed visitors into its eastern walls. The Jewish Quarter was near the sea in the northeastern part of the city. To its west was the Macedonian Barracks, a "museum" (temple to the Muses), and the ancient world's most extensive library. The Lochias Peninsula jutted into the sea with the palace and an elaborate dining hall. The Sema, Alexander's tomb, was either on the peninsula or in the city's center. His tomb was intact until at least 360 CE. Eventually, it was lost to earthquakes, tsunamis, and warfare. The city also had an art gallery, botanical gardens, an observatory, and a zoo.

# Why was the Lighthouse of Alexandria such a famous landmark?

Diodorus Siculus, a first-century BCE historian, wrote that a voyage along the Mediterranean coast from Libya to Syria was long and arduous. He said the only safe landing was Alexandria's Pharos harbor. He pointed out that a hidden sandbank extended along Egypt's coast. Many ship captains thought they had escaped the perilous storms at sea when they saw Egypt's shores. However, they were unaware of the danger lurking in the waters below. Countless ships ran aground on the sandbar and were pounded into oblivion by the relentless waves.[9]

Egypt's low-lying coastline had few landmarks for a ship captain to plan his course. Around 900 BCE, Homer wrote in the *Odyssey* that sailors would look for the island of Pharos and come ashore in the "snug harbor." They knew the lake on the other side of the isthmus had fresh water they could take with them. Homer said that the shape-shifting

---

[9] Diodorus, *Library of History*, Volume I.

Proteus, the "Old Man of the Sea," lived on Pharos island, where he herded seals.[10]

Alexander had envisioned a lighthouse on Pharos, and Ptolemy set out to fulfill his dream. Pharos was already a well-known harbor, and he would capitalize on that. Ptolemy started the project using Sostratus of Cnidus as its architect. Ptolemy I died before its completion, but his son, Ptolemy II, finished the lighthouse, which rose 330 feet into the sky. The workers used marble blocks cemented together with lead mortar.

An artistic representation of the Lighthouse of Alexandria[11]

---

[10] Homer, *The Odyssey,* trans. Samuel Butler. Internet Classics Archive, Book IV, 55. http://classics.mit.edu/Homer/odyssey.html.

The Lighthouse of Alexandria had three stories. The square-shaped lower level was the widest and tallest. The middle story was octagonal and slightly narrower than the bottom level. The top layer was round and had an enormous, curved mirror that reflected the sun by day and a lit fire at night. Sailors could see the lighthouse from thirty-five miles away. At its top was a statue of the Greek god Zeus. The Greek historian Herodotus listed it as one of the Seven Wonders of the World.

The remarkable Lighthouse of Alexandria guided the way to the Pharos harbor through the three centuries of the Ptolemy Kingdom and beyond. It captured Julius Caesar's admiration. He had a small-scale model with a burning light inside built for his triumphal parade through Rome. The top of the lighthouse was reportedly damaged in the Byzantine Era (beginning 395 CE) by treasure hunters who believed jewels were hidden inside. A series of earthquakes caused it to crumble partially, although its lower level still stood in 1182 CE. The Muslims installed a small mosque at its top. In 1375 CE, a devastating earthquake reduced the lighthouse to rubble. Sultan Qaitbay used its stones in the following century to build a fort.

Alexandria, the Jewel of the Mediterranean, survived and thrived to the present day. It reigns as the largest city on the Mediterranean, covering twenty-five miles of Egypt's coastline. In 2015, Egypt's Supreme Council of Antiquities approved a plan to rebuild the Lighthouse of Alexandria.

# Chapter 3: The First Five Ptolemaic Rulers

The Ptolemaic Kingdom's first century was its glory days. The government was efficient, and the economy was healthy. It was a time of stunning scholarly breakthroughs. Greeks relocated to Egypt in droves, doubling its population and dramatically changing its demographics. Yet, eventually, the golden era began unraveling. Debauched kings, inept regents, and messy family feuds all took a toll. Meanwhile, Rome was morphing from a modest city-state into an empire. Egypt didn't notice until it was too late.

## Ptolemy I Soter's Consolidated Kingdom (306-283 BCE)

One of Ptolemy's first acts as Egypt's governor was to execute Cleomenes. He detested Cleomenes's blatant bribery and believed he was a spy for Perdiccas. The Egyptians, who had suffered under Cleomenes, breathed a sigh of relief.

Once word got out that Alexander IV was dead, Antigonus crowned himself king over his vast swathe of Asia in 306 BCE. Ptolemy's officers leaped into action: "If Antigonus can be king, so can Ptolemy!" The other Diadochi quickly followed suit. In 304 BCE, the Egyptians crowned Ptolemy I as their pharaoh. He took the Egyptian throne name Meriamun Setepenra ("beloved of Amun, Chosen by Ra") and minted the first coins with his image.

As the "game of thrones" raged between the Diadochi, Ptolemy occasionally inserted himself. In 304 BCE, Ptolemy rescued the island of Rhodes from an attack by Antigonus and Demetrius. The grateful citizens of Rhodes gave Ptolemy the divine title of "Soter," or "Savior." In 302 BCE, Ptolemy invaded Phoenicia and southern Syria. By 295, Ptolemy controlled Tyre, Sidon, and the island of Cyprus.

Ptolemy I's coin[13]

In 320 BCE, Ptolemy I arrived in Jerusalem on the Jewish Sabbath, pretending he was coming to offer sacrifices. The Jews fell for it. It never occurred to them that Ptolemy intended to take Jerusalem. It was their day of rest, and they offered little resistance. Ptolemy rounded up captives from Judea and Samaria for his military. He gave them citizenship in Egypt if they swore fidelity to him.[11]

Ptolemy wrote a history of how Alexander conquered the Persian Empire. He included the part he played as an officer and eyewitness. This book has been lost. However, it was the primary source for Arrian's second-century CE history of Alexander. Ptolemy respected the Egyptian religion and restored temples the Persians had torn down. He wanted the Egyptians to accept him as their legitimate pharaoh.

## The Last of the Diadochi

Ptolemy's oldest son from Eurydice, his third wife, was Ptolemy Ceraunus (Thunderbolt). He and his brother Meleager were meant to be the heir and the spare. However, Ptolemy then married his fourth wife, Berenice. He elevated Philadelphus, his son with Berenice, over his older sons. A power struggle ensued between the sons of both marriages.

---

[11] Flavius Josephus, *The Antiquities of the Jews,* trans. William Whiston (Project Gutenberg eBook, 2001), Book XII: chapter 1.

Meleager paced back and forth. "We've got to get out of Egypt! Berenice won't stop at anything. Especially you, Ceraunus! You were supposed to be crown prince. You're in mortal danger."

Ceraunus and Meleager fled Egypt, but Philadelphus killed their two younger brothers. Ceraunus escaped to Macedonia, ruled by his father's old friend, Lysimachus. Ceraunus's sister, Lysandra, was the wife of Lysimachus's oldest son, Agathocles. Lysimachus welcomed him warmly. However, Ceraunus soon realized his new situation was just as awkward and dangerous as the one he'd escaped. When Lysandra and Ceraunus were alone, she explained the palace intrigue to her brother.

"It's complicated and dangerous, Ceraunus. King Lysimachus has arranged a marriage between Agathocles's sister, Arsinoe I, and our half-brother, Philadelphus. It gets worse! Lysimachus just married a new wife, and you'll never guess who she is: Arsinoe II!"

"Arsinoe II! Our half-sister and Berenice's daughter?"

"Yes, Ceraunus! She's just as bad as Berenice! She's launched a campaign against my husband, Agathocles. You wouldn't believe the horrible things she's saying about him. Ceraunus, I'm terrified of what will happen!"

Within a few days, Lysandra's worst fears came true. Lysimachus executed Agathocles. He believed his wife over his son. Ceraunus fled with Lysandra to Babylon and the court of Seleucus, another of Ptolemy I's fellow officers under Alexander. Seleucus now ruled western and central Asia.

Their arrival played right into Seleucus's hands. He was looking for an excuse to attack Lysimachus. He also toyed with thoughts of invading Egypt, as Ptolemy I had recently died. In 281 CE, Seleucus and Ceraunus shattered

Seleucus I[14]

Lysimachus's army in the Battle of Corupedium in Anatolia. It was the last battle of the Diadochi. A javelin impaled Lysimachus, killing him. Lysimachus was eighty years old, and Seleucus was seventy-seven.

Seleucus crossed the Hellespont into Europe and took Thrace. His next target was Macedonia, but Ptolemy Ceraunus cut his plans short. As Seleucus was offering sacrifices, Ceraunus stabbed him in the back. Ptolemy Ceraunus then crowned himself king of Macedonia and renounced all claims to the Egyptian throne.

Lysimachus's death left Ceraunus's half-sister Arsinoe II a widow. Despite their hostile history, Ceraunus shockingly proposed to Arsinoe, and she accepted. Why? They both had a tenuous hereditary claim to Macedonia's throne. If they married, it would double the strength of their claim. However, the marriage almost immediately imploded when Ceraunus discovered Arsinoe II and her sons were plotting against him. One account says it was on their wedding day. Ceraunus killed two of Arsinoe's sons, and Arsinoe fled to Egypt and married her full brother, Ptolemy II, who was now Egypt's pharaoh.

Ceraunus's reign as Macedonia's king didn't last long. The Galatians invaded in 279 BCE, and Ceraunus lost his head in the bloodbath.

# Ptolemy II Philadelphus (284-246 BCE)

Ptolemy II Philadelphus[15]

While all the drama played out with Ceraunus in Europe and Asia, his younger half-brother, Philadelphus, began his reign in Egypt. Philadelphus was born in 309 BCE on the island of Kos in the Aegean Sea. Why was he born there and not in Egypt? The other Diadochi were fighting in Babylon, and Ptolemy invaded the Aegean when they were not paying attention. Berenice accompanied him, which seems bizarre given her pregnancy. Perhaps she was nervous about staying in Egypt with her rival, Eurydice.

Three brilliant Greek tutors schooled Philadelphus. Philitas of Cos was a renowned poet who spearheaded the development of the Library of Alexandria. Zenodotus of Ephesus was a student of Philitas and one of the library's first librarians. Strato of Lampsacus was a scholar with a keen interest in natural science. Through their influence, Philadelphus developed a deep appreciation of the arts and sciences. He led Egypt into the golden age of the Ptolemaic Kingdom.

Ptolemy I crowned Ptolemy II Philadelphus as king in 284 BCE when he was twenty-five. Philadelphus co-reigned with his father until Ptolemy I's death two years later. In the same year, Philadelphus's first wife, Arsinoe I (Lysimachus's daughter), gave birth to his oldest son, Ptolemy III Euergetes.

Palace politics took a menacing twist five years later. Ptolemy II's older sister, Arsinoe II, returned to Egypt after Lysimachus's death and her brief marriage to Ceraunus. She brought her son by Lysimachus, Ptolemy Epigonos.

Arsinoe I knew the insidious threat Arsinoe II's arrival presented. However, she was helpless to escape her rival's evil schemes. Arsinoe II convinced Ptolemy II that Arsinoe I was plotting against him. Ptolemy II exiled his first wife to Coptos, Egypt, five hundred miles up the Nile. He then married Arsinoe II, his full sister, and made her his co-regent. The name "Philadelphus" means "sibling-lover" in Koine Greek. The Greeks thought Ptolemy's marriage to his sister was scandalous, but the Egyptians just shrugged. Their pharaohs had been marrying their sisters since the Old Kingdom.

Ptolemy II Philadelphus and Arsinoe II had no children together. They may not have consummated their incestuous marriage. Arsinoe II was already in her forties and may have been past child-bearing age. Ptolemy II adopted Ptolemy Epigonos, her son by Lysimachus. "He will be Egypt's next king!" he promised his sister-wife. He had made Ptolemy Epigonos his co-regent.

However, the relationship fell apart when Ptolemy II sent Epigonos to Miletus in western Anatolia to spy out the political situation there. Epigonos joined forces with the tyrant Timarchus against Ptolemy. Timarchus died in the ensuing war, and Ptolemy II cut Epigonos off as his co-regent. However, he graciously gave Epigonos the city of Telmessos on Anatolia's Mediterranean coast, which had once belonged to Epigonos's birth father, Lysimachus. Epigonos ruled it as a client king under Ptolemy II.

Euergetes, Ptolemy II's oldest son by Arsinoe I, was his heir again. After forty years of ruling Egypt, Ptolemy II died in 246 BCE. He was buried in the Sema, the mausoleum where Ptolemy I had buried Alexander the Great.

A double cameo with Ptolemy II & Arsinoe II[16]

Besides his wives, Ptolemy II also had at least eleven concubines or lesser wives. His Macedonian concubine, Bilistiche, entered the Olympic chariot races and won several events. Ptolemy II created an Egyptian version of the Olympic Games called the Ptolemaieia, which met every four years in Alexandria. Its opening ceremonies included a lavish parade with over one hundred chariots pulled by elephants, antelope, ostriches, gnus, and zebras. Dancers, acrobats, and athletes entertained the crowds. Servants displayed Egypt's war treasures, and Ptolemy II's soldiers marched in full regalia.

Ptolemy II encouraged immigrants to Egypt from Greece, Macedonia, and West Asia. He especially wanted seasoned soldiers, although he also used Egyptian troops. He freed the Jews whom his father brought to Egypt as military conscripts. Some returned to Judea, but others preferred the exciting trade and scholarly hub of Alexandria. He had whole units of Jewish soldiers in his army, now volunteers.

Under Ptolemy II, Alexandria's library became a hotspot for scientists and mathematicians. They discussed and developed new theories, making astounding breakthroughs. Ptolemy II brought famous Greek poets like Apollonius of Rhodes, Callimachus, and Theocritus to Alexandria.

Ptolemy III Euergetes[17]

# Ptolemy III Euergetes and His Remarkable Queen, Berenice II (246-222 BCE)

The name "Euergetes" meant "benefactor" or "one who does good deeds." Ptolemy III earned this name by lifting the Ptolemaic Dynasty to incredible heights in territory and economics. His childhood had been chaotic due to his stepmother forcing his mother into exile. He probably thought he had lost any chance of becoming Egypt's next king. And then it happened! His stepbrother, Epigonos, made the disastrous decision to oppose his father. Suddenly, Euergetes was elevated to crown prince and became engaged to Berenice II.

Berenice was probably the best thing that ever happened to Ptolemy III Euergetes. She was queen of Cyrene, an ancient Greek colony on Libya's Mediterranean Coast. Ptolemy I had captured it and written a new constitution for the city. When Cyrene rebelled, Ptolemy I sent Magus, his stepson by Berenice I of Egypt, to quell the rebels. Magus became Cyrene's governor, and after Ptolemy I died, crowned himself king of Cyrene. He even tried to invade Egypt, which did not go well for him. Yet, Ptolemy II was Magus's half-brother. The two kings reconciled, and Magus held Cyrene.

Berenice II was the only child of Magus and his queen, Apama II. Ptolemy II and Magus arranged for Ptolemy III to marry Berenice. However, after Magus died, his widow, Apama II, broke off Berenice's engagement to Euergetes. Instead, she arranged a marriage with Demetrius the Fair, grandson of Antigonus the One-eyed. Cyrene's citizens disliked her new husband. "He thinks more of himself than he ought. Furthermore, he's too heavy-handed! She should have married Ptolemy III," people whispered. "Demetrius is insufferable!"

Berenice had a hunch that something worse was happening. Her suspicions turned out to be true when she caught her handsome husband cheating on her—with her own mother! She called her guards to her mother's room. As the men burst into the room, Berenice cried, "Spare my mother!"

Apama tried to cover Demetrius with her own body. Nevertheless, it was hopeless. The guards ran Demetrius through as Apama screamed.[12]

"Now I will marry the man my father wanted me to marry," Berenice declared. She sailed to Alexandria, where a delighted Ptolemy III received her.

---

[12] Justinus, *Epitome of Pompeius Trogus' Philippic Histories*, trans. J. S. Watson (1853), 26.3. https://www.attalus.org/translate/justin4.html#26.1.

Ra, the Egyptian god of the sun and kingship, with Ptolemy III and Berenice II[18]

"She murdered her first husband! Is our king safe?" people whispered anxiously. With few friends in Egypt, Berenice had to forge a path for herself, which she did with aplomb. She surrounded herself with poets and scholars at the Library of Alexandria, who enshrined her charm, grace, modesty, and strength of character in dozens of poems. They championed Berenice as a loving wife and excellent mother to her six children—the ideal Greek woman. However, Berenice was also sophisticated and complex, a woman who navigated through treachery, court intrigues, and betrayal by those closest to her.

Yes, it was a political marriage, but it also was a love match—at least, it quickly grew into one. Ptolemy III never married anyone else, although both Egyptian and Macedonian traditions permitted multiple wives. No one ever mentioned him having mistresses or concubines. They had a large family together, and Berenice actively participated in government.

A few months after he married Berenice, Ptolemy III got embroiled in the Third Syrian War. His sister, Berenice Syra, was the wife of Antiochus II Theos, king of the Seleucid Empire in West Asia. After Berenice Syra became pregnant, Antiochus left her for his first wife, Laodice. "You must return to Berenice!" Ptolemy III scolded. "We had a deal!" Antiochus refused and, shortly after, suddenly died.

"He must have been poisoned!" people whispered. "He was barely forty years old!"

"But who would kill him?"

"I'm guessing it was Laodice. I heard he was planning to go back to Berenice, and Laodice was jealous."

"But I thought he only married Berenice for her money. You know, she brought that huge dowry with her."

"Maybe, but Berenice's brother, Ptolemy III, insisted they reconcile, or Antiochus would have had to return the dowry. Laodice feared he would make Berenice's son the next king instead of her son, Callinicus."

Berenice Syra desperately sent messages to her brother Ptolemy to rescue her. "Laodice will murder me and my little son. Come quickly!"

Ptolemy III mustered his army to march north to his sister and nephew in Antioch, Syria. Queen Berenice cut off her hair as a sacrifice for her husband's safe return. She placed her hair in Aphrodite's temple in Alexandria as a votive offering. However, when the priests entered the temple the following morning, the hair had disappeared!

Drachma coin with Berenice II of Egypt[19]

The priests and court were mystified. What happened to the hair? Finally, the court astronomer, Conon of Samos, produced the answer as night fell. "Look! Up in the northern sky, between Leo and Boötes. What do you see? It's a new constellation! Aphrodite placed it there. That's Berenice's hair! The goddess has shown her favor to Berenice for her sacrifice. Her prayers will come true! Her husband and our king will return safely." The poets Callimachus and Catullus both wrote about "Berenice's lock."

Meanwhile, Ptolemy III was leading his army up the Mediterranean coast. When he reached Antioch, he received devastating news. Laodice's henchmen had already killed his sister and her little son, Antiochus. Laodice and her sons were in the north, hiding out in Anatolia. The good news was that the Syrian forces loyal to Berenice had taken Celicia. It served as a buffer zone between Syria and Laodice's army.

Ptolemy III was too late to rescue his sister, but conditions were ripe for taking the rest of the Seleucid Empire. He set out on the most jaw-dropping conquest of any Ptolemaic ruler. With his infantry, cavalry, and war elephants, he captured Syria and Mesopotamia. Crowned "King of Asia," he even claimed to have conquered Persia and Bactria (Afghanistan, Tajikistan, and Uzbekistan). Ptolemy III hunted down the sacred treasures the Persians stole from the Egyptian temples centuries earlier and shipped them home.

Just then, however, he received word of an uprising back home. The native Egyptians had grown weary of the Ptolemaic Kingdom's heavy taxes, which had grown heavier when Ptolemy III needed to fund his new war. Moreover, the annual Nile flooding had failed in 245 BCE. The lakes further south that fed the Nile tributaries had not received enough rain. The Egyptians manipulated the annual Nile flooding to saturate their fields before planting. If the Nile did not flood, they could not grow the crops they depended on for food and trade with other countries.

What disrupted the rainfall south of Egypt? Ice cores from Greenland and Antarctica show that major volcanic eruptions occurred in 247 BCE, triggering cooler air from the ash and sulfur dioxide circulating the earth and filtering sunlight. This cooler air disrupted the African monsoon. Thus, faraway volcanoes triggered a famine in Egypt that forced Ptolemy III to abandon the war and return home—just as he was on the brink of capturing the entire Seleucid Empire.[13]

---

[13] Manning, J. G., et al. "Volcanic Suppression of Nile Summer Flooding Triggers Revolt and Constrains Interstate Conflict in Ancient Egypt," *Nature Communications* 8, no. 900 (2017), https://doi.org/10.1038/s41467-017-00957-y.

The Syrian War ended in 241 BCE when the Ptolemaic Kingdom and the Seleucids agreed to a peace treaty. Ptolemy III kept the land he conquered in Anatolia and Syria. Now, he controlled the Mediterranean coastline from Libya to Anatolia. He also kept Antioch, Alexandria's biggest competitor in trade and scholarly pursuits.

Ptolemy III continued to build up Alexandria's reputation as the Mediterranean's cultural star. He encouraged the works of mathematicians, geographers, and astronomers in his court, like Apollonius of Perga, Conon of Samos, and Eratosthenes.

His father's goal was to include a copy of every book in the world in the Library of Alexandria. Apparently, that library was getting too full, so Ptolemy III built a second one in the Temple of Serapis. He copied every scroll that entered Alexandria's port. He kept the original for his library and gave the copy to the owner. Ptolemy III often had to pay a massive fine for keeping the precious originals. These included the official manuscripts of the Greek tragedy writers Sophocles, Aeschylus, and Euripides.

Ptolemy III died in 221 BCE, and his oldest son, Philopator, became the next king.

Silver coin of Ptolemy IV Philopator[20]

# Ptolemy IV Philopator Purges the Royal Family (221-204 BCE)

Philopator, whose name means "father-loving," became the fourth king of the Ptolemaic Kingdom in his early twenties. He married his full sister, Arsinoe III, and they had one son in 210 BCE: Ptolemy V. Philopator's mistress was Agathoclea. Her brother Agathocles and another friend, Sosibius, were his closest advisors and led him down a dark path. Philopator let these two men run the kingdom while he abandoned himself to a life of ease, indulging his every desire. Sosibius's name appeared on royal documents more than Philopator's.

Philopater might have loved his father, but not the rest of his family. His advisors got annoyed when the king's mother, Berenice II, and other family members questioned what Agathocles and Sosibius were doing. With the king's permission, they poisoned Berenice II. They poured boiling water over Philopater's younger brother, Magus, the army commander. They also killed Lysimachus, Philopater's great-uncle.

The killing spree was not over. Sosibius thought Cleomenes, a king of the Greek city-state of Sparta, presented a threat. He had achieved remarkable reforms and begun conquering the rest of Greece until he lost to the Macedonians and Achaeans. He had fled to Egypt, where Ptolemy III gave him refuge. Ptolemy III died soon after.

Egged on by his advisors, Ptolemy IV put Cleomenes under house arrest. Why? Alexandria's army had many mercenary soldiers from the Sparta area. Ptolemy IV feared the soldiers would be more loyal to Cleomenes than him if Cleomenes sparked a revolt.

Cleomenes did attempt a revolt when Ptolemy IV and his minions were out of town. Cleomenes and the thirteen Spartans with him broke free. With daggers held high, they raced through Alexandria's streets, calling, "Rise up! Be like true Greeks! Champion liberty! Together, we can set up a free state. We'll overturn the Ptolemaic despots!"

The Alexandrians looked curiously at the Spartans. Yes, the Alexandrians were Greeks, but they had been a kingdom for a century. Greek-style democracy was a foreign concept, and revolution wasn't their thing. "These Spartans are rather eccentric, don't you think?" the Alexandrians murmured.

When they saw it was hopeless, Cleomenes and his men fell on their daggers.

Ptolemy IV won an unexpected victory against Antigonus III of the Seleucid Empire. However, rather than pressing his advantage and crippling the Seleucids, he made peace. Ptolemy IV continued to lead successful expeditions in Greece. However, he was disinterested in ruling the Greek states. He merely demanded terms of peace. During this time, the Roman Republic had strengthened and was at war with Carthage on North Africa's coast, west of Egypt. Ptolemy IV kept his options open by remaining neutral yet friendly with both sides.

A drawing of Ptolemy IV's Thalamegos, his luxury, two-hulled catamaran[21]

Around 206 BCE, internal revolts rocked Egypt, just as they had in the reign of Ptolemy III. This time, the Egyptians of southern Egypt declared independence. Their leader, Horwennefer, crowned himself Egypt's new pharaoh in Thebes. Native Egyptians now ruled southern Egypt, and the Greeks ruled northern Egypt.

While all this was going on, Ptolemy IV and his wife died in mysterious circumstances. Some thought Ptolemy IV may have died from something related to his obesity or heavy drinking. Yet, he and his wife died around the same time. Were they poisoned? Some whispered about a fire in the palace. No one knew, especially since Sosibius kept their deaths a secret for weeks.

# Ptolemy V Epiphanes and His Bungling Regents (203-180 BCE)

The two villains, Agathocles and Sosibius, stood in the palace court with five-year-old Epiphanes between them, wearing a miniature royal diadem on his tiny head. Two silver urns rested on a table next to them. The nobility of Alexandria stood waiting. Sosibius cleared his throat and spoke.

"We regret to inform you that our Father-loving gods, King Ptolemy IV and Queen Arsinoe III, have left us for heaven. Their ashes are here, and we will give them a royal burial in the Sema, next to Alexander the Great. Ptolemy V Epiphanes is our new king. Here is Ptolemy IV's will. He has appointed Agathocles and me as guardians of his son. Furthermore, Agathocles will be regent until King Ptolemy V comes of age."[14]

Everyone looked at each other, shaking their heads and whispering. "It's all so sudden! They haven't even explained what happened to our king and queen. And we already hate Agathocles! He's too prideful. It was bad enough when Epiphanes was alive. Now, Agathocles will have free rein for his villainy!"

Agathocles and Sosibius set to work exiling any possible contenders from Egypt. They were nervous that the power vacuum might incite an invasion from Rome, Macedonia, or the Seleucids. Yet, the people had endured enough. The citizens of Alexandria revolted. Led by the army commander Tlepolemus, they dragged Agathocles out of the palace and tore him to pieces. Sosibius had recently died, and his son sided with the revolutionaries. They made

Gold coin of Ptolemy V, the child king[22]

Tlepolemus regent for little Ptolemy V, now seven years old.

---

[14] E. R. Bevan, *The House of Ptolemy* (Methuen Publishing, 1927), chap. VIII, https://penelope.uchicago.edu/Thayer/E/Gazetteer/Places/Africa/Egypt/_Texts/BEVHOP/6*.html.

---

Tlepolemus botched his role as regent. He ignored state affairs and spent too much time partying and playing ball. His neglect destabilized Egypt, so in 201 BCE, Aristomenes of Alyzia took over as regent.

Antiochus III (the Great) of the Seleucid Empire and Philip V of Macedonia jumped at the chance to take advantage of the upheaval. They met in 200 BCE to plot out their strategy.

"Philip, we both know Egypt is weak right now! Their king is only ten years old, and they keep changing regents. The entire Ptolemaic Empire outside of Egypt is ours for the taking."

"I agree, Antiochus! If we attack on different fronts simultaneously, we can divide it between ourselves."

Antiochus smiled. "I'll take Syria, Cyprus, Celicia, and Lycia."

Philip nodded. "And I'll take the rest of Anatolia, Thrace, and the Cyclades."

They launched the Second Macedonian War. Antiochus the Great easily took Syria. When he reached Judea in 198 BCE, the Jews threw open Jerusalem's gates, welcoming him as their conquering hero from the Egyptians. They never expected the horrors his son, Antiochus Epiphanes, would soon bring.

Meanwhile, Philip was making headway in the Aegean. But it didn't all go as planned. Rome got involved, having just wrapped up its war with Carthage. In two battles, the Romans killed most of Philips's men, forcing him to pull out of the war.

Ptolemy V turned fourteen in 196 BCE and was crowned Egypt's pharaoh at Memphis. The Egyptian priests gathered and passed

The Rosetta Stone of Ptolemy V Epiphanes[23]

the "Memphis Decree," carved on the Rosetta Stone. (This monument of polished black granodiorite is almost four feet high. It was once higher, but part of it broke off.) It had identical inscriptions written in three scripts: Egyptian hieroglyphics, Demotic (another Egyptian script), and Greek.

In all three scripts, the priests praised the king's kindness in releasing prisoners, outlawing forced labor, and restoring and rebuilding the Egyptian temples. They proclaimed Ptolemy V's new divine cult and ordered the temples throughout Egypt to install statues of their new king. (Two thousand years later, Napolean's army discovered the monument. The Rosetta Stone unlocked Egyptian hieroglyphics, enabling scholars to translate them.)

Antiochus made peace with Ptolemy V the following year, outraging the Romans. Antiochus kept Judea, Syria, and Anatolia, and Ptolemy got Antiochus's daughter, Cleopatra I ("the Syrian"), as his wife. She was only eight, so they waited two years to marry. The couple had two sons and a daughter, and all three ruled Egypt together.

Ptolemy V successfully took back southern Egypt by 186 BCE. He planned to take back Syria, Phoenicia, and Judea after Antiochus the Great died, but he himself died suddenly in 180 BCE at age thirty. Rumors were that his advisors poisoned him to avoid the heavy taxes needed for a new war. His death marked the beginning of the end for the Ptolemaic Kingdom. It stumbled along for another 150 years but never achieved its early kings' brilliance or massive territory.

# Chapter 4: Cultural Fusion: Greek Influence on Egyptian Society

Ptolemy I's reign laid the groundwork for the unique Hellenistic-Egyptian civilization that would flourish under his successors. The Ptolemaic rulers blended Greek and Egyptian cultures to create a unique societal fabric. What did that look like? Was Greek or Egyptian the most common language? Who were the new gods? Did the Ptolemaic rulers follow Greek or Egyptian administrative styles? This chapter will spend some time answering these questions.

## What was the relationship between Egypt and Greece before Ptolemy I?

From their early history, the Egyptians and Greeks had enjoyed a lively cultural interchange. The Minoans and Mycenaeans traded with Egypt in the Bronze Age (3300-1200 BCE). The Minoans of Crete (an island about halfway between Egypt and Greece) developed a hieroglyphic writing system that looked similar to Egyptian hieroglyphics. Yet, Cretan Hieroglyphic was phonetic and had only eighty-five symbols compared to over eight hundred symbols in Egyptian hieroglyphics.

Through this cultural interchange, some of the Greek and Egyptian mythology intermingled. For instance, the Egyptians had their own twist on Helen of Troy. In the Egyptian version, after kidnapping Helen from Sparta in Greece, Prince Paris meant to take her to Troy. However, a storm blew his ship to Egypt's coast. Helen privately told the Egyptian pharaoh, Seti II, that she had *not* gone with Paris willingly. She loved her husband, King Menelaus.

Seti took pity on Helen and hid her from Paris in a temple. His daughter, a high priestess, called up the god Thoth. He separated Helen's body from her "ka" or spirit. Her ka went with Paris to Troy, but Helen remained in Egypt for ten years while the Trojan War raged. Finally, at the war's end, a storm blew King Menelaus's ship to Egypt, where he reunited with Helen.[15]

About a thousand years before Ptolemy I became king, the Egyptian pharaoh Psamtik I permitted the Greeks of Miletus to establish a colony in Egypt. Their new city was Naucratis, on the westernmost Canopic branch of the Nile, about forty-five miles upstream from where Alexandria would one day be built. It grew into a lively trade center where Egyptian and Greek culture and knowledge interchanged.

Naucratis later became the home base for the Greek military unit. Greek mercenaries fought in the Egyptian forces for hundreds of years before Alexander arrived.

In 460 BCE, the Greeks sailed two hundred ships to Egypt to assist the Egyptian rebel leader, Inaros II, in evicting the hated Persians. The Athenian League had already driven the despised Persians from the Aegean Sea and felt invincible. Initially, they succeeded, killing a hundred thousand Persians and capturing or sinking eighty Persian ships. Yet, the Persians had an inexhaustible source of manpower. They sent three hundred more vessels and two hundred thousand men, viciously crushing the Egyptians and Greeks.

# Who spoke which language?

Ptolemaic Egypt had two official languages: Egyptian and Koine Greek (the "common dialect"). Koine Greek had spread throughout the Middle East after Alexander the Great's conquests. For three centuries, it was the lingua franca of North Africa, West Asia, and Eastern Europe. A common language enabled the ancient Mediterranean world to surge ahead in trade and dramatically impacted the pursuit of knowledge.

Greek, the language of the royal court and the Greek administrators, was the primary language in Alexandria and Naucratis. The Ptolemaic

---

[15] Herodotus, *The Histories*, trans. George Rawlinson (Dutton & Co, 1862), 2:113-120, http://classics.mit.edu/Herodotus/history.html.

rulers imported Greek schoolteachers and gave them tax breaks.

Language divided the Egyptians and the Greeks of Egypt. About half of Egypt's population was still Egyptian. They primarily spoke Egyptian and wrote in the Egyptian Demotic script except for monuments, for which they used ancient hieroglyphics. Egyptian was the language of the temples and priesthood. Cleopatra VII, the last pharaoh, was the only ruler known to have learned the Egyptian language.

Speaking of Cleopatra, the name was Macedonian, not Egyptian. It meant "glory of the father." As you might have noticed, the Ptolemies liked to use the same names over and over. All the kings were named Ptolemy, a popular Macedonian name that meant "warrior." Alexander the Great's sister was Cleopatra, and the name was used repeatedly throughout the dynasty. Cleopatra VII was *the* Cleopatra, the one who married two of her brothers and carried on with Julius Caesar and Mark Antony. Her story is in chapter eight, which unwraps the decline and fall of the Ptolemaic Kingdom. Many other queens and princesses had the name Arsinoe or Berenice. Arsinoe was a Greek word that meant "enlightened woman," and Berenice meant "victory bringer."

As for legal affairs, the native Egyptians continued to follow their traditional laws. However, they also had to follow the royal laws of the Macedonian kings. If they had to write a contract, the language depended on whether it dealt with Egyptian or royal law. If the latter, they used Koine Greek.

Of course, plenty of people in Egypt were bilingual, simply for survival. Many Greeks married Egyptian women, so they had bilingual households. Most Egyptian administrators kept their jobs when Ptolemy I came into power, but now they had to communicate in two languages. Some folks even had two names—one Greek and one Egyptian.

## How did cultural fusion impact architecture and art?

In the three centuries of Macedonian kings, art and architecture reflected both Greek and Egyptian styles. At first, the Ptolemaic kings continued the traditional Egyptian forms. The exception was Alexandria, with its mostly Greek population. This city mainly had Greek-style art and architecture. However, the Ptolemies built Egyptian-style statues of themselves in the harbor and several Egyptian-style temples.

Egyptian sistrum with Ptolemy I's cartouche on the handle[24]

Art and architecture were political in a sense. The Ptolemies wanted to present themselves as a continuation of the Egyptian pharaohs. For example, the Egyptians used a rattle called a sistrum when worshiping goddesses like Isis, Hathor, or Bastet. Ptolemy I had a sistrum made from faience or glazed pottery. His name was on the handle in Egyptian hieroglyphics inside a "cartouche," an oval that signified a pharaoh's name. The face on the rattle was the Egyptian goddess Hathor, and the style of the sistrum was traditional Egyptian. It symbolized Ptolemy I's continuation of Egyptian art and religion.

In the towns and cities where the Egyptians lived, the Ptolemies installed statues of themselves wearing the regalia of Egyptian pharaohs. They wanted to assure the Egyptians of their respect for their culture. Yet, by the second generation of Greek rule, statues had Egyptian poses and clothing but Greek hairstyles and facial features.

Ptolemy I and his successors rebuilt the Egyptian temples in the same style the Egyptians had used for centuries. Ptolemy VI Philometor built a new structure, the Temple of Kom Ombo, dedicated to the Egyptian falcon god Horus and the crocodile god Sobek.

This wall relief from the Kom Ombo temple shows Sobek (l) and the goddesses Isis and Hathor crowning a Ptolemaic pharaoh.[25]

# How did the integration of Greek and Egyptian religions work?

The Egyptians continued to worship their gods, whom the Ptolemies respected. The Macedonian kings supported the temples and attended special ceremonies. The Greek population continued to worship their traditional gods. However, the Ptolemies also started new cults. Ptolemy I introduced the god Serapis to his Egyptian and Greek subjects. Serapis was a fusion of the supreme Greek god Zeus and the Egyptian gods Osiris and Apis. Osiris was the lord of the underworld and the firstborn of Egypt's gods. Apis was a bull and also a god of the underworld.

Serapis had a full beard and looked Greek. He balanced a large cup on his head, representing abundance and new life after death. He became a popular god in Greece and Rome.

According to Plutarch, Ptolemy I had dreamed of a colossal statue of Pluto (Hades), the Greek god of the underworld. Pluto told Ptolemy to bring his statue to Alexandria. Ptolemy was perplexed. He had no idea where the statue was! He started telling his friends about his dream. Finally, he told his friend Sosibius, who had traveled widely.

"Ptolemy! I saw an enormous statue in Sinope! Maybe it was the god in your dream."

"Really? Where is Sinope?" Ptolemy asked eagerly.

"It's on the Black Sea—a long way from here."

Despite the distance and danger of the sea journey, Ptolemy had his men sail to the Black Sea and steal the statue. When they returned to Egypt, Ptolemy called his Egyptian and Greek priests to inspect the statue. They agreed that it represented Osiris (or Pluto). So, Ptolemy built a gigantic temple for his stolen statue, which he named Serapis.[16]

The Egyptians considered their pharaohs to be earthly representations of the god Horus. They believed their pharaohs were part mortal and part god and were intermediaries between them and the gods. The Ptolemies latched on to this and encouraged the Egyptians to consider them divine. Ptolemy II elevated his sister and second wife, Arsinoe II, as the earthly

Serapis [26]

representation of Isis and the Greek goddess Hera. He built a temple for her and held festivals in her honor. He issued coins with Arsinoe II wearing a goddess's diadem.

In 238 BCE, Ptolemy III's little girl, Berenice, died. A little later, Ptolemy III called an assembly of all Egypt's priests. The priests wrote the Decree of Canopus, which honored the dead little girl as a goddess. The decree also lauded Ptolemy III's military prowess. They described how he supported the Egyptian priesthood by returning the idols and other religious artifacts the Persians stole from Egypt. The priests thanked their

---

[16] Plutarch, "Moralia," *Isis and Osiris* (Loeb Classical Library, 1936), https://penelope.uchicago.edu/Thayer/e/roman/texts/plutarch/moralia/isis_and_osiris*/b.html.

pharaoh for importing grain to feed everyone when the Nile went nearly dry and famine struck. Most of the decree dealt with reforms among the priests, but it also added a leap day every four years to the 365-day year.

# What was the bicultural administration like?

The Ptolemies went to great lengths to respect the ancient Egyptian culture, of which the Egyptians were inordinately proud. The Egyptians liked to point out that they had an advanced civilization way back when the "barbarian" Greeks had still not learned how to rid their beards of lice. The Ptolemies knew that trying to force Greek culture on the Egyptians was hopeless. Instead, they pretended to be Egyptians:[17]

> "Given that the maintenance of order depended on the existence of a legitimate pharaoh, the Egyptians were obliged to recognize the prevailing ruler as their Horus-King, for as long as he could not be replaced by another king. Conversely, foreign rulers also had to assume the religious role of the pharaoh, if they were to secure their success ... the Ptolemies took particular care to act as culturally relevant kings and, thus, gain acceptance (whenever possible) as the central figure of Egyptian religion."[18]

When dealing with the Egyptians, the Ptolemies used the title pharaoh and dressed in Egyptian clothing.

In Alexandria, the Greeks called their rulers "basileus," which meant "monarch" in Greek. The Greeks had experimented with several styles of government since emerging from their Dark Ages. Athens had developed an early form of democracy. Sparta had two kings. Thebes had an oligarchy, or a council of aristocrats. Tyrants ruled Corinth for a few years. Macedonia had a traditional monarchy, the model the Ptolemies chose. A monarchy was also the system that Egypt had under their pharaohs until the Persians invaded.

Alexander the Great had rarely changed the existing systems in the conquered regions unless they weren't working. He usually kept what was already in place and tweaked it a bit. The Ptolemaic pharaohs did the same, mostly continuing the administrative system the Egyptians already

---

[17] Philip Matyszak, *Greece Against Rome: The Fall of the Hellenistic Kingdoms 250–31 BC* (Pen & Sword Military, 2020).

[18] Günther Hölbl, *A History of the Ptolemaic Empire*, trans. Tina Saavedra (Routledge, 2000), 1.

had in place. For instance, their marriage and property laws stayed the same.

The Egyptians followed Egyptian law, while the Greek citizens followed Greek law and had their own courts. However, the Greeks were at the top of the administrative ladder and had special rights and privileges.

Most people in Egypt had always been farmers. The government, temples, and nobility owned nearly all the land, and the farmers worked as serfs. This system stayed the same in the Ptolemaic kingdom, except now the aristocrats and government were the Greeks.

# How were Greek agricultural techniques blended with traditional Egyptian farming practices?

Ptolemy II and Ptolemy III rewarded their Macedonian military with land grants and established farm colonies for their Macedonian veterans. One large colony was Crocodilopolis (near today's Faiyum) in the lake region about eighty miles southwest of Memphis. It was named after the pet crocodile the local Egyptians worshiped and decorated with gold and gems. The Greeks also had garrisons around the country, with the surrounding land farmed by the Macedonian soldiers.

Egyptian farmer[27]

Egypt already had excellent farming techniques that took advantage of the annual Nile flooding. The Macedonians introduced some of their methods, and Egypt's agricultural production soared to new heights. For instance, in Crocodilopolis, the Greeks drained the swampland to use for fields. They built longer canal systems so farms could thrive further away from the Nile. The Ptolemies learned early on that the Nile sometimes didn't flood as it should, which devastated agricultural production and left the people starving. To offset this, the Ptolemaic rulers started stockpiling grain in the years of plenty to use during famines.

The Greeks brought new crops, like durum wheat, and increased sheep and goat herding for wool. The Egyptians liked drinking beer, but the Greeks preferred wine, so they introduced vineyards.

# Chapter 5: The Great Library of Alexandria

As Alexander the Great shared his vision for Alexandria, he wanted it to rival Athens. "You must build a library and dedicate it to the Muses!" The first three Ptolemies made Alexander's dream a reality. They created the world's most extensive collection of scrolls, an incredible intellectual legacy. The Library of Alexandria transformed the city into the ancient world's creative hub. It drew scholars and poets from the Greek, Jewish, Roman, and Syrian cultures.

## How was the library established?

As mentioned, the dream had started with Alexander, yet Ptolemy I and his immediate descendants put it into action. Ptolemy I built the "Museum" of Alexandria. In those days, a museum wasn't a collection of artifacts but a temple of the Muses—the nine Greek goddesses who inspired knowledge in the arts, literature, and science. The Alexandrian Museum was like a modern research university, where great minds came together to discuss the latest ideas and research.

Demetrius of Phalerum was a Greek philosopher and historian. For ten years, he was the governor of Athens under King Cassander of Macedon. Then, the political scene in Athens shifted. Forced into exile, Demetrius joined Ptolemy I in Egypt. The historian Strabo said that Demetrius created the museum, patterning it after Aristotle's school in Athens. The museum featured a covered walkway and a communal dining room. Most importantly, it had the library with thousands of carefully organized scrolls.

What the Great Library of Alexandria may have looked like[28]

No library in the ancient world came close to the Library of Alexandria's staggering collection. Its librarians zealously hunted down "every book in the world." One day, Ptolemy II met with his librarian, Demetrius of Phalerum.

"How many scrolls are in the library now?"

"Sire, we have more than two hundred thousand. I'm working day and night to reach my goal of a half million."

By Ptolemy III's reign, Callimachus, the librarian and poet, updated the count. "We now have four hundred thousand mixed scrolls and ninety thousand unmixed." A "mixed" scroll probably meant it contained a collection of works. An "unmixed" scroll was one book. They had almost achieved Demetrius's goal of a half-million scrolls.

Many classical works, including those of Homer, Plato, and Aristotle, were preserved, copied, and studied in Alexandria. These texts were later translated into Latin and Arabic, ensuring their survival through the Middle Ages.

## How did its vast collection of scrolls contribute to various fields of study?

Scholars gathered to read the scrolls, translate works into Greek, and discuss them with other mental giants. The library's scholars surged ahead in the sciences, math, philosophy, and literature. It was a society of savants making unprecedented strides. With their brilliant minds, the library's resources, and a cross-disciplinary approach, they made one breathtaking breakthrough after another.

The scholars and intellectuals clustered in Alexandria's library fostered a vibrant academic community. As "Fellows of the Museum," they got free housing and didn't have to pay taxes. Chapter nine dives into the legacy of these scholars, including Euclid and Eratosthenes, who made strides in geometry. The mathematician and engineer, Hero of Alexandria, taught at the Museum in the Roman era. The Alexandrian Pleiad was a group of poets and writers of Greek tragedy that clustered at the library. Among

Demetrius of Phalerum[29]

them were Alexander Aetolus, Homerus the Younger, Lycophron, Philiscus of Corcyra, and Sositheus of Alexandria.

# Who were some of the librarians?

The date for the library's founding is unclear, and sources disagree on who the first librarian was. Like Strabo, some say it was Demetrius of Phalerum, while others say it was Zenodotus of Ephesus. However, Zenodotus wasn't appointed the chief librarian until 284 BCE, a year before Ptolemy I died. Demetrius died in 280 BCE, so Demetrius and Zenodotus possibly served together for several years.

Zenodotus was an epic poet who edited Homer and organized and cataloged other poets. He divided Homer's poems into twenty-four books and gave lectures on Hesiod, Anacreon, and Pindar. His assistants were Alexander the Aetolian, who edited the Greek tragedies, and Lycophron, who worked with the comedies. Zenodotus assigned different literature genres to various rooms of the library and then organized them alphabetically. Each scroll had a small tag hanging from its end. It had the author's name and other information so the librarians could return it to the correct place. In addition to his librarian work, Zenodotus tutored Ptolemy II's children. Instructing the royal children became part of the job for future librarians.

Callimachus of Cyrene was a librarian during the reigns of Ptolemy II and III. However, no one mentioned he was the head librarian. Still, he did create a reference guide, something like a card catalog. Callimachus took Zenodotus's alphabetization to the next level by writing the *Pinakes*, a systematic list of the bibliographic information of every scroll in the library. The bibliographic information in the *Pinakes* filled 120 books. The shelves and bins holding the scrolls had tablets over them with their bibliographic information drawn from the *Pinakes.*

In addition to organizing the library, Callimachus was a prolific writer, producing over eight hundred poems, hymns, and works of prose. His favorite topic was the nature of beauty, as evidenced in his "Hymn to Apollo":

> "Begin, young men, begin the sacred song.
> Wake all your lyres, and to the dances throng,
> Rememb'ring still, the Pow'r is seen by none
> Except the just and innocent alone;
> Prepare your minds, and wash the spots away,
> That hinder men to view th' all-piercing ray,
> Lest ye provoke his fav'ring beams to bend
> On happier climes, and happier skies ascend"

Callimachus probably worked under Eratosthenes of Cyrene, who became the lead librarian toward the end of Ptolemy II's reign. Eratosthenes lived well into his eighties and continued as the librarian through the reigns of the subsequent three kings. He was a literary and scientific genius in multiple fields, including astronomy, math, geography, poetry, and music. He is best known for figuring out the earth's circumference. (Chapter nine digs into that.)

## What scripture translation went into the library?

The library included scriptures from many religions translated into Greek. However, one was missing. In the "Letter of Aristeas," written around 180 BCE, one of Ptolemy II's courtiers told how he visited the library with the king one day.

Demetrius, the librarian, spoke up. "Sire, I'm told that the laws of the Jews deserve a place in your library."

Ptolemy II frowned. "What's prevented you from doing this?"

"They need to be translated," answered Demetrius. "You see, their scriptures are written in their ancient Hebrew language. It's similar to the early Syrian script, but hardly anyone uses it today."

Ptolemy II nodded and sent a letter to Eleazer, the high priest in Jerusalem:

> "Greetings and salutations. Many Jews live in our realm of Egypt, who the Persians carried off from Jerusalem. My father brought thousands more into Egypt as soldiers with a high wage. Others came as enslaved people. I have freed more than one hundred thousand captives and made reparation. Thousands of Jews are now in my army and official positions. I want your sacred law translated from Hebrew to Greek and added to my library. Please select six elders from each tribe who are skilled in your law and interpretation. I am sending a hundred talents of silver as an offering for your temple and its sacrifices."[19]

---

[19] *The Letter of Aristeas to Philocrates*, trans. R. H. Charles (1913), https://www.attalus.org/translate/aristeas1.html.

Some scholars question the authenticity of the Letter of Aristeas. However, Aristobulus of Alexandria included part of the letter in his writings about eighty years later Philo of Alexandria also mentioned the letter.

Ptolemy II housed the Jewish scholars on the island of Pharos. They translated the Torah (the first five books of the Old Testament) into Greek, and it went into the Library of Alexandria. Hebrew scholars translated the rest of the Jewish Tanakh (Old Testament) over the next few decades. The Greek translation is called the Septuagint (The Translation of the Seventy) in honor of the Jewish scholars sent to Egypt to begin its translation. Based on language analysis, the Greek translation of the Torah took place in the third century BCE.

The Greek translation of the Tanakh served as a valuable tool for Judaism in Egypt and elsewhere.

Tens of thousands of Jews lived in the northeastern Jewish quarter of Alexandria, which took up about a fifth of the city then. Even the Jews in Judea were rapidly becoming Hellenized under Ptolemaic rule. Their languages were Koine Greek and Aramaic (a relic of the Babylonian captivity).

Before long, synagogues in Egypt, Judea, and the rest of the eastern Mediterranean were using the Greek Septuagint version. Jesus read from the Greek Septuagint in the synagogue at Nazareth (Luke 4:16-21). The apostle Peter quoted from the Greek Septuagint (Acts 2:17-21), as did most New Testament writers.

# Chapter 6: Ptolemaic Economy

Of all the Diadochi kingdoms, Egypt was the longest-lasting and, ultimately, the richest. Egypt's strategic position at the crossroads of major trade routes facilitated trade between Africa, Asia, and Europe. Egypt's grain was the gift of the Nile. The Ptolemies enhanced its production, so there was enough to feed Egypt plus export to Greece and Rome. The Ptolemaic Kingdom's stellar economic strategies grew and sustained its prosperity. The Ptolemaic kings used this wealth productively through financing infrastructure and promoting scholarly and cultural advances. They enhanced life for their people and built their influence in the ancient world.

## Egypt Starts Using Money

Before the Greeks arrived, Egypt's use of coins was spotty. Most of the time, they just traded one item for another. Since most Egyptians were farmers, they exchanged wheat or barley for other goods. They did have copper, gold, and silver for trade. However, they didn't mint it into coins. If they wanted to buy something, they weighed out the metal. During the two centuries before Ptolemaic rule, the Egyptians began minting coins that imitated coins from Athens. They used a gold stater coin to pay Greek mercenaries.

When the Persians conquered Egypt, they banned Greek-style coins in favor of Persian coins. However, most people continued using a barter system or weighing out precious metals. When Alexander the Great arrived, he quickly introduced coins. He had gold and silver drachma coins minted in Egypt, mainly used by the upper-class Egyptians and Greeks.

Most of the working-class Egyptians and Greeks still used a bartering system. However, they now had receipts written on potsherds in either Greek or Egyptian.

Ptolemy I was the first ruler to issue Egypt's own minted coins. Egypt's new money impacted how buying and selling happened. It also promoted the Ptolemaic royal family, whose faces were imprinted on the coins. Egypt had its own copper and gold mines for making coins, but silver had to be imported from Cyprus, Crete, or Persia. Instead of opting out of silver coins, Ptolemy I made them 20 percent smaller, so less silver was needed. As the later Ptolemaic kings faced economic crises, they reduced the amount of gold and silver used in coins even more.

A Ptolemy III gold drachma coin[30]

The Ptolemaic kings quickly banned the use of coins from other countries. Foreign trade conducted in Egypt had to use Egyptian money. Of course, as the kings began using smaller percentages of precious metals in their coins, they profited from exchanging money from countries that used standard amounts of gold and silver in coins.

Ptolemy IV reduced the weight of even the bronze coins. This hurt the working classes, who were paid with bronze coins. Ptolemy V redid the money system with bronze coins in varying amounts. In 53 BCE, Ptolemy XII reduced the silver content in drachma coins to only one-third to pay off his debt to Rome. The last Macedonian ruler, Cleopatra VII, reduced the silver in a drachma by more than half. Supposedly, the reason was for a direct exchange with the Roman denarius.

# How did the kingdom's strategic position facilitate trade?

Seas and rivers were the primary trade conduits in the world at that time. The Nile River was Egypt's internal highway. Goods arriving in ports along the Mediterranean Sea could be transported upstream the entire length of the country. If the Nile was swollen and flowing swiftly, sailors had to tow the ships upstream using pack animals or teams of workers from the bank. Fortunately, the prevailing winds usually blew south (and the Nile flows north), so they could sail upstream most of the time. Egypt also used the Nile for trade with Nubia to the south (in today's Sudan).

The Mediterranean was the connection to points near and far. If someone wanted to travel to other places in North Africa, like Libya or Carthage, they usually went by sea rather than risking getting lost in the desert or attacked by fierce Berber tribes. Over a thousand years earlier, the Greeks had established trade colonies around the Mediterranean. Socrates said they were "like frogs around a pond." Early Greek colonies extended as far west as Spain and France.

The Ptolemaic Kingdom sailed its merchant ships around the entire Mediterranean Sea. Ptolemaic coins have even been found in Britain, so the British must have been trade partners. Ptolemaic merchant ships also sailed around the Ionian, Aegean, and Black Seas.

Egypt had yet another water highway. At its eastern border was the Red Sea, which passed along Arabia's shores to the Arabian Sea. From there, ships sailed up the Persian Gulf to Mesopotamia and Persia or south to the Indian Ocean.

The Ptolemaic Kingdom easily accessed the Silk Road's water route from China. Most of East Asia's silk and spice trade did not go overland. Formidable high mountains and lethal deserts lay in the way, overrun with bandits. Typically, the Chinese merchants sailed from the South China Sea to the Indian Ocean and then up the Red Sea. Alternatively, they crossed over the Himalayas to India and then up the Persian Gulf.

Egypt's ships sailed to much of the eastern hemisphere. The trade possibilities were endless.

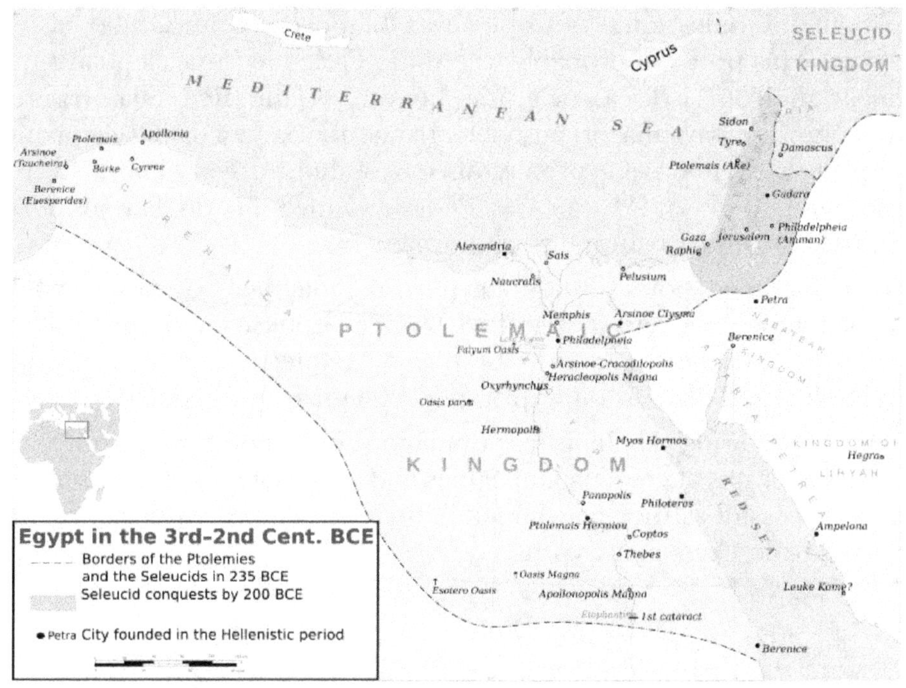


Ptolemaic Kingdom[31]

# How did Alexandria and other major ports enhance Egypt's economy?

Alexandria enabled the Ptolemies to expand their overseas influence. The Lighthouse of Alexandria beckoned incoming ships into its secure, double harbor. The harbor also connected the Mediterranean to the Nile.

The Ptolemaic kings multiplied the amount of trade that Egypt had always had. Alexandria was the primary hub, yet the Ptolemies built other new ports or took possession of ports already in existence. Pelusium continued as another Egyptian port on the Mediterranean. However, it began silting over after about a century of Ptolemaic rule. Ptolemy II founded the port of Berenice Troglodytica in southern Egypt, which grew into a prosperous hub on the Red Sea. Ships laden with frankincense crossed the Red Sea from Arabia. Other ships brought silver from the Near East and silk from China. A road with regular watering stations connected the Red Sea port with the port of Coptos on the Nile. Coptos was a strategic port because it was near the Red Sea, and the area was rich in gold and quartz.

About 150 miles south of Coptos was the port of Kom Ombo, also on the Nile. This port was probably where the Ptolemies' war elephants were brought in from Eritrea, near the bottom of the Red Sea. (Eritrean elephants were savanna or bush elephants, the largest living elephants.) The ports in southern Egypt were also a conduit for ivory and gold from central and southern Africa. The Ptolemy Kingdom was famous for its intricately carved ivory furniture and ornaments.

In addition to ports around Egypt, the Ptolemaic Kingdom had the port of Itanos on Crete. It also had ports at Ephesus and Samos in the Aegean Sea. Its ports along West Asia's Mediterranean coast included Nea Paphos and Salamis on Cyprus and Ptolemais in Phoenicia.

Egypt's growing Hellenistic population demanded fine wine. The people's attempts at growing grapevines and producing wine in Egypt were not as successful as they had hoped. Thus, they imported fine wines and ceramics from Crete and Cyprus.

Drawing of Ptolemy IV's Tessarakonteres ship, perhaps the world's largest in its day[32]

Under Ptolemy I, the Ptolemaic Kingdom morphed into the naval powerhouse of the eastern Mediterranean. It could protect its ports and sea highways from nefarious pirates and hostile nations. Naval bases dotting the Aegean and eastern Mediterranean protected the Ptolemaic maritime empire.

Egypt's navy attracted mercenaries from around the Greek world, as the Ptolemies had a reputation for paying the best wages for their navy. In his "Idyll 14," the Greek poet Theocritus mentions this when he writes about a man named Thyonichus meeting his friend Aeschines (paraphrased):

"I'm ill at ease," Aeschines complained.

"Well, that explains why you're thin, your mustache is unkept, and your curls are dry," Thyonichus observed.

"You can joke, but I've been suffering. I'm about to go stark mad."

"You've always been that way, my friend." Thyonichus was unsympathetic. "What's your grievance this time?"

"I was dining with my friends, Apis and Cleonicus, and serving my best wine from Byblos. When we were deep in our cups, we played a drinking game. We each had to name the woman we loved and then drain our cup. So, I named Cynisca. She was sitting right there! We've been together for two months. However, she said nothing! I named her as my true love, and she said nothing! Someone asked her if she'd seen a wolf, and she blushed and answered, 'Shrewdly guessed.' The man beside me whispered, 'A wolf *has* charmed her—the neighbor's tall, handsome son!' If only I could *un*love, Thyonichus! The only cure is to take to the seas. My friend Simus joined a mercenary crew, which cured him of his hopeless love. I, too, shall sail the seas!"

"Well, I hope your love life runs smoothly," Thyonichus said to comfort his friend. "Yet, if you really mean to hire yourself out for someone's navy, Ptolemy II is the best paymaster."

"What else is he?"

"A gentleman. He's witty and has good taste. He's very generous with his money. If you insist on wearing a military cloak and going to war, you should hire yourself to Egypt."[20]

Theocritus's story illustrates the mentality in the Greek world at that time. When a young man encountered seemingly insurmountable issues or wanted a better life, he would hire himself out to one of the Hellenistic armies or navies. The Ptolemaic military offered the best deal. In addition to competitive pay, the Ptolemies gave their military men land grants. They could farm their own land and support a family. Emigrating to Egypt was an attractive option for young men willing to become mercenary soldiers.

---

[20] Theocritus, "Idyll XIV" in *The Project Gutenberg EBook of Theocritus,* https://www.gutenberg.org/files/11533/11533-h/11533-h.htm#IDYLL_XIV.

# How was the Ptolemaic economic system organized?

Ptolemaic Egypt's economic chief was the *dioketes*, appointed by the king. He was in charge of establishing and maintaining financial policies. All the ministers of agriculture, finance, and record-keeping answered to him. Egypt had thirty-six provinces called *nomes*. Each nome had an administrator who handled things like currency, land management, and taxes.

The Ptolemaic economy maintained a delicate balance between the Greek monarchy and the Egyptians at the local level. The Greeks introduced agricultural innovations that benefited everyone. However, corruption reared its ugly head, with bureaucrats exploiting their position to enrich themselves. Many of the lower classes ended up in debt to the government because of unfair administrators. It got so bad that when a new Ptolemaic king came to the throne, he magnanimously forgave all debt owed to the Crown so that the victims of corruption could have a clean slate.

The Ptolemaic king owned between one-third to one-half of Egypt's agricultural land, and the temples owned a sizeable slice of the rest. Serfs farmed the land belonging to the Crown and the temples. However, Egypt did have private land ownership, both among the native Egyptians and the Greek military men who received land grants.

Egyptians harvesting papyrus[88]

# How did taxes work?

Taxes were the Ptolemaic monarchy's primary income. Usually, landowners paid taxes on their farmland with the grain, fruit, or vegetables they grew. Artisans paid taxes with a percentage of the pottery, fabric, or other goods they produced. The government also taxed each person, taking a regular census to get an accurate count. Each family head had to pay taxes for his wife, children, and any enslaved people.

The Greeks had lower taxes than the Egyptians and other ethnic groups. Greeks living in Alexandria had even lower taxes. Greek schoolteachers and the scholars at the Alexandrian Museum did not have to pay taxes at all. The lower classes of the Egyptians had a reduced tax rate. If farmers owned their land, they got a tax discount on the harvest if they paid for the planting with their own money.

The Ptolemies labeled all priests as "Hellenes," even if they were ethnically Egyptian, so they could get the tax break. The same held true for Egyptian soldiers serving in the Ptolemaic military. Even Egyptian actors and other artists got a tax break if they used their art to promote Hellenistic culture.

# What were the key economic activities?

Agriculture was the most significant economic venture. Greece lacked enough arable land to feed its population, so Egypt shipped grain there. Also, it increasingly supplied Rome's need for grain, especially in the Ptolemaic Kingdom's last century. Papyrus reeds were native to Egypt's wetlands, especially the Delta, and were used to make paper, which became another export. Egypt also shipped out luxury items like dyed cloth, jewelry, and artwork.

Egypt was well-known for manufacturing glassware. Egyptian faience was a vivid blue or green transparent glass used for jewelry or as a glaze on pottery. Items made with faience became a notable export.

A Ptolemaic-er falcon with faience glaze[34]

The Egyptians preferred wearing thin, comfortable linen, but the Greeks liked wool. Thus, the Ptolemies increased herds of sheep and goats to produce clothing, rugs, and tapestries. They were woven with brightly dyed wool into patterns reflecting an exciting fusion of Egyptian and Greek designs.

Egypt had always been a significant manufacturer of perfumes, cosmetics, and medicine. It had natural resources, like natron for soap and antiseptics and malachite for eye makeup.

# What were the economic policies of the early Ptolemies?

Ptolemy I avoided jumping into wars that wasted manpower and money without positive economic outcomes for Egypt. Instead, he invested his people and resources into building a better and stronger Egypt. When Ptolemy I inserted himself into the Wars of the Diadochi, his main objective was gaining control of the coastal regions of Syria, Phoenicia, and Judea, which had a two-pronged benefit. For one thing, they acted as a buffer zone for Egypt. A protected and secure Egypt was a more prosperous Egypt. Secondly, controlling West Asia's coast meant controlling its fantastically wealthy trade, giving Egypt the upper hand economically.

Ptolemy II's completion of the Lighthouse of Alexandria increased ship traffic into Alexandria, and his economic endeavors expanded tax revenue. J. G. Manning, a history professor at Yale University, believes Ptolemy II was the wealthiest person in the world in his day.[21]

Unfortunately, Ptolemaic Egypt could not sustain the peak of wealth it enjoyed in its first century. Climate change caused cooler weather some years, leading to less rainfall at the Nile sources. Decimated agricultural output meant Egypt had trouble feeding its people, much less shipping grain to Greece and Rome. The devaluation of coins created issues with international trade, and the cost of wars emptied the treasury. Nevertheless, despite all its woes and depleted wealth, Ptolemaic Egypt maintained one of the world's most significant economies until it fell to Rome.

---

[21] J. G. Manning, *Land and Power in Ptolemaic Egypt* (Cambridge University Press, 2007), 129.

# Chapter 7: The Ptolemaic Wars and Strategies for Survival

The cornerstone of the Ptolemaic state was its military. The army was the engine that drove the Ptolemies' expansion efforts, blended Greeks and Egyptians into one unit, defended Egypt from attack, and protected it from internal uprisings. "The Ptolemaic Army ... was at all times a military body structured for armed conflict, a colonizing and occupying presence mainly in Egypt, and a reflection and auxiliary of the monarchic project of the Ptolemies themselves."[22]

The Ptolemies' Hellenistic culture influenced them to establish a highly organized, disciplined, and well-equipped force. The Ptolemaic dynasty not only survived longer than the other Hellenistic kingdoms, but thrived. What strategies and conflicts defined the Ptolemaic Kingdom's efforts to maintain and expand power? How did their recruiting system and military innovations defend the kingdom? This chapter will look at these topics in more detail.

## Who served in the Ptolemaic military?

The soldiers serving in the Ptolemaic army, both Greek and Egyptian, were privileged people. They got tax breaks and free land, and the higher status of the military provided incentives to join.

---

[22] Paul A. Johstono, *The Army of Ptolemaic Egypt 323-204 BC: An Institutional and Operational History* (Pen & Sword Military, 2020).

Ancient Egypt did not always have a standing army. The farmers were also the infantry, so Egypt went to war when its people were not in the middle of planting or harvesting. However, the Ptolemaic royal army had permanent units that always stood ready to mobilize.

Mosaic of Ptolemaic Egypt's Greek soldiers[35]

The army included soldiers with a proud heritage, the descendants of the men who fought with Alexander the Great. It also included Greeks who immigrated to Egypt by the thousands. They saw Egypt as a bright, Hellenistic land full of opportunities. They were masters of Greek weaponry and the phalanx formation, which the Ptolemies continued using.

Beginning with Ptolemy II, native Egyptians flooded into the army. As we've mentioned, the Ptolemies carefully portrayed themselves not as conquerors but as a continuation of the ancient pharaohs. As one scholar writes, "The 'marriage' between army and temple, incorporating Greeks, Greco-Egyptians, and Egyptians, became one of the pillars of Ptolemaic power and survival in the latter part of the Hellenistic era."[23]

Some of the Ptolemaic army's professional, full-time soldiers were mercenaries from other countries who lived in Egypt year-round. If no wars were going on, they manned the forts and garrisons around the country, spending their time in training. The next and largest group were military settlers. They had farms and families but served in the military regularly in the off-season for agriculture. The government gave them land

---

[23] Hans Hauben, "Review of 'Army and Society in Ptolemaic Egypt: From Invasion to Integration,' by Christelle Fischer-Bovet," *The Bulletin of the American Society of Papyrologists* 53 (2016): 395–409, http://www.jstor.org/stable/44968458.

allotments called *klerouchoi* (cleruchs). The Egyptian soldiers got about ten acres, and the Greeks got fifteen. Allotments for cavalry riders (of any ethnicity) went up to fifty acres, and officers usually got more. The last group was foreign mercenaries who did not live in Egypt but signed on to fight in a specific war. They received a generous salary but no other benefits.

## How were new soldiers recruited?

The Ptolemaic kings had *xenologoi,* army recruiters who went abroad to enlist new soldiers, most of whom were volunteers. Most recruits were Greek, but the recruiters also hired soldiers from North Africa, Arabia, and Syria. Celtic-speaking tribes, including the Galatians, flooded into Macedonia, Thrace, and the Black Sea region in the Ptolemaic era. They were fierce fighters without particular allegiance to anyone, making them ideal mercenaries. Cavalry recruits mostly came from Anatolia, Judea, Persia, and Thrace.

Another source of recruits were prisoners of war, such as those brought by Ptolemy I into Egypt from Judea and Gaza. Despite not being voluntary soldiers, they still got plots of land.

## How was the military organized?

The king was the top military leader. After consulting with his generals and advisors, he decided when and where to go to war. He was expected to lead his men into battle and fight with them. Following the tradition of Alexander the Great, the king usually led the elite cavalry forces. He had the flexibility to move around the battlefield and direct cavalry or infantry to areas needing assistance.

Directly under the king were the generals, called *strategoi.* Some generals served as governors of the Ptolemaic provinces, which meant they were there if war broke out in the region. The infantry formed units of about one thousand men, called *chiliarchies,* led by a commander called a *hegemon.* The *máchimoi* were native Egyptian soldiers. The Greek historian Herodotus said they were a particular caste in Egypt (predating the Ptolemaic and Persian rule). Under Ptolemaic rule, they served as guards, police, and military.

**An Egyptian máchimos**[36]

The cavalry formed units of around five hundred horseback riders called *hipparchies*. The cavalry unit commander was a *hipparch* with a status similar to a hegemon. The Ptolemaic army had elite units, such as the *agema*, with three thousand cavalry and *hypaspist* infantry. The hypaspist infantry were a legacy of Alexander the Great and his father, Philip II. They were chosen from the working class for their determination, ability, and fast movement. Their armor and weaponry were lightweight, giving them speed and agility for lightning-fast strikes or fighting on rough terrain.

Another elite unit was the royal guard surrounding the king. Among them were his bodyguards, who were also his military advisors. The royal guard had seven hundred heavy cavalry stationed in Alexandria when not at war. Heavy cavalry used large warhorses with body armor, like breastplates. The riders carried heavy swords, lances, and battle axes. The heavy cavalry typically engaged in shock charges, mowing down the opponents and smashing them with the heavy weaponry.

The Ptolemaic kings were proud of their herd of war elephants, meant to shock and awe. However, the African breed they used did not work out well in battle, as discussed later in the chapter. Eventually, they gave up on using elephants in war.

# What about the navy?

Ptolemy I focused on building an exceptional navy while the other Diadochi fought over Greece, Macedonia, and Asia. The two primary naval bases were at Cyprus and Alexandria. Ptolemy commanded his navy in person and initially was the dominant force in the eastern Mediterranean. In 306 BCE, disaster struck when he suffered a brutal loss off the coast of Salamis, Cyprus.

Ptolemy I had earlier taken control of Cyprus. He put his brother, Menelaus, in charge of the island. He used it as his base for attacking Antigonus I in Syria and Turkey. Antigonus sent his son Demetrius to neutralize Cyprus as a Ptolemaic operations center. Demetrius landed in Cyprus, marched overland, and met Menelaus in battle five miles out of Salamis. Menelaus lost the first clash, then hunkered down in Salamis while desperately messaging Ptolemy for help. He nervously waited as Demetrius began building deadly siege engines: massive battering rams, catapults, and a siege tower on wheels that was 150 feet high.

In a ferocious attack, Demetrius smashed part of Salamis's wall. However, Menelaus's men snuck out by night and burned Demetrius's siege engines, buying the city some time. Meanwhile, Ptolemy was sailing to his brother's rescue from Alexandria. He had 140 warships and 200 transport ships carrying 10,000 troops. Demetrius had at least 180 ships, which he had not yet used in his invasion. He had 15,000 soldiers and 500 cavalry surrounding Salamis.

Ptolemy I messaged Demetrius, "Leave Cyprus now!"

Demetrius replied, "I will leave if you remove your garrisons from Corinth and Sicyon in Greece."

Ptolemy snorted at this, then sailed around the island by night, hoping to launch a sneak attack offshore of Salamis, where his brother had sixty ships. Yet, Demetrius was one step ahead of him. Guessing what Ptolemy would do, he armed his ships with missile throwers and stationed them outside Salamis's harbor. At dawn, Ptolemy sailed in to see Demetrius's fleet floating between him and Salamis.

Demetrius left ten of his ships at the harbor's narrow entrance, blocking Menelaus from deploying his ships. He sailed the rest of his fleet out to meet Ptolemy. The two navies bore down on each other, using their battering rams to smash the enemy ships. Sometimes, the ram impaled the side of another vessel, holding the two boats together, and the men jumped aboard to fight hand-to-hand. Another trick was sailing just next to another ship, shearing off its oars and leaving it dead in the water. The two forces sent hails of arrows and javelins at their opponents. They flung rocks with their *ballistae*, catapults with levers powered by torsion springs.

Ballista[37]

Ptolemy's men were able to board Demetrius's ship, killing or severely wounding his bodyguards. Nevertheless, Demetrius fought like a tiger, throwing missiles and spearing anyone who got close. Projectiles hit him, but his armor protected him. Demetrius and his men finally forced Ptolemy's troops off the ship. The sea battle raged on as Demetrius shattered the right wing of Ptolemy's navy. From his position on the left wing, Ptolemy saw a horrifying sight. His ships on the far right were sinking, and his vessels in the middle were sailing away from the battle. Ptolemy had no choice but to swing around and follow the rest of his ships in flight.[24]

---

[24] Diodorus, *Library of History*, Volume X.

It took Ptolemy I ten years to rebuild his navy and retake Cyprus. Ptolemy II fought and lost several battles in the Aegean Sea. Eventually, military activities shifted from sea battles to land battles in Syria and Egypt. The navy had become defunct by the beginning of Ptolemy V's reign.

# Why was Antigonus's attempt to annex Egypt an abject failure?

Inspired by Demetrius's naval victory, his father, Antigonus I, decided he could take Egypt with a dual assault by land and sea. In the winter of 306 BCE, Antigonus marched on Egypt while Demetrius sailed his navy to Alexandria. In this attack, Ptolemy discovered a new advantage of having Alexandria in the Nile Delta as his capital. The Delta was swampland with several branches of the Nile barring the way from an army arriving from West Asia. It was too boggy for Antigonus's land army, not to mention the logistics of crossing multiple rivers.

Getting provisions for the land army was a nightmare. Antigonus had depended on Demetrius to deliver supplies by sea. However, storms kept Demetrius from arriving at the expected time. When his navy finally arrived at Alexandria, Demetrius faced unexpected resistance. Ptolemy held him off, thanks to his harbor design. Meanwhile, Antigonus's army was starving and had to abandon the expedition as Demetrius sailed away from Africa's coast.

## Alexandria's Ingenious Harbor

Alexandria's primary harbor was the island of Pharos. The secondary harbor was the peninsula jutting out from the mainland to the east of Pharos, where the palace was. Ships also moored in the freshwater Lake Mareotis just south of Alexandria's walls, which connected to the Nile via canals. Alexandria's challenge with ship traffic was offshore waves and wind that abruptly changed directions. If the waves or wind from the east were too disruptive, the ships could move to the secondary harbor, where the peninsula protected them, or to Lake Mareotis.

The Heptastadion causeway from the city to Pharos Island enabled foot and cart traffic from the harbor to the city. It also offered protection from wind and waves from the west. When designing the Heptastadion, Dinocrates ingeniously placed several canals through which ships could pass. If Alexandria was under attack by sea, it enabled the vessels in the harbor to move around to safety. It also meant that the military could post catapults and archers on Pharos and the causeways, launching missiles at attacking ships and preventing access to the mainland.

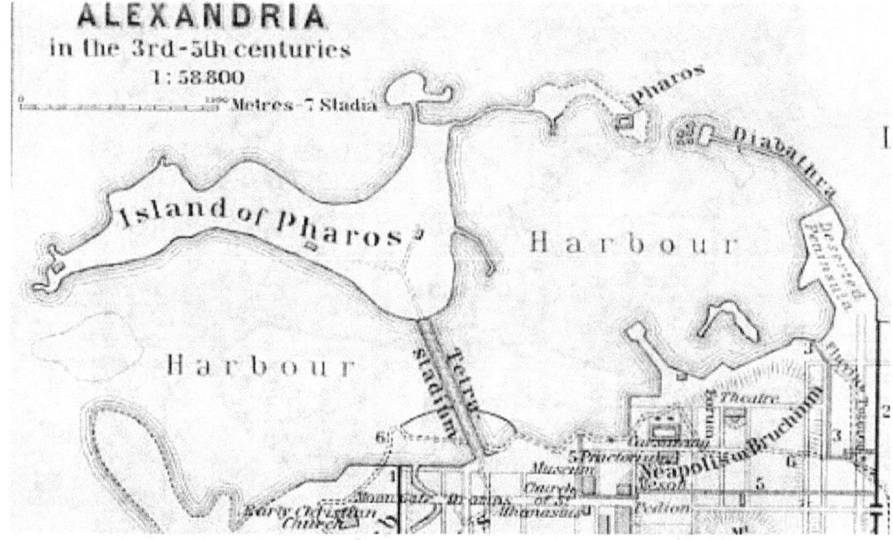

Alexandria's Harbor[38]

# The Great Battle of Rafia on the Border of the Sinai and Gaza Strip

In 217 BCE, one of history's most extensive land battles raged between the Sinai Desert and Gaza. It was the final clash of the Fourth Syrian War. Ptolemy IV had about seventy-five thousand men, and Antiochus III had nearly as many. Their troops faced off, with the front lines extending for miles. The Greek general Polybius wrote a detailed account of the great clash between the Titans. His report opens a window into the Ptolemaic army's organization, command units, divisions, and battle tactics.

Ptolemy IV commanded his left wing, which had Egypt's elite forces. Seven hundred of his three thousand cavalry were his highly trained palace guards, and the rest were Libyan and Egyptian horseback riders. Forty African war elephants bellowed and stomped as they waited for the battle to begin. He had three thousand light infantry from Crete and five thousand infantrymen. Of these, two thousand were Thracian *peltastai*, skirmishers who carried crescent-shaped shields, javelins, and swords. The rest were the *agema*, the royal squadron that surrounded the king.

A peltast infantryman with his crescent shield[89]

On the right wing of Ptolemy IV's army were six thousand more foot soldiers from Galatia and Thrace, thirty-three more war elephants, two thousand Greek cavalry, and more mercenaries. The regular infantry lined up in a phalanx position in the center of the Ptolemaic army. It numbered twenty thousand Egyptians, eight thousand Greek mercenaries, twenty-five thousand Macedonians, and three thousand Libyans. The Greeks developed the rigid discipline of the phalanx position, with the foot soldiers forming rows where they stood shoulder to shoulder. Their shields overlapped slightly, and long spears extended from the front row. The soldiers behind the first row held their shields over their heads, forming a ceiling of shields. The arrows shot by the enemy simply bounced off. If an infantryman on the front line fell, the man behind him stepped into his place.

The phalanx had been the core of Alexander's army, and the Ptolemies continued the tradition. The Macedonian phalanx usually had sixteen soldiers in a row, yet it was flexible. Depending on the terrain or how the opposing army lined up, it could have as few as eight in a row or up to thirty-two. The shorter lines worked well for quick mobility if the phalanx had to move to the side quickly in situations like an elephant or scythed chariot charging them.

As mentioned earlier, Ptolemy IV was guilty of ignoring matters in Egypt while indulging his every whim. He had left his corrupt advisors, Sosibius and Agathocles, to deal with the government. The Seleucid king, Antiochus III, took advantage of Ptolemy's inattention to invade Syria and Phoenicia. Egypt's naval commander, Theodotus, defected to Antiochus, bringing part of Ptolemy's navy with him. Ptolemy IV had not been recruiting new soldiers or properly equipping his army. They were in no shape to fight the Seleucids.

Ptolemy IV had no idea what to do, but his advisors rose to the occasion. Sosibius reached out to Antiochus, who agreed to a temporary ceasefire. They convinced Antiochus that Ptolemy had no interest in fighting and wanted to discuss peace terms, using nearby governors as intermediaries. While the negotiators traveled back and forth from Egypt to Syria for months, the Ptolemaic Kingdom briskly prepared for war. It sent out recruiters for Greek mercenaries, stockpiled supplies, and trained its men. The recruiting efforts went splendidly, bringing in nearly twenty thousand soldiers from abroad.

The kingdom also recruited two stellar leaders. Polycrates of Argos, the governor of Cyprus, drilled the troops, pumping them full of enthusiasm. In the Battle of Raphia, he rode with Ptolemy IV in the left wing, commanding the cavalry. Andromachus of Aspendus drilled the infantry in the phalanx maneuvers and led them into battle.

Meanwhile, Antiochus III continued in his delusion that Egypt did not want war. Winter was approaching, so he left Syria for his winter quarters in Seleucia. He did not even bother to drill his troops during the winter months. Negotiations for a settlement dragged on through the winter while Ptolemy's crew whipped his army into shape.

When spring arrived, it finally dawned on Antiochus that Ptolemy IV intended to take Syria back. He heard that Ptolemy had rallied his men at Alexandria and was marching toward Gaza. Ptolemy and his sister-wife, Arsinoe III, rode their horses along their front lines, calling the troops to arms. Ptolemy IV had no glorious achievements of his own to fire up the troops, so he tried to inspire them with what their ancestors had done. He also promised extraordinary rewards if Egypt won the battle.

Meanwhile, Antiochus rallied his troops and marched south. He also had his Macedonian-style phalanx in the center with mercenaries from Greece and Crete. He had sixty elephants on his right wing, directly across from Ptolemy IV's elephants. Behind the elephants and angling off were four thousand cavalry. He had another two thousand cavalry on his left wing, with javelin throwers, three thousand light infantry, and the rest of his elephants. His Arab troops were between the cavalry and the phalanx.

War elephants[40]

The two armies collided at Raphia, at the border of Gaza. The battle began with an elephant charge from both sides, which was cringeworthy for Ptolemy IV. Most of his elephants refused to fight. The remaining elephants crashed into the opposing elephants' foreheads, locking tusks. It was then a battle of strength, with each massive creature trying to wrestle the other to the ground or turn them around. If one elephant could swipe another's trunk so it turned around, the stronger elephant would gore the other in the rear end. Each elephant had a tower on its back where men with spears rode. As the elephants wrestled, the spearmen tried to impale the enemy spearmen on the other elephants.

The problem for Ptolemy IV was that he had African elephants. They were bigger and more aggressive than the Indian elephants used by Antiochus. However, they could not stand the smell of the Indian elephants, which is why most of them turned and rushed off the battleground. While this fiasco played out, the Seleucid cavalry charged the Ptolemaic cavalry led by Polycrates. On the other end of the line, the elephants threw Ptolemy's Thracian infantry into disarray. Ptolemy's entire left wing was in retreat.

However, Echecrates, a commander in Ptolemy IV's right wing, saw the left wing falling apart. He ordered the Greek mercenaries to attack the enemy on their left wing. At the same time, he led the cavalry in a charge, flanked the enemy elephants, and chased off the enemy cavalry.

Ptolemy IV's phalanx stood nervously in the middle, uncertain what to do. Suddenly, Ptolemy raced just ahead of their front lines, leading them in a charge. They lowered their spears, and the opposing infantry fled the field.

Meanwhile, Antiochus thought he had won the day after his elephants crashed through Ptolemy's troops. He was chasing down a few stragglers when he realized most of his army was racing off the battlefield, with Ptolemy's men in hot pursuit.

Night was falling, so both sides retreated to their camps. The next morning, they buried their dead. At first, Antiochus planned to face off for battle again. He did not realize how dreadful things were. Most of Antiochus's surviving men had hidden in Gaza, so he had to round them up. When he began burying his men, he discovered he had lost 13,000. Ptolemy IV had captured another 4,000. Ptolemy lost 2,200 men and most of his elephants.

Antiochus offered the rites of honor over his dead soldiers, then rounded up the living ones and returned to Seleucia. Ptolemy IV took back Gaza, Syria, and Phoenicia. His victory astonished his citizens, who were unaccustomed to their king accomplishing anything.[25] The momentous battle temporarily arrested the Ptolemaic Kingdom's downward spiral.

Polybius believed that when the native Egyptians mobilized en masse at the Battle of Raphia, it awakened them to a new reality. They now held sway! Before Raphia, the Egyptians only comprised a fraction of the Ptolemaic military. Now, they played a vital role. This self-awareness simmered for about a decade as they considered what they could do with their newly realized power.

Beginning with Ptolemy V, internal struggle derailed Egypt's military operations outside the country. The royal family spent more time fighting each other than fighting outside threats like Rome, and uprisings and civil war rocked the kingdom.

---

[25] Polybius, *The Histories* (Loeb Classical Library Edition, 1923), Book V, https://penelope.uchicago.edu/Thaer/E/Roman/Texts/Polybius/5*.html.

# Chapter 8: Decline and Fall of Ptolemaic Rule

What led to the weakening and eventual collapse of the Ptolemaic Kingdom? It involved internal issues like civil wars and the treasury going bankrupt. External threats, like Egypt's conflict with rival Hellenistic states, led Rome to insert itself. However, the ultimate death blow came from a string of weak rulers and the loss of centralized control. This chapter unwraps how it all played out.

## The Rising Threat of Rome

When Ptolemy I became Egypt's king, Rome was a modest republic ruling central Italy. However, during Ptolemy II's reign, Rome began attacking the ancient Greek colonies in southern Italy. King Pyrrhus of Epirus (northwestern Greece) sailed to the rescue. Ptolemy sent twenty war elephants to help drive the Romans out of southern Italy. Pyrrhus initially won two costly "Pyrrhic" victories. Nevertheless, he lost the war, and Rome took southern Italy. Oddly, Ptolemy II sent an embassy to Rome two years later with gifts, pledging friendship.[26]

---

[26] Mary Siani-Davies, "Ptolemy XII Auletes and the Romans," *Historia: Zeitschrift Für Alte Geschichte* 46, no. 3 (1997): 308. http://www.jstor.org/stable/4436474.

It was not long before Rome launched its first offshore war in Sicily, which meant it had to build a navy. Despite never before fighting at sea, Rome trounced Carthage in the world's largest naval battle. Rome won Sicily in 241 BCE, during Ptolemy III's reign. Rome continued its empire building in Ptolemy IV's reign, capturing Spain and destroying Carthage in North Africa. The legendary sea empire had to give up its navy and pay tribute to Rome.

When Ptolemy V was ruling Egypt, Rome began attacking Greece and Macedonia.

Ptolemy VI Phlometor[41]

Inconceivably, the Ptolemaic leaders seemed oblivious to the threat Rome presented. It never seemed to dawn on them that Rome might one day attack Egypt. Instead, the Ptolemaic royal family regarded Rome as the playground nanny. They ran to the Roman Senate with their dynastic disputes, asking for arbitration. In so doing, they ultimately gave Rome a foothold.

## A Tale of Two Brothers: Ptolemy VI Philometor and Ptolemy VIII Physcon

When Ptolemy V dropped dead at age thirty, his oldest son by his queen and co-ruler, Cleopatra Syra ("the Syrian," daughter of Antiochus III the Great, ruler of the Seleucid Empire), was Ptolemy VI Philometor. He was only six years old. Ptolemy VI ascended the throne in 180 BCE, with his mother as his regent.

Cleopatra Syra became the first queen of the Ptolemaic Kingdom to rule when her husband was not living. Ptolemy V had been preparing to invade the Seleucid Empire, but his death cut those plans short. Cleopatra's first act as queen regent was to call off the war against her homeland. She did not want to fight her brother, Seleucus IV, now the ruler of the Seleucid Empire. Three years later, Cleopatra suddenly died.

"She was young!" people whispered. "Not even thirty yet."

"Do you think she was poisoned?" others wondered.

"Who will be the boy king's regent now?"

"She named Lenaeus and the eunuch Eulaeus as co-regents on her deathbed."

"Who are they?"

"Nobody! They're not Greek—they're barbarians.[27] Both were slaves. They came with Cleopatra Syra to Egypt. Eulaeus is Ptolemy VI's tutor."

"They must be the only ones she trusted."

Eulaeus and Lenaeus knew they had to declare Ptolemy VI an adult quickly. Otherwise, Rome would insert itself into Egyptian politics. Ptolemy VI celebrated his *anaklētēria* or coming-of-age ceremony in 172 BCE when he was fourteen. Two years later, he married his sister, Cleopatra II, making her his co-ruler. Eulaeus and Lenaeus still ran things as advisors.

By this time, Ptolemy VI's uncle, Antiochus IV Epiphanes, had seized the Seleucid throne at his brother's death. Eccentric and unhinged, he refused Ptolemy VI's demand to return Coele-Syria to Egypt. Coele-Syria, which included Judea, was Cleopatra Syra's dowry when she married Ptolemy V. Eulaeus and Lenaeus sent an army to Syria. However, before it reached Gaza, Antiochus Epiphanes charged south and crushed the army in the Sinai Desert.

Antiochus crossed the Sinai and marched into Egypt, capturing Pelusium and then Memphis. This was the first foreign invasion of Egypt since Antigonus I's failed attempt over a century earlier. Ptolemy VI tried to sail out of Alexandria to safety, but his uncle Antiochus captured him, taking him prisoner.

Antiochus Epiphanes had himself crowned king by Egypt's priests. He loved play-acting and was well-known for strange and unconventional behavior. This "crowning" seems to have been an absurd joke, not to be taken seriously.

The Greeks in Alexandria tired of rule by foreign regents while Antiochus held their king captive. They staged a revolt in 170 BCE, overthrowing Eulaeus and Lenaeus. Since Ptolemy VI was still his uncle's

---

[27] For the ancient Greeks, the word βάρβαροι (barbaroi) meant "babbler," or people who spoke a language that was not Greek. It was a catch-all label for non-Greek people.

prisoner in Memphis, they made his younger brother, Ptolemy VIII, the next king. His nickname was "Physcon," or "fatty." Why did they jump from Ptolemy VI to Ptolemy VIII? Who was Ptolemy VII, and what happened to him? He was apparently a son of Ptolemy VI who may have briefly ruled (as a small child) before being murdered by his uncle, Ptolemy VIII Physcon.

Ptolemy VIII was only fourteen when he took his older brother's place in Alexandria. Antiochus Epiphanes still held Memphis and the eastern Delta for another year. However, he returned to Syria in 169 BCE, leaving Ptolemy VI as king of Memphis. Egypt was divided between two brothers. However, their sister, Cleopatra II (Ptolemy VI's wife), negotiated an agreement where all three would rule together.

Ptolemy VI and Cleopatra II[42]

This plan enraged Antiochus Epiphanes, who wanted Egypt divided and weak. He invaded Egypt again, stopping off in Jerusalem on his way. Antiochus had been imposing Hellenistic culture and religion on the Seleucid Empire. His predecessors promoted Greek ways while respecting the culture and religion of their conquered people. Yet, Antiochus Epiphanes harbored nothing but disrespect for the Jews. They had adopted some Hellenistic ways, but they insisted on worshiping their one god and no one else. Antiochus appointed a Hellenistic Jew named Menelaus as Jerusalem's new high priest. Menelaus was willing to syncretize Judaism with the Greek gods. Antiochus helped himself to the temple treasure to pay for his war and headed to Egypt in 168 BCE.

Antiochus Epiphanes retook Memphis, and his next target was Alexandria. At this point, Rome got involved, pretending to be a negotiator. Their motive was to prevent the spread of the Seleucid Empire. As Antiochus Epiphanes approached Alexandria, the Roman proconsul, Popillius, intercepted him:

"I have orders from the Roman Senate. Leave Egypt at once or face war with Rome."

Antiochus stared in stunned shock as the elderly envoy drew a circle around him in the sand. "Stay there in that circle until you give me an answer for the Senate!"

Trembling in humiliation and rage, Antiochus left Egypt. He had to go through Judea on his way back to Syria. His fury knew no bounds when he found out that the Jews had reinstalled their former priest in the temple. Antiochus Epiphanes launched a three-day killing spree, massacring forty thousand Jews, including women and children. He outlawed Judaism, put Zeus's statue in the Jewish temple, and slaughtered a pig on its altar. These outrages spawned the Maccabean Revolt, in which the Jews won independence from the Seleucid Empire. Their new state provided a buffer zone between Egypt and Syria.

For the next five years, Ptolemy VI and VIII ruled with their sister, Cleopatra II. Ptolemy VI Philometor was gentle and accommodating, happy to coexist with his younger brother. Yet, Ptolemy VIII Physcon's unbridled ambition got in the way. His friend, Dionysius Petosarapis, convinced him to launch a mob on Philometor's palace to kill him. The plot fell through, and Philometor gave Physcon the option to abdicate.

Ptolemy VIII Physcon[48]

Physcon tried to convince his older brother of his innocence. "My brother! I knew nothing about this uprising. I swear!"

Philometor believed him, and the two appeared together before the people on the palace portico.

Dionysius realized he needed to get out of town fast. He swam naked across the Nile and hid among the native Egyptians, plotting a renewed revolt. In 164 BCE, the rebels forced Ptolemy VI Philometor to flee to Rome, ending the five years of double kingship.

When Philometor presented his case to the Roman Senate (still masquerading as arbitrators), it played right into their hands. Just like Antiochus Epiphanes, they wanted a divided and weaker Egypt. They proposed dividing the Ptolemaic Kingdom. Ptolemy VI Philometor would get Egypt and Cyprus, and Ptolemy VIII Physcon would get Cyrene. Philometor sailed to Cyprus to await Rome's negotiations with his brother. However, in Philometor's absence from Egypt, Physcon became a ferocious tyrant, inciting an uproar. If the Romans had not intervened, Egypt's people would have torn Physcon limb from limb. They begged Philometor to return, which he did, as Physcon sailed off to Cyrene in 163 BCE.

For the rest of his life, Ptolemy VI Philometor and his queen, Cleopatra II, were Egypt's only rulers. However, Ptolemy VIII Physcon was still stirring up trouble. He visited Rome and complained to the Senate: "It isn't fair! You gave Egypt *and* Cyprus to Philometor. All I got was Cyrene."

The Senate agreed that Physcon should also have Cyprus. When the Roman envoys traveled to Egypt to convince Philometor to concede Cyprus, he refused. Rome let the matter drop, and Cyprus remained in Philometor's hands.

In 146 BCE, Ptolemy VI invaded Syria. The Jews allowed his army to pass through Judea on his way. Ptolemy VI conquered all the coastal cities belonging to the Seleucid Empire, and the leaders of Antioch crowned him Asia's king. However, Ptolemy VI worried that Rome would interfere if he snatched the entire Seleucid Empire. He kept Syria, once part of the Ptolemaic Kingdom. Shortly before returning to Egypt, he fell from his horse, fracturing his skull, and died five days later.

Ptolemy VI's teenage son had recently died, and his only other son was seven. The door was open for Ptolemy VIII to take back Egypt. He had maintained friendly relations with the Roman Senate. Confident they had his back, he sailed to Egypt in 145 BCE. He married his sister and Ptolemy VI's widow, Cleopatra II. She gave birth to their only child, Ptolemy Memphites, in 143 BCE. Ptolemy VIII viciously purged everyone who had supported Ptolemy VI over him.

While still married to Cleopatra II, he married her daughter by Ptolemy VI, Cleopatra III. An infuriated Cleopatra II initiated an uprising. After the Alexandrians set fire to the palace, Ptolemy VIII escaped to Cyprus with Cleopatra III. A native Egyptian named Harsiesi took advantage of the chaos to generate a rebellion in southern Egypt and take control. Eventually, Ptolemy VIII and Cleopatra III returned to Egypt with their children and settled in Memphis in 130 BCE. His forces were able to kill Harsiesi and reunite Egypt.

Ptolemy VIII killed Memphites, his son by Cleopatra II, chopped him up, and sent the body parts to the boy's mother on her birthday. Cleopatra II grabbed the royal treasury and sailed to Syria, where Demetrius II was ruler of the Seleucid Empire. His wife was her daughter, Cleopatra Thea. However, inexplicably, Cleopatra II returned to Egypt and reconciled with her second husband and brother in 124 BCE. They co-ruled until Ptolemy VIII died in 116 BCE.

Ptolemy IX[44]

# Ptolemy IX Soter and Ptolemy X Alexander I Continue the Messy Family Politics (116-81 BCE)

When Ptolemy VIII died, his son, Ptolemy IX Soter, became king. He co-ruled with his grandmother, Cleopatra II, and his mother, Cleopatra III. Cleopatra II died the following year after sixty years as Egypt's queen. Before becoming king, Ptolemy IX had married his full sister, Cleopatra IV, and they had two children together. However, after Cleopatra II died and Cleopatra III gained more power, she forced her son to divorce Cleopatra IV. Apparently, the mother and daughter had fallen out. She had Ptolemy IX marry his other sister, Cleopatra Selene.

Ptolemy IX followed his mother's orders, but tensions grew between mother and son. Cleopatra IV sailed to Cyprus, where her younger brother, Ptolemy X, was governor. She married her cousin, Antiochus IX, ruler of the Seleucid Empire. In Egypt, Ptolemy IX and Cleopatra Selene had a daughter named Berenice III in 114 BCE.

Finally, the unpredictable Cleopatra III ejected Ptolemy IX from Egypt in 107 BCE, forcing him to divorce Cleopatra Selene. Cleopatra III made her younger son, Ptolemy X, the next king and had him marry Cleopatra Selene. In exile, Ptolemy IX took control of Cyprus.

Ptolemy X and his mother allied with Antiochus VIII Grypus, son of Cleopatra Thea and Demetrius II. Grypus was fighting his half-brother, Antiochus IX Cyzicenus, for control of the Seleucid Empire. Cleopatra III forced Ptolemy X and Cleopatra Selene to divorce as part of the deal. Why? Cleopatra Selene now had to marry her third husband, her cousin Antiochus VIII. By 101 BCE, Ptolemy X's anger finally boiled over at his mother's mechanisms, and he arranged her murder.

# Berenice III, a Strong-Willed and Beloved Queen (101–88, 81–80 BCE)

After killing his mother, Ptolemy X married his thirteen-year-old niece, Berenice, the daughter of his brother, Ptolemy IX, and sister, Cleopatra Selene. Berenice became his co-ruler. By this time, he was a hopeless drunk and so fat he could not walk without his servants holding him up. Ptolemy X had to deal with the uprisings of native Egyptians in 91 BCE. They took control of Thebes and cut off Ptolemy X's interactions with Nubia.

**Berenice III**[45]

The citizens of Alexandria became increasingly dissatisfied with Ptolemy X's botched attempts at running the country. His army staged a coup, forcing him and Berenice out of Egypt in 88 BCE. They then recalled Ptolemy IX to be their king again. Ptolemy X raised a mercenary army in Syria and got his throne back. However, needing money to pay his soldiers, he raided Alexander the Great's tomb and melted down his gold coffin. The Greeks were appalled at this dreadful sacrilege. His scandalized subjects drove Ptolemy X out of the country again, and he died in a naval battle off Cyprus.

Now a widow, Berenice returned to Egypt, where her father, Ptolemy IX, was king again. He made Berenice his co-regent, and some sources say he married her. His death a few months later left Berenice as Egypt's first female ruler without being the wife or mother of a king. Her subjects thought she was a model queen. She properly worshiped the Greek and Egyptian gods, was unpretentious, and respected the growing Jewish population (now about 25 percent of Alexandria's population).

Her subjects loved Berenice but felt she should be married. Berenice knew she needed to stabilize her shaky throne, but who would she marry? The Roman dictator Sulla suggested that she marry Ptolemy XI Alexander. He was Berenice's half-brother, as Cleopatra Serene was their mother. His father was Ptolemy X, so Berenice had also been his stepmother. Ptolemy XI was the only living legitimate male of the Ptolemaic family.

The marriage lasted only nineteen days. Ptolemy XI murdered Berenice, perhaps angry that she did not make him the full king of the Ptolemaic Kingdom. The horrified Alexandrians chased him into the gymnasium and killed him, leaving Egypt with no ruler.

# Ptolemy XII Auletes, the Illegitimate Son (80–58, 55–51 BCE)

The Ptolemy family had run out of legitimate offspring. Who would become the next ruler? Ptolemy XII Auletes, Ptolemy IX's son by a non-royal mother, became king. He married his relative, Cleopatra V, making her co-regent. They had five children, but their second-oldest daughter, Cleopatra VII, was the famous Cleopatra who got involved in sultry affairs with Julius Caesar and Mark Antony.

Ptolemy XII immediately faced multiple challenges. Egypt was plunging into decline, and its relations with Rome were precarious. In 75 BCE, Rome grabbed Cyrene, a major grain producer, which had been part of the Ptolemaic Kingdom since its first king. Rome was careful about seizing new provinces. It did not usually annex new lands without the assurance that political consequences, if any, would be minimal. They were right. Ptolemy XII let the province go. He was in no position to fight Rome.

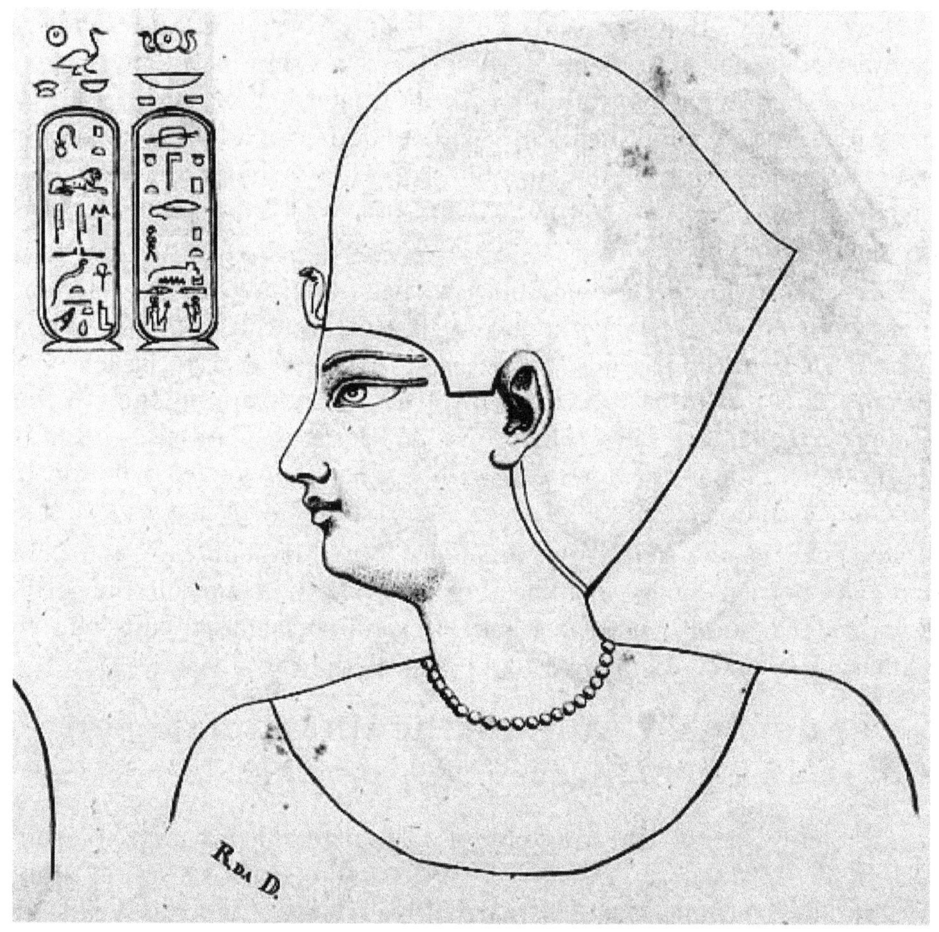

**Ptolemy XII**[46]

In 65 BCE, the Roman censor Crassus recommended annexing Egypt itself. "When Ptolemy X died, he left Egypt to Rome in his will!"

Julius Caesar, a rising political star, supported Crassus.

Nevertheless, the senators shot it down: "Crassus! You know it was only valid if he had no surviving sons. Ptolemy XI Alexander was his son! Furthermore, no one here in Rome has ever seen that will. It's probably just a rumor. At any rate, trying to take Egypt at this point is too risky. "

Nevertheless, Ptolemy XII began bribing the Roman senators to ensure their vote against attacking Egypt. Meanwhile, General Pompey had been sweeping through Anatolia and Syria, making them part of Rome's empire. His next target was Judea. Ptolemy XII sent a gold crown to Pompey and paid for eight thousand cavalry to use in his war against his neighbor. He did not want to be Pompey's next target.

Pompey, Caesar, and Crassus formed the First Triumvirate, which got Caesar elected as Rome's consul. Ptolemy XII traveled to Rome to cement recognition from Rome of his kingship. He bribed Caesar and Pompey with six thousand talents (Egypt's annual revenue) and won the title *socius et amicus* (ally and friend) by the Senate's decree. Rome and Egypt made a formal alliance.

Most of Egypt disapproved of the bribery scheme. For one thing, it broke Egypt's bank, leading to crushing taxes. Secondly, it was embarrassing that Egypt was groveling before Rome. Even worse, the Romans ignored the alliance when they snatched Cyprus the following year. Even when Ptolemy XII's brother, the governor of Cyprus, committed suicide, Ptolemy XII did nothing.

The Alexandrians poured into the streets in protest, calling for Ptolemy XII's expulsion from Egypt. Even before the Cyprus debacle, the priesthood and military had grown to loathe Ptolemy XII. The king fled to Rome in 58 BCE, leaving most of his family behind. The Alexandrians placed his oldest daughter, Berenice IV, on the throne. Cleopatra IV, either another wife or daughter, ruled with her. His second daughter, Cleopatra VII, "the" Cleopatra, went with him to Rome.

Most senators turned their backs on Ptolemy XII in Rome despite him being an ally. However, Pompey took him and Cleopatra VII into his villa and interceded for him with the Senate. He finally persuaded the Senate to restore Ptolemy XII to the throne. Nevertheless, they had a peculiar problem. An ancient oracle said that if Rome got involved in attacking Egypt because an Egyptian pharaoh asked for help, disaster would come down on Rome.

In Egypt, Berenice IV continued ruling, but Cleopatra VI either died or withdrew from politics. Berenice's position was tenuous, as she had no husband, which the Alexandrians felt was improper. They found her a husband, Archelaus, from the house of Mithridates. However, he was only her husband, not co-ruler.

In Rome, Ptolemy XII borrowed money heavily to fund his restoration to Egypt. He paid ten thousand talents to Aulus Gabinius, a Roman general and proconsul of Syria, to attack Egypt. Since Archelaus's "pirate" fleets had allegedly been stealing grain shipments to Syria, the feeling was that now, war was justified. It was not so much about restoring the old king as removing the man behind the piracy.

Gabinius successfully attacked Egypt, killed Archelaus, and restored Ptolemy XII to the throne in 55 BCE. The twists and turns of politics sometimes meant that friends ended up fighting each other. Archelaus's friend, Mark Antony, led Gabinius's cavalry in the invasion yet gave Archelaus a proper burial.

The Alexandrians were still rioting, so Gabinius enslaved the ringleaders. Ptolemy XII wasted no time getting revenge on his enemies. He even killed his daughter, Berenice IV, who had ruled Egypt in his absence. He replaced the city's leaders with unsuitable and unrefined men.

Now, Ptolemy XII had a new problem. He had borrowed a fortune from Rome's creditors, and they wanted repayment. Emptying Egypt's treasury would not be enough. Ptolemy XII appointed Rabirius Postumus, a Roman banker, to be Egypt's new treasurer. Postumus confiscated the wealth of the Alexandrians who opposed Ptolemy XII to pay back the debt. Then, he imposed more taxes. This riled up the Alexandrians again, and Postumus fled to Rome.

Not everyone in Rome got their money back. When Julius Caesar sailed into Alexandria in 48 BCE, he presented an outstanding debt of 17,500,000 denarii, demanding the heirs of Ptolemy Aulete pay 10,000,000, possibly Caesar's share of the loan.[28]

Ptolemy XII died in 51 BCE. His will stated that his son Ptolemy XIII and his daughter Cleopatra VII should get married and be the next rulers. He sent a copy of his will to Rome, and it ended up in Pompey's hands. Rome was in the midst of a civil war, leaving Egypt to its own devices for the time being.

## Cleopatra VII and Ptolemy XIII Fight for Power

Ptolemy XIII and Cleopatra VII married immediately. The bride was eighteen, but the groom was only eleven. Cleopatra ruled in her own right, and the eunuch Pothinus acted as Ptolemy's regent. The couple's relationship quickly turned sour as each vied for total control. Cleopatra was getting the upper hand. Documents and coins only represented Cleopatra, not Ptolemy. By 48 BCE, a civil war erupted between brother and sister. Ptolemy was winning, so Cleopatra fled to Syria and recruited an army to fight her brother.

---

[28] Siani-Davies, "Ptolemy XII Auletes," 31.

At this point, Pompey arrived in Egypt. Once close friends and co-conspirators, Pompey and Julius Caesar had fallen out and were now bitter rivals. Caesar was chasing Pompey down, intent on becoming Rome's sole ruler. Ptolemy XIII welcomed Pompey to Egypt, feigning friendship. Nevertheless, he quickly ordered the great general's murder. Ptolemy thought he had a better chance of allying with Julius Caesar than Pompey. Caesar sailed into Egypt shortly after, and Ptolemy XIII greeted him with Pompey's head. It did not have the effect he'd hoped.

"Where's the rest of his body? Find it! Give him a proper Roman burial," Caesar barked. He wept at the funeral of his one-time friend, vowing to avenge his death.

Ptolemy XIII escaped, but Caesar killed the eunuch Pothinus and the two men who had stabbed Pompey. Caesar was now Rome's dictator, and Cleopatra VII, who had just arrived back in Egypt, wanted him on her side. She used her feminine wiles to make that happen. Caesar and Cleopatra became lovers and joined their armies against Ptolemy XIII.

From December 48 to February 47 BCE, the two forces clashed. Sadly, the Library of Alexandria caught fire in the fighting. Caesar and Cleopatra won, and while escaping, Ptolemy drowned in the Nile. Caesar placed Cleopatra back on Egypt's throne with her younger brother, twelve-year-old Ptolemy XIV, as her co-regent and new husband. Rather than rushing back to Rome, Caesar enjoyed two months with Cleopatra, and she conceived their child, Caesarion.

Caesar returned to Rome, where he ruled until 44 BCE as consul and dictator. Although they liked his reforms, the Senate feared he would return Rome to a monarchy. As he entered the Senate on March 15, 44 BCE, the senators surrounded him and stabbed him to death. Cleopatra was staying at Caesar's villa in Italy with her little son, Caesarion. She immediately left for Egypt. Several months later, when he was three years old, she declared Caesarion her co-ruler.

Cleopatra VII and Caesarion[47]

Mark Antony was Rome's consul and Caesar's right-hand man at the time. Holding Caesar's bloody toga, he presided over Caesar's funeral. The conspirators who had murdered Caesar had fled, leaving Antony as Rome's de facto leader. However, Caesar's will shook things up. He named his nephew, Octavian, as his heir. Antony expected to step into Caesar's shoes, but now he had a nineteen-year-old contender. The Romans liked young Octavian better. He eventually became Rome's next consul and, as Caesar Augustus, ruled Rome for the rest of his life.

As part of a deal with Octavian, Antony became the ruler of all Rome's eastern provinces. In 41 BCE, while in Tarsus, Anatolia, Antony asked Cleopatra to meet with him. Egypt was still technically independent, and he wanted to work out an alliance with Rome. Cleopatra arrived in style, sailing into Tarsus in a splendid boat with purple sails and silver oars. The sound of flutes and lyres drifted through the air as little boys dressed as Cupids fanned their queen, who was dressed as Aphrodite.

Antony instantly fell under her sway and sailed back to Alexandria with her. The following year, she gave birth to twins, Cleopatra Selene and Alexander Helios. Eventually, Antony's jealous wife, Fulvia, Rome's most powerful woman, began stirring up trouble in Italy. Antony left Egypt to sort things out. Fulvia died suddenly and suspiciously, and weeks later, Antony married Octavian's sister, Octavia.

Of course, it was just a political marriage. Antony got annoyed when Octavian did not send him enough troops for his Parthian expedition. He returned to his lover, Cleopatra, who had plenty of soldiers to help him. In 36 BCE, Cleopatra had another son with him, Ptolemy Philadelphus.

In Rome, Octavian found Antony's secret will and discovered Antony planned to give some of Rome's provinces to his sons with Cleopatra. In the will, he called Cleopatra his "queen" and gave instructions to bury him with her in Alexandria.

What alarmed Octavian the most was that Antony declared that Caesarion was Caesar's biological son and heir. Octavian was only Caesar's "son" by adoption. Caesarion presented a grave threat to Octavian's inheritance and political ambitions. Octavian had the Senate declare war on Cleopatra, yet a third of the Senate went over to Antony's side.

## The Battle of Actium

In 31 BCE, the naval Battle of Actium was the decisive showdown. Antony and Cleopatra fought against Octavian and his naval commander, Agrippa. The battle occurred in the Ionian Sea off Actium on Greece's western coast. Octavian's army had 3,000 archers, 80,000 troops, and 12,000 cavalry. His navy had 400 lightweight and easily maneuverable ships carrying catapults. The catapults launched harpoons, which hooked the Egyptian ships, enabling the Romans to pull them close and board.

The Egyptians had 480 ships, 70,000 infantry, and 12,000 cavalry. However, the Egyptian ships were heavier and more challenging to maneuver, although they made good platforms for archers. Several kings fought with Antony, including those from Libya, Cilicia, and Thrace. Other kings sent armies to help, including King Herod the Jew and King Malchus of Arabia.[29]

A strait that led into the Ambracian Gulf divided the opposing land forces, so they did not engage. Plutarch said that Antony's infantry and

---

[29] Plutarch, *Plutarch's Lives*, trans. Bernadotte Perrin (Harvard University Press, 1920), chap. 6, https://www.perseus.tufts.edu/hopper/text?doc=Perseus%3Atext%3A2008.01.0007%3Achapter%3D6.

cavalry were superior to Octavian's, so Octavian purposefully did not fight him on land. Antony did not press the matter because Cleopatra insisted on a sea battle. Even so, she did not position her ships in the most strategic places to win. Instead, she had them where they could most easily escape if the battle did not go well.

When the battle began, the plan was for Antony's ships *not* to go into the open sea but to stay in the gulf and the narrows. They could launch arrows and other projectiles without being surrounded by the Roman's smaller and faster ships. However, some of his ship captains thought their size made them unapproachable. They got irritated by the delay and sailed out into open water, much to Octavian's glee. His smaller vessels had the speed and agility to surround them and get close. However, they couldn't use the harpoons to catch the ships and board. The Egyptian ships were too high, and their hulls were too hard.

Battle of Actium by Laureys a Castro[48]

Although neither side had the upper hand in the sea battle, Cleopatra suddenly gathered her sixty ships and sailed south, away from the battle. The Romans dropped their jaws in surprise. When Antony saw her leaving, he sailed after her with forty ships. The rest of his vessels were tangled with the Romans and could not leave. Antony sent word to his land forces, "Retreat! Cross over to Anatolia. Keep going to Syria."

After Cleopatra and Antony abandoned the battle, their remaining ships fought fiercely but were overwhelmingly outnumbered. A squall blew in high waves that shattered some vessels. Five thousand troops defending Egypt died, and Caesar captured three hundred ships. Meanwhile, Antony's infantry and cavalry kept waiting for him to arrive, even though he had messaged them to leave immediately. Finally, after a week, they surrendered to Rome.

## The Final Downfall

Back in Egypt, Cleopatra paced back and forth, trying to make plans. Antony sat staring into space, depressed and drinking heavily. In July of 30 BCE, Octavian arrived, spurring Antony into action. At first, Antony was winning the battle, but then his troops began deserting, realizing that resistance was futile. Antony fell on his sword, dying in Cleopatra's embrace. Cleopatra killed herself, probably by poison or snakebite, on August 30, 30 BCE. Octavian buried them together in Alexandria. He gave Cleopatra's younger children to his sister to raise, yet killed her oldest son, seventeen-year-old Caesarion—the last pharaoh of Ptolemaic Egypt. Egypt was now a Roman province.

# Did the Romans follow the Ptolemaic administration model in Egypt?

The Ptolemies and Romans had similar ways of doing government. Both had a strong central government and a hierarchy of administrators. Both governments followed strict procedures. Egypt had been divided into nomes (territories) from ancient times. The Persians adopted this system, followed by the Ptolemies and then Rome. The Romans did not make many changes in Egypt. They replaced a few Greek administrators with Romans but kept many Greeks in office. They put the Roman legal system into play. The Ptolemies already had a highly organized taxation system, which the Romans adopted. Greek continued to be the administrative language, with Latin added in.

# Chapter 9: Legacy of the Ptolemaic Kingdom Beyond Egypt

The Ptolemaic Kingdom left a profound legacy on history and culture. Its enduring influence spread far beyond its heartland, Egypt. The world owes a debt to the stunning breakthroughs of the mathematicians and scientists at Alexandria's Library. Alexandria's poets, tragedians, and other literary giants lifted the world to new creative heights. As great minds came together and exchanged ideas, they sparked astonishing strides in intellectual growth.

## Mathematics, Science, and Astronomy

Euclid of Alexandria made mind-blowing progress in geometry and logic in Ptolemy I's reign. He wrote a mathematical treatise called *The Elements*. It contained thirteen books on geometry, number theory, and mathematical proofs, including the work of earlier mathematicians. Euclid took earlier theories and developed them further, providing solid proofs. He explained parallel postulates, the Pythagorean theorem, and Euclidian geometry. *The Elements* is the world's oldest mathematical collection that still exists today.

Aristarchus of Samos moved to Alexandria to study natural science under Strato of Lampsacus. Aristarchus specialized in astronomy. He was the first to suggest that the Earth traveled with other planets around the sun each year. Most people believed that the Earth was the center of the universe, but Aristarchus said that the sun was the center. However, he could not convince other scholars. Eighteen centuries later, Nicolaus Copernicus presented the idea again, and it finally caught on. Aristarchus also taught that the Earth turned on an axis each day and that the stars were far-away suns.

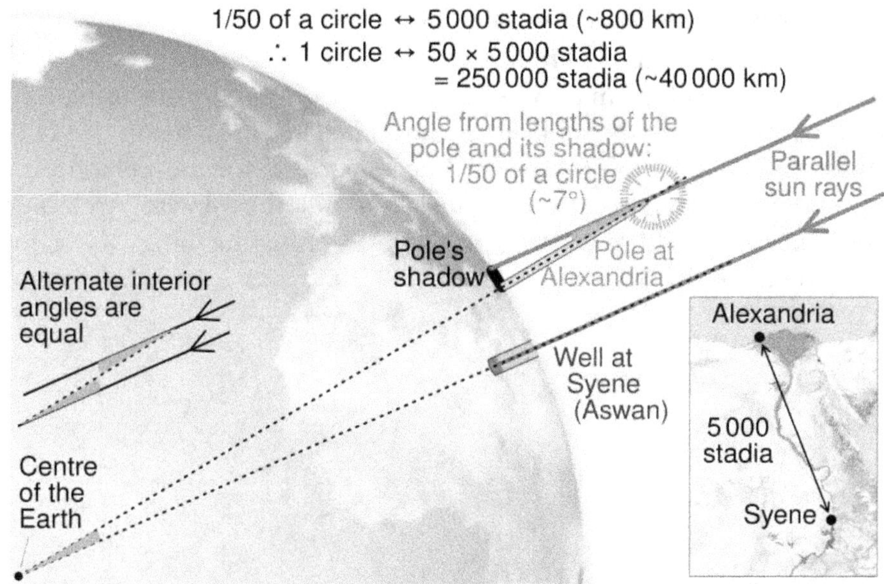


**How Eratosthenes estimated the Earth's circumference**[49]

By this time, Greek philosophers were realizing that the Earth was not flat but a sphere. Eratosthenes, head of the Library of Alexandria in Ptolemy II's reign, figured out the Earth's circumference. In Alexandria, Eratosthenes went outside at noon on June 21 and stuck a stick in the ground. He noted a shadow with a seven-degree angle. Meanwhile, he had sent a man to Syene, down the Nile from Alexandria. His assistant measured the distance between the cities and the shadow cast by a stick in the ground in Syene at noon on June 21. Comparing these measurements, Eratosthenes calculated that the Earth's circumference was 250,000 stadia (28,000 miles). He was incredibly close! Today's calculations place the distance around the Earth at 24,901 miles.

As a teen, Archimedes of Syracuse traveled from Sicily to study at the Library of Alexandria, where he rubbed shoulders with Eratosthenes. Archimedes would get so engrossed in mathematical calculations that he forgot to eat. After his studies, he returned to Sicily but maintained a lively correspondence with Alexandria's scholars. He was ancient history's greatest mathematician, making staggering advances in calculus and geometry.

Archimedes used geometry to estimate square roots and figured out a theoretical calculation of pi ($\pi$) – the ratio of circumference to diameter in a circle. By drawing polygons inside a circle, he came up with an approximation between 3.14285 and 3.14084. Today's mathematicians put pi's first ten digits as 3.1415926535.

Another brainchild of Archimedes was the "Law of the Lever." He discovered that even a small person could lift a heavy weight using a rock and a long stick—something like a seesaw. The closer the heavy object is to the fulcrum or center of the seesaw, the easier it is for the person on the other end to push down on the stick and lift the object. Archimedes claimed anyone could apply this principle to lifting anything: "Give me a place to stand, and I shall move the earth!"

Archimedes's Law of the Lever[50]

Archimedes' interest in moving heavy objects also led to his invention of the first compound pulley, which he used to move a ship. He discovered that a sphere's volume is two-thirds the volume of a cylinder surrounding it. (Think about a ball fitted inside a can that has both ends open.) Archimedes was so proud of this calculation that he asked for it to be inscribed on his tomb (and it was).

## Poets and Tragedians

Greek poets and drama writers clustered at the Library of Alexandria. In Ptolemy II's reign, seven of the most brilliant writers formed the "Alexandrian Pleiad." The name came from the Pleiades constellation, which has seven stars the human eye can see. The Alexandrian Pleiad included Philiscus of Corcyra. As a priest of Dionysus, Philiscus marched in Ptolemy II's coronation procession. He wrote forty-two tragic dramas.

Another Pleiad writer was Lycophron, who organized the comedy section of the Library of Alexandria. He wrote both comedies and tragedies. Lycophron probably wrote *Alexandra*, in which the Trojan priestess Cassandra prophesies that the Trojan descendants (Romans) would rule the earth and sea.

A third Pleiad author was Sositheus, who wrote satyr plays combining comedy and tragedy. His play *Daphnis* is the tale of Daphnis, the shepherd, searching for his true love. He encountered Lityerses, the "Reaper of Men," who forced him into a competition. Who could reap the fastest? The loser would die! The hero Heracles came to the shepherd's rescue and killed Lityerses. Theocritus, another Pleiad poet at Alexandria, picked up Daphnis's story. Unfortunately, the shepherd died of lovesickness, taunted by Aphrodite, the goddess of love: "You tried to 'bend' love, but instead, it bent you."

Alexander Aetolus was another member of the Pleiad. He assisted in the mammoth task of organizing and revising the classical Greek literature collection at the Library of Alexandria. He was a poet with a range of styles but was mainly known for his tragedies. One of his plays was the *Astragalistai*, meaning "Knucklebone-players." It tells the story of the child Patroklos, who later became a hero of the Trojan War. Patroklos argued with his playmate Clysonymus over a game of dice, accidentally killed him, and was exiled.

# Philosophy

The philosopher Strato (Straton) taught Ptolemy II and Aristarchus. He focused on natural science, taking the teachings of his mentor Aristotle to the next level. Aristotle believed in the eternal, unchanging, perfect "unmoved mover." However, Strato did not believe in a creator god. Instead, he thought the divine yet unconscious force of nature caused creation.

Strato believed natural law kept the universe running without the gods doing anything. He believed that hot and cold temperatures, especially heat, made things happen. He said the stars were made from "fiery stuff" and had to obey the laws of gravity like everything else. Strato believed the moon and some "stars" (planets) reflected the sun's light. Strato taught that a child was conceived by "γονή" (semen or reproductive material) from both its mother and father. A child's gender was determined by which parent had the most potent "semen."

Unlike Strato, most Greeks and Egyptians in Ptolemaic Egypt believed in many gods. They thought these deities controlled the universe and intervened in the lives of humans. However, as mentioned, up to a quarter of Alexandria's population were Jews who believed in only one god. Most Ptolemaic rulers gave religious freedom to the Jews. The grateful Jews even dedicated synagogues to the Ptolemaic kings.

Philo of Alexandria[51]

Aristobulus of Alexandria was a Jewish philosopher in the reign of Ptolemy VI. He fused Judaism and Hellenism. His life mission was to drive home his belief that Judaism influenced Greek thought, even as far back as Homer and Hesiod. Philo of Alexandria was a Jewish philosopher in the final days of Ptolemaic rule. He taught that true existence only happens when a person recognizes he or she is nothing without God, the source of *logos* (reason).

# Conclusion

A fascinating aspect of the Ptolemaic Kingdom was that the Greeks invaded and liberated Egypt simultaneously. The Egyptians had suffered horrifically under the harsh Persian rule. Undoubtedly, the Egyptians would have preferred self-rule, but that was not an option. If they had to be ruled by foreigners, they preferred Greek administration over Persian.

The only Persian ruler they liked was the third: Darius I. He improved Egypt's agriculture through irrigation projects and enhanced trade by completing a canal to the Red Sea. He also rebuilt their temples and honored their priests. After Darius, Persian rule mainly went downhill for Egypt. The Persians took Egypt's best and brightest—their skilled artisans, architects, and doctors—to Persia. They placed crushing taxes on the remaining Egyptians and disrespected their temples. By contrast, the Greeks and Egyptians had enjoyed a primarily friendly and beneficial relationship for over a millennia. They traded, shared culture, and defended each other against common enemies.

Although the Greeks held the political reins, they did not consider themselves more enlightened or cultured. They valued and embraced aspects of Egyptian culture while maintaining their own traditions. They initiated new cults revolving around the Ptolemaic kings, but even that was an Egyptian tradition. They translated Egyptian histories, medical books, and literature into Greek. The Ptolemies were champions of compromise and cultural blending.

The lively Ptolemaic economy benefited all of Egypt, both Greeks and Egyptians. With Alexandria as a hub, trade around the Mediterranean skyrocketed. New crops and improved irrigation led to abundant food to feed the rapidly doubling population and sell to foreign countries. The Ptolemaic Kingdom also initiated a cultural revival that took the world by storm. The Library of Alexandria drew razor-sharp scholars from around the ancient world who shared ideas and developed thrilling new ones.

What if the Ptolemaic Kingdom never ruled Egypt? What would the world have lacked? One can only imagine the stimulating cultural and economic growth the Mediterranean region would have missed without Ptolemaic rule! The astounding breakthroughs achieved by the scholars at the Library of Alexandria would not have happened. How many centuries would the world have needed to wait for such incredible advances in science and mathematics?

Furthermore, while his fellow Diadochi were grabbing up as many provinces as possible, Ptolemy I saw Egypt as a desirable land in and of itself. He envisioned what Egypt could be, with its water highways reaching most of the known world. He put his vision into play, and Alexandria became the jewel of Alexander's one-time empire.

Hundreds of years later, Egypt persisted as a major player in the Roman Empire. It became Rome's primary source of grain. Alexandria continued as a trade center and cultural hub. Today, with a population of five million, it is the largest city on the Mediterranean Sea. The "Bride of the Mediterranean" still reigns as a major port and industrial center.

# Part 2: Cleopatra

*An Enthralling Guide to a Life of Power, Politics, and Seduction from Ancient Egypt to Rome*

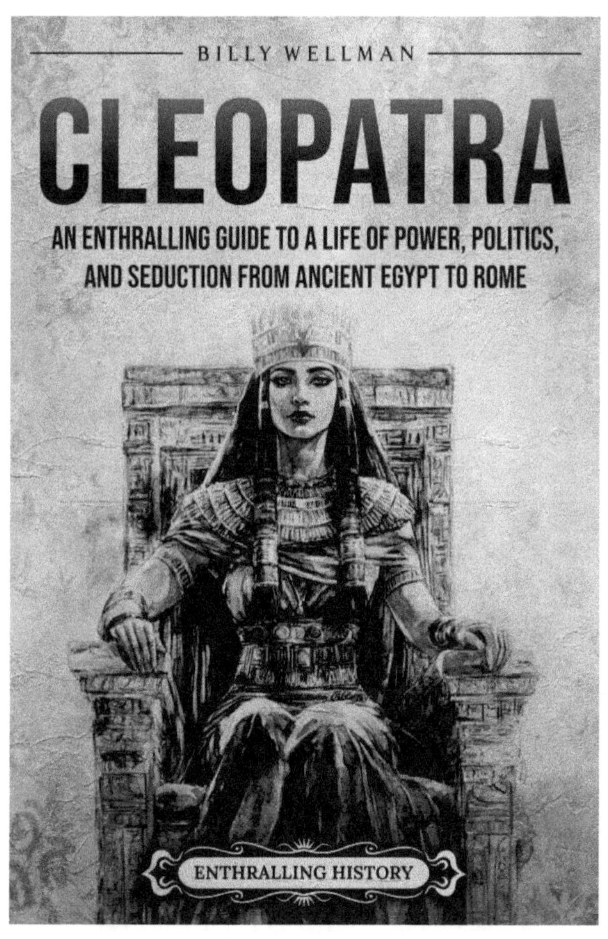

# Introduction

In the annals of ancient history, there are few figures who captivate the imagination quite like Cleopatra. She is undoubtedly the most famous Egyptian ruler, but how much do we really know about the human behind the myth?

Cleopatra VII Thea Philopator was the queen of Ptolemaic Egypt from 51 to 30 BCE. She was the last active ruler of the Kingdom of Egypt before it was swallowed up by the Roman Empire. Born in 69 BCE, Cleopatra's life spanned one of the most tumultuous periods in Mediterranean history, bridging the twilight of the Hellenistic era and the dawn of the Roman Empire. Her reign, marked by political intrigue, military alliances, and romances, continues to fascinate scholars, artists, and the public more than two thousand years after her death.

Cleopatra's education and intellect set her apart from many of her contemporaries. She was fluent in multiple languages; in fact, she was the only Ptolemaic ruler to learn and converse in the ancient Egyptian language. She was well versed in philosophy, astronomy, and mathematics, thanks to her rich upbringing. This intellectual prowess, combined with her charisma and political acumen, made her a formidable leader and master negotiator.

Her education and political instinct helped her not only in fending off the Roman Republic but also in ruling over Egypt. She skillfully used Egyptian religious and cultural traditions to legitimize her rule despite her Macedonian Greek heritage. Cleopatra embraced the role of pharaoh, presenting herself as the living embodiment of Isis, the Egyptian goddess of love, healing, fertility, and the moon.

Of course, it wouldn't be a book about Cleopatra without talking about Julius Caesar and Mark Antony. These alliances had far-reaching consequences for Egypt and Rome. Was Cleopatra a harlot, using her allure to manipulate these men, or were they legitimate romantic relationships and tragedies in their own right? According to history, they have been both, depending on who was writing them. The most famous account is still Shakespeare's play *Antony and Cleopatra*, a tragedy that follows the relationship of Mark Antony and Cleopatra against the backdrop of the advancing Roman Empire. The play is not meant to be a historical record; instead, it examines themes like love, betrayal, honor, shame, and the tension between the "East" (Cleopatra's Egypt) and "West" (Octavius's Rome). The play culminates with the Battle of Actium in 31 BCE and the tragic aftermath of Antony and Cleopatra's failed defense against Rome.

We'll explore Cleopatra's life, from her early years ruling alongside her father, Ptolemy XII, to her famous romantic relationships, to the downfall of her kingdom in the face of the growing Roman power. We'll also take a look at her lasting legacy through the world of art and theater and see how these stories have colored the way we look back on her reign. We'll also put into context what the Kingdom of Egypt was like during her reign and see just how old the kingdom really was. Finally, we'll explore the unique challenges faced by a female ruler in a male-dominated ancient society.

As we explore the life and legacy of Cleopatra, we will encounter themes that resonate across history: the struggle for power, the role of women in politics, the clash of cultures, and the impact of individual personalities on the course of historical events. We'll explore how Cleopatra approached these challenges, making decisions that would be remembered, reinterpreted, and retold. Cleopatra lived in the complicated landscape of the ancient Mediterranean, so her legacy has been placed in the context of European and British history. These broad interpretations of her life change how we view it, and since it has been so long since she lived, it becomes harder and harder to find unbiased accounts that aren't colored by a particular historian's view. That being said, we'll try to take an objective look at why Cleopatra, the last ruler of the Kingdom of Egypt, was so important and why she is perhaps the most remembered and celebrated woman of the ancient world.

# Chapter 1 – The Ptolemaic Dynasty: Egypt's Greek Rulers

## Who Were the Ptolemies?

The Ptolemies were the dynastic family that Cleopatra belonged to. They were a Macedonian-Greek dynasty, founded by Ptolemy I Soter, the childhood friend (and possibly illegitimate brother) of Alexander the Great.[30] He later became one of his most trusted generals and advisors. Ptolemy was by Alexander's side as he conquered most of the ancient world, from the Greek islands into the Persian Empire and all the way to what is now the Punjab region of Pakistan and India.

When Alexander the Great died in 323 BCE, he left his empire without an heir, and his generals began to carve the former Alexandrian territories for themselves. It was during this tumultuous period that Ptolemy I Soter claimed Egypt for himself, taking the city of Memphis. At first, he titled himself the satrap (governor) of Egypt. In 305, he declared himself pharaoh of the Kingdom of Egypt, establishing the Ptolemaic dynasty. The Ptolemies ruled over Egypt for centuries. However, there were a few rulers who stood out from the rest. These rulers provided the foundation for Cleopatra's rule.

---

[30] Ptolemy I was very likely not Alexander's half-brother. Ptolemy likely came up with this story to provide legitimacy to his rule.

## Ptolemy I Soter (305–282 BCE)

In order to legitimize his rule and make himself popular with the Egyptians, Ptolemy I established a unique approach, blending elements of Greek and Egyptian culture. He retained the Egyptian religion and had himself declared pharaoh by the priests at Memphis. This helped establish trust between himself and the Egyptians, enabling him to move the capital to the more strategic (and more Greek) city of Alexandria on the banks of the Mediterranean. He developed the city into a hub of learning and culture by establishing the Library of Alexandria, which became the biggest and most important institution of scholarship in the Hellenistic world.

Ptolemy's bureaucracy and foreign policy helped establish and defend the Kingdom of Egypt from the rulers of Alexander the Great's former territories. While he maintained Greek as the official language and staffed senior positions with Greeks, he respected Egyptian traditions and religious practices, even preserving the high priests of Ptah at Memphis. Ptolemy also made strategic alliances with the noble families in Egypt, bringing them into his court. This approach helped validate his rule among both the Greek settlers and the native Egyptians, keeping the balance of power and not showing favor to either culture.

When it came to navigating foreign policy, Ptolemy was known for his cautious and strategic thinking, a quality he had demonstrated earlier during Alexander the Great's conquests. Ptolemy engaged in the Wars of the Diadochi, the conflicts between Alexander's successors over his conquered territories, but he avoided direct military confrontations. Instead, he focused his energy on securing and expanding his control over Egypt and its surrounding territories. His successful defense of Rhodes against Antigonus I Monophthalmus in 304 BCE earned him the epithet "Soter" ("Savior"), the name by which he was referred to during his lifetime.

Ptolemy I had several wives and consorts, including the Persian princess Artakama and his mistress Thaïs. His marriage to Berenice I produced his successor, Ptolemy II Philadelphus, and in 285 BCE, Ptolemy II was made his co-regent, the first in a line of co-regents that ensured a smooth transition of power.

Ptolemy I Soter died in 283 or 282 BCE at the age of eighty-four, leaving behind a stable and prosperous kingdom.

### Ptolemy II Philadelphus (285–246 BCE)

Ptolemy II Philadelphus continued his father's legacy. His reign marked the zenith of Ptolemaic power and prestige, cementing Egypt's position as a rich and dominant force in the Hellenistic world.

One of his most notable achievements was his patronage of the arts and sciences, which transformed Alexandria into the true intellectual capital of the ancient world. He expanded the Library of Alexandria, turning it into practically a legend. He also completed the Mouseion of Alexandria, an institution that served as a sort of university during the Hellenistic period. Under his rule, Alexandra became more than a strategically placed capital city. It became a hub of literary and artistic production, as Philadelphus patronized poets and writers, supporting their work and contributing to what is now known as the golden age of Alexandria.

In addition to his patronage, Philadelphus was a highly skilled diplomat and leader. He implemented a complex bureaucratic system to govern Egypt and its territories. This was influenced by the Greek system. Philadelphus oversaw the expansion of Ptolemaic rule through a combination of military campaigns and strategic alliances in the territories surrounding Egypt. He successfully expanded their influence into Asia, Syria, and the Aegean Islands, with a network of dependencies that enhanced Egypt's power and wealth.

Philadelphus took the land and influence that his father had started and improved upon it. He introduced new crops and irrigation systems to the Egyptians. He also encouraged trade around the Mediterranean. With all this innovation came the need for a new monetary system. Ptolemy II built on his father's monetary reforms, expanding and stabilizing the coinage system by issuing silver tetradrachms and overhauling bronze currency, laying the foundations for a truly monetized economy.

As a tactic to maintain his popularity at home, Philadelphus followed his father's footsteps in incorporating Egyptian customs into his rule, further cementing the unique Greco-Egyptian culture that would come to define the Ptolemaic dynasty. He continued the Egyptian tradition of ruler worship (pharaoh as a god), deifying himself and his wife (and sister), Arsinoe II, as the Theoi Adelphoi, or "Sibling Gods," drawing inspiration from both the Greek and Egyptian pantheon of gods. In Greece, Hera and Zeus were believed to be siblings and the king and queen of the gods. In Egypt, Iris and Osiris held the same role.

Philadelphus's marriage to his sister shocked Greek sensibilities, but it was already commonplace among Egyptian pharaohs. Marrying his sister served a strategic and symbolic purpose. Philadelphus could keep power within his own family and also appease the Egyptians by seeming to assimilate to their ancient traditions. By maintaining his popularity and power within Egypt, Philadelphus could focus on external threats to his land and power rather than balancing foreign diplomacy with domestic struggles. The practice of marrying siblings continued, with a few exceptions, until Cleopatra's reign.

Ptolemy II Philadelphus's reign was significant for establishing the Ptolemaic dynasty as a major Hellenistic power, transforming Alexandria into a cultural and intellectual powerhouse, and creating a unique Greco-Egyptian culture that would influence the Mediterranean world for centuries. His policies and achievements laid the foundation for Ptolemaic Egypt's golden age, setting standards of royal patronage, administrative efficiency, and cultural synthesis that would be emulated by later Hellenistic rulers and even Roman emperors.

### Ptolemy V Epiphanes (205–180 BCE)

The beginning of the Ptolemaic period brought stability, prosperity, and wealth to the Kingdom of Egypt. The pharaohs expanded their territories and secured the region's economy while managing to keep infighting at bay. However, that all changed during the reigns of Ptolemy IV and V. The reign of Ptolemy V offers a glimpse into that turmoil, particularly through one of the most significant historical artifacts of the period, the Rosetta Stone.

Ptolemy V ascended to the throne at the tender age of five after the suspicious deaths of his parents, Ptolemy IV Philopator and Arsinoe III. The cause of Ptolemy IV's death is not known, though it is suspected that he was murdered at the hands of corrupt advisors who likely hoped to influence Ptolemy V's decisions. After the murder of Arsinoe III, the people of Alexandria rioted and lynched one of the court advisors who was implicated in her death. This marked the beginning of a period of instability within the kingdom, as Ptolemy V had to contend with conflicts within his court and external threats to the Kingdom of Egypt.

During his reign, the Ptolemy dynasty's rivals, Antiochus III of the Seleucid Empire and Philip V of Macedon, took advantage of the king's young age, the infighting with his advisors, and the instability in Egypt to conquer and divide parts of the Ptolemaic lands outside of Egypt. This power grab contributed to the outbreak of the Fifth Syrian War (202–195 BCE). Egypt lost much of its territory to the east, in Asia Minor and the Levant, including the highly strategic area of Coele-Syria (according to modern geography, this would be the territories stretching from southern Syria through Lebanon to northern Israel). At the same time, Ptolemy V faced a widespread Egyptian revolt that began in the southern part of the kingdom. The rebellion, led at first by the self-proclaimed pharaoh Horwennefer and later by Ankhwennefer, resulted in the loss of much of Upper Egypt for over two decades; it was only regained after a prolonged and costly military campaign.

Because Ptolemy V lost control of the lucrative Coele-Syria region, the Kingdom of Egypt had to operate with less economic power and wealth than ever before. This meant he began to impose heavy taxes on the people of Egypt, likely influencing the rebellion. The kingdom would find peace again, especially once Ptolemy V married the Seleucid princess Cleopatra I and could reaffirm his alliance with Antiochus III. However, he would not regain the power or influence Egypt had at the beginning of the Ptolemaic period.

## The Decline of the Ptolemaic Dynasty

As his kingdom and influence weakened, Ptolemy V's rule gradually underscored the fragility of the Ptolemaic state. By marrying Cleopatra I, the daughter of Antiochus III of the Seleucids, he aligned Egypt more closely with the Seleucid dynasty—a move that alarmed Rome, which had recently checked Seleucid power. Ptolemy V died in 180 BCE under mysterious circumstances (he was possibly poisoned) and left behind a kingdom with a minor heir and growing internal and external pressures.

What followed over the next century was a turbulent era: the reigns of his successors (from Ptolemy VI onward) were frequently marred by power struggles, regencies, sibling rivalries, and civil strife. These internal divisions, combined with foreign threats and increasing Roman intervention, steadily eroded the strength of the Ptolemaic dynasty.

## Ptolemy VIII Physcon (c. 184–116 BCE)

The most dramatic example of this dysfunction can be seen in Ptolemy VIII's reign. He was nicknamed "Physcon" (which means "Potbelly") for his obesity and reputation. He was the younger brother of Ptolemy VI Philometor. The two were supposed to rule together peacefully after their father's death; instead, they spent years locked in a rivalry for sole control of Egypt. In 164 BCE, Ptolemy VIII managed to force his brother to flee and briefly seized power, but by the following year, the opposition and external pressure forced him out. He was sent to rule Cyrenaica (modern-day Libya) as a consolation.

When Ptolemy VI died in 145 BCE, Ptolemy VIII returned to Egypt and married his sister Cleopatra II (his brother's widow), establishing himself as king. Some years later (around 141 or 140 BCE), he married his niece, Cleopatra III, the daughter of Ptolemy VI and Cleopatra II, while keeping Cleopatra II as co-queen. This arrangement, acceptable under Ptolemaic dynastic tradition, triggered deep internal tensions.

From 132 to around 126 BCE, Egypt was plunged into civil war. Cleopatra II commanded Alexandria (backed largely by Greek and Macedonian residents), while Ptolemy VIII and Cleopatra III held sway over much of the rest of Egypt, where they gained support from many native Egyptians. Ancient accounts portray Ptolemy VIII as especially ruthless. He allegedly murdered his own son, and later sources accuse him of purging opponents and driving out intellectuals from Alexandria. By the time he reconsolidated power (around 124 BCE), Egypt was politically fractured, and its institutions had been severely weakened.

Ptolemy VIII died in 116 BCE. In his will, he left the throne to Cleopatra III, with instructions that she choose one of her sons—either Ptolemy IX Soter or Ptolemy X Alexander I—as co-ruler. This set the stage for yet another round of dynastic instability and internal conflict.

### Ptolemy IX Soter (Lathyros) (c. 140-81 BCE)

Cleopatra's grandfather, Ptolemy IX Soter II, nicknamed "Lathyros" ("Chickpea"), had one of the most turbulent reigns in the dynasty's history. He was the eldest son of Ptolemy VIII and Cleopatra III. When his father died, pressure forced Cleopatra III to associate Ptolemy IX with the throne, even though she appeared to favor his younger brother. She forced him to divorce his first wife, his sister Cleopatra IV, and marry his other sister, Cleopatra Selene, instead.

For a time (from 116 to 107 BCE), mother and son ruled together, but tensions mounted. In 107 BCE, his mother deposed him, and he fled Egypt. He ended up governing abroad in Cyprus. Meanwhile, his younger brother (later known as Ptolemy X Alexander) became co-ruler with Cleopatra III.

After years in exile, Ptolemy IX was recalled by the Alexandrians and restored as king in 88 BCE. He ruled again until his death in 81 BCE.

During that final reign, there was unrest in Upper Egypt (including a revolt around Thebes). He did not designate an heir to succeed him. His daughter Berenice III briefly ruled, but soon a new king, Ptolemy XI Alexander II, was installed.

Ptolemy XI married Berenice III, but he reportedly murdered her just nineteen days after their wedding. The Alexandrians rioted and lynched him. Afterward, the throne passed to an illegitimate branch of the family, eventually leading to Ptolemy XII, the father of Cleopatra VII.

### Environmental and Economic Collapse

On top of all this political chaos, Egypt was suffering from environmental disasters. The Nile's floods, the lifeblood of Egyptian agriculture, became increasingly unreliable during this period. When the Nile failed to flood year after year, crops failed, families went hungry, and people were forced to sell their land just to pay the ever-increasing taxes. The Ptolemies kept raising taxes to fund their civil wars and pay for Roman support, creating a vicious cycle that made the Egyptian people resent their Greek rulers even more.

The dynasty also kept losing territory. By the time Ptolemy XII came to power around 80 BCE, Egypt had long since shed most of the far-flung territories that once made the Ptolemies a great Mediterranean power. Lands such as Cyrenaica, Coele-Syria (the Levant), and other overseas holdings had slipped from Ptolemaic control, leaving the kingdom reduced largely to Egypt proper (the Nile valley and delta).

By the time Ptolemy XII sat on the throne, Egypt had suffered almost a century of chaos. The kingdom was a shadow of what it had been under Ptolemy I and II. It was economically weakened, militarily dependent on Rome, and ruled by a dynasty that had lost the respect of both the Greek and Egyptian populations. As we'll see, Ptolemy XII would only make matters worse, driving Egypt even deeper into debt and dependence on Rome, leaving his daughter Cleopatra with the nearly impossible task of restoring Egyptian independence and prosperity.

# Chapter 2 – Birth of a Queen

Cleopatra VII Thea Philopator, better known to us simply as Cleopatra, was born in 69 BCE during the final decades of the Ptolemaic dynasty. At the time, the Mediterranean world was being turned on its head by the expanding Roman Republic. Cleopatra's life was marked by periods of exile and war, as well as threats to the throne from both the Roman world and within the Egyptian court. She was likely the second of five children born to Pharaoh Ptolemy XII Auletes, the others being Berenice IV (Cleopatra's elder sister), Arsinoe IV, Ptolemy XIII, and Ptolemy XIV. Her early life was characterized by an education that reflected her Macedonian Greek heritage and emphasized Hellenistic culture. Her early exposure to royal politics would inform her decisions later in life when she ruled Egypt as pharaoh.

### Cleopatra's Birth and Family Life

Cleopatra's early life is still shrouded in mystery, in part because of how long ago she lived, but also due to the Roman effort to discredit her after her death. We know that she was the daughter of Ptolemy XII. She was likely not the eldest, though the exact birth order remains unclear. Her mother is believed to have been Cleopatra V Tryphaena, but that is difficult to confirm. If her mother had been Cleopatra V, some wonder whether Cleopatra should have been numbered Cleopatra VI instead of VII. However, these numeric designations are modern conventions, not ancient ones, so they were not consistently applied in antiquity. Some historians once speculated that Cleopatra VI Tryphaena might have been either identical to Cleopatra V or a separate daughter of Ptolemy XII, possibly a co-ruler with Berenice IV. This confusion reflects the limited and often contradictory sources from this period, as well as the common reuse of royal names in the Ptolemaic dynasty. Whether Cleopatra V and VI were the same person or distinct individuals does not change the complex relationships among Cleopatra VII, her siblings, and her father.

A Hellenistic depiction of Ptolemy XII. [52]

## Siblings and Status

The relationships Cleopatra had with her siblings weren't what we would consider "typical" by today's standards. In Ptolemaic Egypt, it was customary for members of the royal family to marry their siblings and rule as co-regents. This practice became a hallmark of the Ptolemaic dynasty and was intended to preserve dynastic purity and reinforce legitimacy. Although the idea may seem strange today, these sibling relationships were typically formal and politically driven rather than affectionate. They were often marked by rivalry and a continuous struggle for power.

We will talk about this in more detail, but over the course of her life, Cleopatra either opposed or outlasted all of her siblings. Berenice IV was executed by their father, Ptolemy XII, upon his return to power.

Cleopatra later co-ruled with her younger brothers, Ptolemy XIII and Ptolemy XIV, both of whom died under suspicious circumstances—Ptolemy XIII drowned during a civil war, and Ptolemy XIV was likely poisoned, possibly on Cleopatra's order. Arsinoe IV, her younger sister, was executed in Ephesus years later on Cleopatra's command. Each sibling presented a potential threat to Cleopatra's rule, and the political environment of the Ptolemaic court offered little room for family loyalty.

Her path to power changed dramatically after her father's exile and the ascension of Berenice IV to the throne in his absence. Early in life, Cleopatra might have been expected to marry a foreign or dynastic ally, as royal daughters often served diplomatic roles in marriage. However, with the death of Berenice and her father's restoration, Cleopatra emerged as the likely heir. She would go on to marry her brothers in turn, as was customary for Ptolemaic queens, and rule as pharaoh. Egypt, unlike many other ancient societies, did not prohibit female rulers, and co-regency with male relatives became a normalized practice over the three centuries of Ptolemaic rule.

### Education, Politics, and Culture

No matter what her status was in her family, Cleopatra was always bound to have a robust education, fitting for a woman of her status in the ancient world. She was born and raised in Alexandria, the intellectual center of the Hellenistic world, and had the massive Great Library at her fingertips. Though she was raised in Egypt, her family still considered themselves Greek, so Cleopatra would have had a classical Greek education. Some later sources suggest she was tutored by prominent scholars, though historians today aren't certain who they were or how reliable those claims are. Still, it's clear she had a strong foundation in literature, science, politics, and both Greek and Egyptian religion. When she was older, she might have studied with scholars affiliated with the Mouseion, a kind of scholarly academy in Alexandria, where she likely studied languages, culture, math, science, Egyptian religious practices (including her ceremonial roles), and the workings of power.

Cleopatra was known for her grasp of languages. She was a polyglot and is said to have spoken multiple languages, including Greek, Egyptian, Aramaic, at least one Persian language, and possibly others, like an Ethiopian dialect. She likely picked up some Latin too. While her reputation for speaking nine or more languages might have been exaggerated for political effect, there's no doubt that she stood out for actually learning Egyptian—something no Ptolemaic ruler had done. It was a smart political move. Being able to speak directly to her subjects without a translator would have helped her connect with them and appear more legitimate in their eyes.

She likely learned about Greek political systems during her studies, but her real education came from her life. She lived through power shifts, court intrigues, and cultural tensions. Her early life shaped her into a ruler who was clever, adaptable, and deeply aware of the mistakes her family had made—and how not to repeat them.

## Ptolemy XII: The Flute Player Who Ruined Egypt

One of the last male pharaohs of Egypt was Cleopatra's father, Ptolemy XII. His reign would set the stage for everything that came after. Born around 115 BCE, Ptolemy XII came to power under a cloud of uncertain legitimacy that would haunt him his entire life, and his desperate attempts to secure his throne left Egypt politically and financially weakened.

When Ptolemy XI was lynched by an angry Alexandrian mob in 80 BCE for murdering his wife, Berenice III, he left no legitimate heir. The only surviving male descendants of Ptolemy I were the illegitimate sons of Ptolemy IX. They had been born to an unknown concubine. As the eldest, Ptolemy XII was installed as king by the Alexandrian elite.

But there was a problem. Roman sources later claimed that Ptolemy XI had left Egypt to Rome in his will, giving the Romans a pretext to assert control, though no such will has ever been found. However, the Roman Senate was divided and unwilling to take on the expense and complications of annexing Egypt, so it allowed Ptolemy XII to rule, at least for the moment. The new king knew his position was precarious. He wasn't legitimate in the traditional sense, and Rome could change its mind at any moment.

Ptolemy XII took the cult name "Neos Dionysus" ("New Dionysus"), associating himself with the god of wine, music, and divine ecstasy. This wasn't just religious devotion; the Ptolemies had long revered Dionysus, who in Greek mythology conquered Asia and was seen as a counterpart to the Egyptian god Osiris. But ancient writers mocked him mercilessly for it, giving him the derogatory nickname "Auletes" (meaning "the Flute Player") because of his fondness for playing the aulos at musical competitions and Dionysian festivals. This was considered beneath the dignity of a king by many. It was low-class entertainment that, to his critics, made him look weak.

## Buying Rome's Friendship

From the beginning, Ptolemy XII's reign was marked by one overriding obsession: securing Roman recognition of his legitimacy. He married his sister, Cleopatra V Tryphaena (in accordance with Ptolemaic tradition), and was crowned in Alexandria according to Egyptian rites in 76 BCE. But that wasn't enough. In 65 BCE, some Roman politicians raised the issue of his illegitimacy and invoked a supposed will of his predecessor, claiming that Egypt should be annexed. Ptolemy XII panicked.

His solution was simple, if ruinous: he would buy Rome's support. In 59 BCE, when Julius Caesar became consul, Ptolemy XII promised him six thousand talents—an absolutely staggering sum—in exchange for a law recognizing him as an "ally and friend of the Roman nation." Caesar passed the law, and Ptolemy XII was officially recognized. But where was an already-struggling Egypt supposed to find six thousand talents? Ptolemy XII didn't have it, so he borrowed it from Roman moneylenders at high interest rates.

To pay these debts, he raised taxes dramatically across Egypt. The burden on farmers and laborers grew unbearable. The Egyptian population, who were already resentful of their Greek rulers, grew furious. And the bribes kept coming. Ptolemy XII sent troops and money to support Pompey the Great in Palestine, paid for the upkeep of Roman forces, and continued showering Roman officials with gifts. However, when he asked for Roman military protection in return, he was repeatedly rebuffed. The Romans were happy to take his money, but they weren't about to commit legions to defend him.

## The Cyprus Disaster and Exile

In 58 BCE, disaster struck. A Roman politician named Publius Clodius Pulcher proposed the annexation of Cyprus, which was still a rich Ptolemaic possession, saying that the king of Cyprus had offended Rome by failing to ransom Clodius from pirates. The pretext was enough. The Roman Republic moved to seize the island. Cato the Younger was sent to carry out the annexation. He offered Ptolemy of Cyprus, the younger brother of Ptolemy XII, a choice: abdicate and accept a comfortable retirement as a priest at the Temple of Aphrodite in Paphos or face war. Ptolemy chose suicide instead.

For many in Egypt, this was a humiliating blow. Not only had a vital Ptolemaic territory been handed over to Rome, but Ptolemy XII Auletes had failed to protect his brother or preserve the island. In 58 BCE, riots broke out in Alexandria. The Alexandrian elite and other factions declared Ptolemy XII had been deposed and proclaimed his eldest daughter, Berenice IV, as queen. (Some sources indicate she ruled jointly with Cleopatra V Tryphaena; others suggest Tryphaena was already dead.) By 57 BCE, Berenice IV stood as the sole monarch in Alexandria.

Ptolemy XII fled Egypt. He reportedly took one of his younger daughters, likely the future queen Cleopatra VII, with him. They sought refuge in Rome or some nearby allied territory. In exile, he turned to political maneuvering and bribery, hoping to win back the throne with Roman backing.

### Three Years in Exile

According to later accounts, Ptolemy XII took up residence at Pompey's villa in the Alban Hills outside Rome. He lavished gifts and promises on Roman senators, cultivating allies and calling in favors. When envoys from Alexandria arrived in Rome to oppose his restoration, Ptolemy had some of them quietly eliminated.

Despite his efforts, the bribes didn't produce swift results. By late 57 BCE, the Roman Senate expressed support for his return, but when a controversial "prophecy" was presented warning against providing active military aid, the Romans hesitated. A frustrated Ptolemy departed Rome and moved to Ephesus, taking shelter in the precinct of Artemis.

Meanwhile, in Alexandria, his daughter Berenice IV staked her claim to the throne and searched for a husband to legitimize her reign. The first candidate, Seleucus, a man of obscure origins, was so despised for his vulgar manners that the Alexandrians nicknamed him "Kybiosaktes" ("the Salt-fish-monger"). Berenice had him strangled after only a few days. Eventually, she married a Cappadocian nobleman named Archelaus.

### The Brutal Return

In 55 BCE, Ptolemy XII finally got what he wanted. He bribed Aulus Gabinius, the Roman proconsul of Syria, with a huge sum in return for a Roman army to invade Egypt and restore him to the throne. Gabinius, encouraged by Pompey the Great and enticed by the payment, marched into Egypt with Roman forces. Among them was a young cavalry officer named Mark Antony, who would later become important in Cleopatra's story. According to tradition, Mark Antony might have first encountered Cleopatra at this time (Cleopatra would have been about fourteen years old, while Mark Antony would have been almost thirty).

The invasion was swift. The forces of Berenice IV's consort, Archelaus, tried to resist, but his troops mutinied. Archelaus was killed, and the palace surrendered. In spring 55 BCE, Ptolemy XII was restored to the throne by Roman military might. One of his earliest acts was to eliminate his daughter Berenice IV and her supporters. She had usurped his rule, and he showed no mercy.

After being restored, Ptolemy XII ruled with the backing of roughly two thousand Roman soldiers and mercenaries (the Gabiniani), who were stationed in Alexandria. Their presence meant that Rome held effective leverage over Egypt. The debts he had incurred to pay for his restoration weighed heavily on the treasury. To meet these financial obligations, heavy taxation fell on his subjects, deepening Egypt's economic troubles. The kingdom had effectively become a client state of Rome.

## The Final Years and the Co-Regency

In 52 BCE, with her father growing older, Cleopatra VII was formally made regent, a move that marked the beginning of her immersion in the business of kingship. For a time, she was being prepared to rule. She must have learned about the responsibilities she would carry as the proper ruler during that regency (though sources are scant). This hands-on learning gave her a head start when the throne passed to her.

When Ptolemy XII died in 51 BCE, his will left Egypt to Cleopatra VII and her younger brother Ptolemy XIII as joint monarchs. They were to be co-regents and spouses. However, Cleopatra, who was about eighteen, quickly became the dominant presence at court.

She inherited not only the throne but a kingdom deeply in distress. The state finances had been drained, public trust had eroded, and Rome's influence and debt obligations loomed over Egypt. This was a fragile inheritance. Cleopatra assumed power as queen in a state that needed careful, tactful rule to survive.

The foundation of her later political skill—the alliance-building, the public-relations instincts, the delicate dance between Greek, Egyptian, and Roman interests—began in those early, turbulent years following her father's death. What she would later attempt with Roman generals, foreign diplomacy, and internal reform all had their roots in the crumbling legacy she inherited.

# Chapter 3 – The Struggle for the Throne

**Marriage and Co-Regency with Ptolemy XIII Philopater**

As per tradition, Cleopatra and her younger brother Ptolemy XIII were designated co-rulers of Egypt after their father's death. They were likely supposed to be spouses under Ptolemaic custom, though there is no firm contemporary record that confirms their marriage. Cleopatra was about eighteen, and Ptolemy XIII was around ten. This age gap gave Cleopatra the advantage in experience, maturity, and political awareness.

Because of his youth, Ptolemy XIII was surrounded by regents and advisors who were expected to manage affairs until he came of age. These advisors soon grew wary of Cleopatra's talents and influence, particularly as she had already seen how rulership worked under her father and might have had some strong ideas about governance. Their suspicions about her loyalty and ambitions would ultimately spark a bitter rivalry that would tear the kingdom apart.

In practice, though nominally co-rulers, Cleopatra appears to have been the dominant figure. When official documents began listing her name first, it signaled that she held the actual power. Ptolemy XIII's advisors began to plot. The co-regency, which might have offered a stable transition of power, instead became a dangerous power struggle.

### The Three Men Who Controlled the Boy King

To understand why Cleopatra's co-regency was doomed from the start, we need to understand the three men who controlled her brother. This wasn't just a sibling rivalry; it was a power struggle between an experienced, ambitious queen and a triumvirate of advisors who held the real power.

Pothinus (sometimes spelled Potheinous) was the most powerful of the three. A eunuch who had been appointed as Ptolemy XIII's official regent, he controlled the palace administration and Egypt's finances. Eunuchs were common in royal courts throughout the ancient world because they couldn't father children, thus posing no dynastic threat. As regent and minister, Pothinus managed Egypt's resources and debts—the key levers of political power in a kingdom drowning in obligations to Rome.

Achillas commanded Egypt's military forces, including the garrison in Alexandria and the armies stationed throughout the kingdom. Ancient sources describe him as leading substantial infantry and cavalry forces, more than enough to make him a kingmaker in times of turmoil. His appointment as one of Ptolemy's guardians gave him both military and political authority. Control of the army meant control of the kingdom, and Achillas knew this.

Theodotus of Chios was a Greek rhetorician; he was basically a professional teacher of public speaking and persuasion. He served as Ptolemy XIII's tutor. In the Hellenistic world, rhetoric was considered one of the most important skills for a ruler or statesman. As the king's tutor, Theodotus shaped not only how the young king spoke and made decisions but also how the court presented itself to Greek elites and foreign powers. His influence over Ptolemy XIII gave him considerable sway in policy decisions.

With the palace, the army, and the king's education under their control, these three men held the machinery of the state. Cleopatra had intelligence, experience from her year as co-regent, and legitimacy as the designated heir, but the triumvirate controlled the resources that could make or break a ruler in ancient Egypt.

Cleopatra understood the need to solidify her position. Early in her reign, she made public appearances, issued decrees, and worked to present herself as the rightful monarch to both Egyptians and Greeks. Although the surviving evidence for her earliest acts is limited, inscriptions and later accounts suggest she aligned herself with Egyptian religious tradition and fulfilled the ceremonial duties expected of a pharaoh. These efforts helped her cultivate support among the Egyptian populace and elites. Cleopatra knew that the goodwill of the people and the perception that she respected Egyptian customs could prove crucial in the power struggle unfolding around her.

## Cleopatra vs. Ptolemy XIII

Apart from their differences in age and experience, the co-regency between Cleopatra and Ptolemy XIII was unstable from the beginning due to political and personal tensions. Cleopatra increasingly aligned herself with Rome, recognizing its growing power and the advantages of cultivating strong ties with Roman leaders. Her understanding of Roman politics was shaped in part by her father's reliance on Roman support during his reign and exile. She aimed to preserve Egypt's autonomy not by resisting Roman influence outright but by leveraging it strategically to maintain what remained of her family's rule.

In contrast, the advisors who surrounded Ptolemy XIII, particularly Pothinus, Theodotus, and Achillas, opposed Cleopatra's independent rule and likely viewed her Roman connections with suspicion. These men saw Rome's deepening involvement in Egyptian affairs as a threat to their own authority at court. They preferred the young and inexperienced Ptolemy XIII, since they could more easily manipulate him, over a politically astute queen who acted on her own initiative.

In many respects, the conflict between Cleopatra and her brother can be better understood as a power struggle between Cleopatra and the ruling council in Alexandria. These men were not accustomed to a monarch, especially not a woman, who governed with such authority and independence. Cleopatra was multilingual, politically savvy, and confident in her decision-making, which diminished the influence of the court advisors who had held sway under her father and brother. Though there had been women in power before her, including her older sister Berenice IV, the patriarchal norms of Ptolemaic society likely played a role in the council's hostility toward Cleopatra's assertive leadership.

## A Kingdom in Crisis

The power struggle between Cleopatra and her brother's advisors played out against a backdrop of environmental and economic stress. Egypt was entering a period of mounting crisis, and the instability gave Pothinus and his allies a convenient opportunity to turn court opinion against the young queen.

The lifeblood of Egypt had always been the Nile's annual flood. Every summer, monsoon rains in the Ethiopian Highlands would swell the river until it overflowed its banks and flooded the surrounding plains. When the waters receded, they left behind fertile silt. But if the flood was too low, crops would fail. If it was too high, it could destroy infrastructure and livestock. The entire kingdom's survival depended on the Nile flooding at just the right level. During Cleopatra's early reign, the floods were reportedly poor.

Modern scientific research has revealed what the ancient Egyptians couldn't have known. Volcanic eruptions around the world might have disrupted the climate. When volcanoes erupt, they release sulfur dioxide into the atmosphere, forming aerosols that reflect sunlight and cool the climate. This cooling could have altered precipitation patterns, reducing the monsoon rainfall in Ethiopia that fed the Nile. Recent studies have linked major eruptions in the mid-1$^{st}$ century BCE to decreased Nile flooding, and their effects on Egypt might have been significant.

Without adequate flooding, the harvest would have suffered. Without a harvest, famine could follow. And with food in short supply, tax collection would falter. The government still needed revenue to pay back the enormous debts left by Ptolemy XII to Rome. The result could have been a vicious cycle. Crop failures put pressure on state revenues, which led to increased taxation, which in turn might have forced some rural families into debt or land sales, prompting migration into cities and fueling unrest.

Cleopatra did what she could. She couldn't control the Nile's floods, but she reportedly took steps to stabilize the countryside, perhaps by issuing guidance on irrigation or working to check the abuses of local officials. However, the crisis was likely too large for any one ruler to manage, especially a young queen still consolidating her power.

Pothinus saw his opportunity. It was easy to pin Egypt's troubles on Cleopatra. She was young, female, and making decisions independently without deferring to the "experienced" council. In Egyptian tradition, the pharaoh was expected to uphold ma'at (cosmic order and balance). If the Nile failed to flood properly, some might have interpreted it as a sign of divine displeasure. Whether through religious undertones or court politics, Pothinus and his allies began to circulate the idea that Cleopatra's assertiveness and her failure to share power with her brother, as their father's will had outlined, had brought misfortune to the kingdom.

By 49 BCE, after several years of instability and hardship, Cleopatra's position had weakened. Though the environmental crisis was not her fault, it became a weapon in the political battle that drove her from power.

During the first few years of her reign, Pothinus and his followers continued to resist Cleopatra's growing independence and diplomatic overtures to Rome. By 48 BCE, they had gained the upper hand in Ptolemy XIII's name. With military backing and control of Alexandria, they forced Cleopatra to flee the capital. This exile tested her resilience and political instincts, but it ultimately proved to be a turning point in her campaign to restore her authority.

### Exile from Alexandria

Cleopatra was only about nineteen or twenty years old when she found herself ousted from the place she called home. Ptolemy XIII's advisors, led by Potheinous, succeeded in forcing her from power, and she fled Egypt for Syria.

In 49 BCE, Syria was under Roman influence, which offered Cleopatra a degree of safety from her brother's forces. While this was her first exile, she had witnessed political turmoil during her father's reign and understood the power of Roman backing.

In Syria, Cleopatra began to gather support for her return. Though ancient sources don't detail her alliances in the region, she likely tried to revive political networks first built during her father's reign. However, the Roman world she inherited had changed.

While the extent of local support is unclear, Cleopatra began to raise a force to reclaim the throne. She also had her younger sister Arsinoe IV with her, which might have added legitimacy to her claim, presenting her not as a lone exile but as a contender representing another branch of the royal family.

### Building an Army

The key to Cleopatra's return was military force. Ptolemy XIII controlled Alexandria and commanded the Egyptian army under Achillas, so Cleopatra needed to raise her own. Ancient sources tell us only that she assembled a force during her exile, likely drawing on the wide networks of mercenaries active throughout the eastern Mediterranean. This region was home to many professional soldiers—Greeks, Thracians, Arabs, and others displaced by the constant wars between Hellenistic states. These men hired themselves out to whoever could offer to pay them and had a plausible chance of victory.

Cleopatra might have carried some money with her when she fled Egypt, but more importantly, she had royal legitimacy. Her claim to the throne had been endorsed by her father's will and, originally, by Rome. That credibility could have made her an appealing patron to mercenaries and regional leaders who stood to benefit if she regained power.

Some later sources suggest she might have sought support from neighboring Arab groups, possibly Nabataean or other tribal forces from the east or south of Judea. These would not have been large professional armies but smaller contingents tied to local rulers who might have seen political advantages in backing Cleopatra's return.

## The Return to Egypt

By the spring of 48 BCE, Cleopatra had gathered enough forces to make her move. But she was strategic about it. She didn't march directly on Alexandria; that would likely have been disastrous. Ptolemy XIII controlled the capital and had the Egyptian army, including a sizable force of infantry and cavalry, under his control through Achillas. Instead, Cleopatra positioned her forces at Pelusium, the fortress city on Egypt's northeastern frontier. This was a calculated move for several reasons.

First, Pelusium controlled the main land route into Egypt from the east. By holding it, Cleopatra could secure her entry point and shield herself from immediate retaliation while she remained outside the heart of the kingdom. Second, it placed her close enough to Egyptian territory to assert her claim to the throne but not so deep inside the country that she risked being surrounded or cut off if her campaign failed. Third, Pelusium was where many arrivals from the eastern Mediterranean, possibly even fleeing Romans, would have landed when entering Egypt.

She couldn't have known it at the time, but this positioning would soon become significant. Within months, the Roman civil war between Caesar and Pompey would reach Egyptian shores, and Cleopatra's presence at Pelusium placed her near the epicenter of what followed. For the moment, though, she and her brother were in a tense standoff. These two rival factions were confronting one another along the eastern edge of Egypt, neither able to decisively defeat the other.

Cleopatra had clawed her way back from exile to the gates of her homeland. She had raised an army, cultivated key alliances, and positioned herself with care. However, she still lacked the power to unseat her brother and reclaim her throne. For that, she would need support from Rome—and that support was about to arrive in the form of Julius Caesar.

A sculpture of Julius Caesar. [53]

# Chapter 4 – Alliance with Caesar

### Caesar's Arrival in Egypt

While Cleopatra and Ptolemy XIII were locked in a stalemate on Egypt's frontier, the Roman Republic was tearing itself apart in a civil war. Julius Caesar and Pompey the Great—once allies in Rome's First Triumvirate—had become bitter enemies, each vying for control of Rome. After Caesar defied the Senate and crossed the Rubicon in 49 BCE, the two generals clashed across the Mediterranean. Though Caesar's forces were smaller, his bold strategy and loyal legions delivered a series of victories that ultimately forced Pompey to flee.

In September 48 BCE, after his crushing defeat at the Battle of Pharsalus, Pompey arrived at Pelusium seeking refuge. He had enjoyed close ties with Ptolemy XII, had played a role in ratifying the late king's will, and likely believed that Egypt, which was now under the rule of his son, Ptolemy XIII, would offer sanctuary. It was a fatal miscalculation.

Pothinus, Achillas, and Theodotus faced a difficult choice. To shelter Pompey risked Caesar's wrath. To reject him invited danger from a desperate and cornered general. According to ancient accounts, Theodotus argued that neither course was safe—only assassination would remove the threat. On September 28th, 48 BCE, as Pompey's boat approached the shore, Achillas and a Roman officer named Lucius Septimius rowed out to meet him. They murdered him in the boat and severed his head.

Two days later, Caesar arrived in Alexandria with a fairly small force. Pothinus and his allies presented him with Pompey's head and signet ring, expecting gratitude. Instead, Caesar responded with revulsion. According to some sources, he wept. However, Caesar's reaction was not just sentimental; it was also political. He had built his image on mercy toward defeated enemies, a strategy that had earned him a lot of support in Rome. Pompey's murder had robbed him of the chance to offer forgiveness publicly, and it ensured that Pompey's sons would continue the war rather than accept defeat.

The assassination had backfired. If anything, it pushed Caesar closer to Cleopatra's camp and set the stage for a new chapter in the power struggle for Egypt.

## The Carpet Meeting

Recognizing the opportunity of Caesar's presence, Cleopatra made her boldest move yet. Caesar was staying in the royal palace in Alexandria as an honored guest of Ptolemy XIII. Cleopatra couldn't simply walk through the palace gates. Achillas controlled the city, and she risked arrest or death if discovered. She needed to reach Caesar without being detected.

The story of what happened next comes from Plutarch, who wrote more than a century later. According to his account, Cleopatra enlisted the services of a Sicilian merchant named Apollodorus. She climbed into a large sack, likely a bedding sack used for linens. Apollodorus tied it up and carried it through the palace. Once inside Caesar's private chambers, he unrolled the sack, and Cleopatra emerged.

The popular image of a "carpet" likely stems from a later mistranslation. Plutarch's original Greek describes a bedding sack or linen bag, but 18th-century translators, such as John Langhorne, rendered it as a "carpet," possibly due to a lack of an exact English equivalent or for dramatic flair. The carpet version stuck and was immortalized in paintings and films. But whether it was a sack or a rug, the core truth remains: Cleopatra smuggled herself into Caesar's chambers in a dramatic, risky gambit.

According to Plutarch, Caesar was immediately captivated by her boldness and charm. We don't know what they discussed that night, but we know the outcome. Caesar soon threw his support behind Cleopatra. The next day, he summoned both siblings and announced that they would rule together as co-regents, just as their father's will had specified. But everyone understood that Caesar was backing Cleopatra.

For Cleopatra, this was everything. Caesar commanded battle-hardened Roman legions. His endorsement gave her legitimacy in the eyes of Rome and the Alexandrian elite. For Caesar, the alliance made sense too. Cleopatra was intelligent, experienced, and politically astute. She would be a reliable ally who could keep Egypt's grain flowing to Rome. Ptolemy XIII's faction, by contrast, had just demonstrated its instability and short-sightedness by murdering Pompey.

## The Alexandrian War

Pothinus and Achillas were outraged. They hadn't assassinated Pompey and controlled Egypt for months just to hand power back to Cleopatra on Caesar's say-so. They began plotting immediately.

Caesar had only about 3,200 soldiers with him—a tiny force by military standards. Achillas commanded the Egyptian army, which some modern estimates suggest might have numbered around twenty thousand men, though this figure is not confirmed in ancient sources. Either way, the Egyptians vastly outnumbered the Romans. In late 48 BCE, Achillas brought his forces into Alexandria and launched an attack on the royal quarter where Caesar was staying with his soldiers and the Ptolemaic royal family.

What followed was urban warfare in one of the ancient world's greatest cities. Caesar managed to hold the royal palace and the harbor, giving him access to the sea and potential reinforcements. His troops fought the Egyptians in Alexandria's streets and in naval skirmishes in the harbor.

## The Battle for the Harbor

One of Caesar's first priorities was securing his naval position. Much of the Egyptian fleet was docked in the harbor when the siege began, possibly undergoing routine maintenance, with crews likely dispersed throughout the city. Caesar moved quickly, sending his men to burn the Egyptian ships before they could be used against him. The fires spread. According to some ancient sources, the fires reached part of the famous Library of Alexandria, though the extent of the damage remains debated by historians.

The Egyptians weren't finished. They managed to preserve a portion of their naval force and continued to outfit additional ships. The Egyptian forces launched a particularly cunning attack. They cut off the freshwater supply to the Roman-held section of the city. Caesar's soldiers were close to panic until he ordered them to dig wells, which successfully found fresh water beneath the city.

## The Fight for Pharos Island

Caesar understood that controlling Alexandria's harbor meant controlling the island of Pharos, home to the famous lighthouse and one of the Seven Wonders of the Ancient World. The lighthouse wasn't just a marvel of engineering. It also stood on a fortified island that commanded the entrance to the harbor. If Caesar could hold Pharos, the Egyptians couldn't blockade him.

He led an amphibious assault on the island, landing troops from small boats while his fleet provided covering fire. The fighting was fierce. The island was defended by a Ptolemaic garrison and possibly some local inhabitants. Eventually, Caesar's troops forced the defenders to retreat into the town on Pharos, and the Romans captured most of the island.

However, holding it proved harder than taking it. The island was connected to the mainland by the Heptastadion—a causeway about three-quarters of a mile long, with channels or passages at key points. Caesar needed to control this causeway to prevent the Egyptians from attacking his positions. The next day, he landed more troops and began fortifying his position on the causeway.

The Egyptians launched a sudden two-pronged counterattack by land and sea. Caesar's light infantry, caught between the Egyptian assault from the mainland and enemy ships attacking from the water, was quickly overwhelmed by the better-armed Ptolemaic soldiers. In the chaos, Caesar's men began a panicked retreat to their boats.

Caesar himself was caught in the melee. His small ship was swamped by fleeing soldiers trying to escape, and it began to sink. According to Plutarch, Caesar, wearing his distinctive purple cloak that made him an easy target, threw himself into the water. He swam about two hundred paces to safety, reportedly holding important documents above the water with one hand while swimming with the other. Some sources say he dragged his purple cloak through the water with his teeth to prevent the Egyptians from capturing it as a trophy.

The battle ended in defeat. Caesar lost control of the causeway and suffered about four hundred legionaries killed. Another four hundred sailors drowned, according to later sources. It was one of his rare setbacks, though he maintained control of most of Pharos Island itself.

## The Siege Drags On

During the fighting, Caesar had Pothinus executed. Ancient sources say he discovered the eunuch was sending messages to Achillas and possibly conspiring with the Egyptian forces. Some later accounts suggest he might have tried to poison Cleopatra. His death created a power vacuum in the Egyptian command structure that Cleopatra's younger sister would attempt to fill.

Arsinoe IV, who was probably around fifteen or sixteen years old at the time, had been held with her siblings in the palace when the siege began. At some point early in the conflict, she managed to escape from Caesar's custody and made her way to the Egyptian forces besieging the palace. The army proclaimed her queen, making this a three-way civil war. Now Cleopatra (with Caesar), Ptolemy XIII (nominally in Caesar's custody but still a figurehead for the loyalists), and Arsinoe were all claiming the throne.

Arsinoe brought her chief advisor, a eunuch named Ganymedes, with her to the Egyptian camp. Almost immediately, she and General Achillas began quarreling over who should command the army. The power struggle ended when Arsinoe had Achillas assassinated. Ganymedes took over military command of the Egyptian forces. Under Ganymedes's leadership, the Egyptians launched some of their most effective attacks, including the cunning scheme to cut off the freshwater supply to Caesar's forces that nearly caused panic among the Roman soldiers.

For months, the siege continued, with Arsinoe and Ganymedes leading the Egyptian forces. Caesar was trapped in the palace quarter with dwindling supplies and no way to break out. The Egyptians couldn't dislodge him, but he also couldn't advance. Both sides settled into a stalemate. There was street fighting, occasional naval skirmishes, and artillery exchanges. Alexandria's citizens were caught in the middle, their city becoming a battlefield.

Interestingly, a delegation of Alexandrians eventually approached Caesar, asking him to release Ptolemy XIII. They claimed they were tired of being ruled by Arsinoe and Ganymedes. Whether this represented genuine popular sentiment or was orchestrated by Ptolemy's remaining supporters is unclear. Caesar agreed, apparently calculating that releasing the boy might divide his enemies. It didn't work as planned. Ptolemy XIII immediately took command of the Egyptian forces from Arsinoe and renewed the attacks with fresh determination. What happened to Arsinoe at this point is unclear. She seems to have been sidelined when her brother took over, but she remained with the Egyptian forces.

## The Relief and Final Victory

Finally, in early 47 BCE, Roman reinforcements arrived from the east under Mithridates of Pergamum. He brought a mixed force of Roman troops and allied soldiers, including a Jewish contingent contributed by High Priest Hyrcanus II, which was led by Antipater; later sources say it numbered around three thousand men. Mithridates stormed the fortress city of Pelusium on Egypt's eastern frontier and then began marching toward Alexandria.

Ptolemy XIII took much of his army out of Alexandria to intercept Mithridates before he could link up with Caesar. Caesar, seeing his chance, broke out of the city with his troops and marched to join forces with Mithridates. The two armies met somewhere in the Nile Delta region.

In the decisive Battle of the Nile, in late January or early February 47 BCE, Caesar's combined forces crushed the Egyptian army. The battle was a rout. Ptolemy XIII fled the battlefield and attempted to escape by boat across the Nile, but in the chaos, his vessel was reportedly overloaded with panicked soldiers. It capsized and sank. The fifteen-year-old king drowned, weighed down by his armor. His body was later recovered from the river.

With Ptolemy XIII dead and Arsinoe captured, the war was over. Caesar marched back to Alexandria, and the city surrendered without further resistance. Arsinoe was taken prisoner, and she would later be paraded in Caesar's triumph in Rome before being exiled to the Temple of Artemis at Ephesus.

With her rivals defeated, Cleopatra was installed as the sole ruler of Egypt. To maintain the appearance of traditional Ptolemaic co-regency, she married her youngest brother, the twelve-year-old Ptolemy XIV, and made him her nominal co-regent. However, everyone understood he ruled in name only. Cleopatra was the undisputed queen of Egypt, and she had Caesar to thank for it.

## Caesar Lingers in Egypt

The Roman civil war wasn't over. Pompey's sons were still fighting in North Africa and Spain. Caesar's presence was urgently needed back in Rome, where his absence had created political chaos. Yet Caesar didn't leave Egypt immediately after his victory.

Modern scholars believe he stayed for approximately two to three months, roughly from late January or early February until April or May of 47 BCE. Ancient sources offer various explanations. Perhaps he was resting after the exhausting siege, waiting for favorable sailing winds, or simply enjoying his time with Cleopatra. The truth was likely a combination of political necessity, practical concerns, and personal desire.

The relationship between Cleopatra and Caesar was both political and personal, though where one ended and the other began is impossible to say. Their partnership was built on mutual necessity and mutual benefit, but ancient sources also make it clear that genuine affection developed between them. They were well matched intellectually; both were brilliant, ambitious, and politically astute. Ancient writers describe how they would talk late into the night and how Caesar was fascinated by her intelligence and charm.

Politically, Caesar needed to ensure Cleopatra's regime was stable. He couldn't afford to have Egypt descend into another civil war the moment he left. He left behind three Roman legions—about fifteen thousand soldiers—to garrison Egypt and protect the new queen. This was a substantial force that demonstrated Rome's commitment to Cleopatra's rule while ensuring Egypt would remain under Roman influence. He also returned the island of Cyprus to Egyptian control, a gesture that helped legitimize Cleopatra's rule in the eyes of her subjects. Cyprus had been annexed by Rome years earlier under her father's troubled reign.

For Cleopatra, Caesar's support was everything. His military power had secured her throne. His endorsement gave her legitimacy in the eyes of both Egyptians and the wider Mediterranean world. His protection meant that no one—not rival Ptolemies, not ambitious courtiers, not foreign enemies—would dare challenge her while Caesar lived. Egypt needed Rome's backing to survive, and Caesar was Rome's most powerful man.

For Caesar, the alliance made equal sense. Egypt was the wealthiest kingdom in the Mediterranean, and its grain exports were critical for feeding Rome's population. By backing Cleopatra, he secured a reliable, grateful ally who would ensure that grain kept flowing to Rome at stable prices. He also gained access to Egypt's vast wealth without having to spend the time, money, and manpower to conquer it. A friendly Egypt was far more valuable than a hostile one.

There were also practical matters to attend to. Caesar made plans for construction projects in Alexandria, including a monument to himself that would later be called the Caesareum. Though he wouldn't have time to complete it, Cleopatra would take on the project after his departure. He likely spent time meeting with scholars at Alexandria's famous library and museum, discussing mathematics, astronomy, and geography.

In the spring of 47 BCE, Caesar joined Cleopatra on a lavish cruise up the Nile. The stated purpose was to show the Egyptian people their queen, to visit temples, and to reinforce Cleopatra's connection with Egyptian religion and tradition. Cleopatra styled herself as the living incarnation of Isis, the Egyptian goddess of fertility, motherhood, and protection.

There was no strategic reason for Caesar to join this cruise. He had urgent business in Rome. Yet he stayed, traveling with Cleopatra on her opulent royal barge. Ancient sources describe the vessel as spectacular. It was like a floating palace with dining halls, gardens, and elaborate decorations. Each night brought lavish banquets. The cruise allowed Caesar to see Egypt's wealth firsthand—its ancient monuments, its fertile farmland, and its resources. But more than that, it was an extended interlude of luxury and romance, far from the battlefields and political games.

Eventually, duty called Caesar away. In mid-47 BCE, he left Egypt to deal with a rebellion in Anatolia (where he would famously declare "Veni, vidi, vici"—"I came, I saw, I conquered"). A few months after his departure, Cleopatra gave birth to a son. She named him Ptolemy XV Philopator Philometor Caesar, but he was known to history by his nickname, "Caesarion," or "Little Caesar."

Though Caesar never formally acknowledged Caesarion as his son, he never denied it either, and he treated the boy with affection during Cleopatra's later visit to Rome. For Cleopatra, Caesarion represented a potential dynasty, a link between Egypt's throne and Rome's power.

### Cleopatra in Rome

In 46 BCE, Cleopatra traveled to Rome with her co-ruler, the young Ptolemy XIV, and possibly her son, Caesarion. She stayed in Caesar's villa across the Tiber River, which was a very public statement of their relationship.

She came to strengthen Egypt's alliance with Rome, to gain formal recognition from the Senate, and to pursue her long-term goal of recovering Egyptian territories lost by previous Ptolemaic rulers. Her lavish entourage made a powerful impression, reminding Romans that Egypt was wealthy and sophisticated, not just another conquered province.

Personally, she came to be with Caesar and, perhaps, to have him acknowledge their son. Caesar commissioned a golden statue of her in the Temple of Venus Genetrix, reportedly depicted in the guise of Isis-Venus. This sparked a cultural fascination with Egypt among Rome's elite—the latest outbreak of what we now call "Egyptomania." Egyptian motifs appeared in Roman art and architecture. Egyptian fashion influenced Roman dress. The worship of Isis and Serapis spread through Rome.

But not everyone was enchanted. The orator Cicero described Cleopatra with contempt in his letters, calling her arrogant and detailing his disdain for her. Many Romans were scandalized by Caesar's relationship with a foreign queen and his treatment of Caesarion. Some feared Cleopatra's influence over Caesar was leading him toward creating a monarchy, a concept that Romans despised.

The most lasting contribution often associated with Cleopatra's Roman visit was the Julian calendar. The Egyptian solar calendar of 365 days had been in use for millennia and was far more accurate than Rome's confusing lunisolar calendar. Caesar, impressed by its precision, reformed the Roman calendar. He consulted the Alexandrian astronomer Sosigenes to work out the details. The resulting Julian Calendar—365 days divided into 12 months, with a leap year every fourth year—became the standard in the Western world for over 1,600 years.

### The Ides of March

On March 15th, 44 BCE, Julius Caesar was assassinated. A group of senators, led by Brutus and Cassius, stabbed him to death during a Senate meeting. They called themselves the Liberators and claimed they were saving the Roman Republic from tyranny. Earlier that year, Caesar had been appointed dictator for life, and the conspirators feared he intended to make himself king.

Cleopatra was in Rome when it happened. Ancient sources don't record her immediate reaction, but given what followed, one can infer that she was shocked and shifted into survival mode. She remained in Rome for a few weeks, apparently hoping to have Caesarion acknowledged as Caesar's heir. However, Caesar's will named only his grand-nephew Gaius Octavius (better known as Octavian and later known as Augustus) as his heir. Caesarion was not officially mentioned.

Realizing that Caesarion would likely gain no recognition under Roman law, Cleopatra spent her remaining time in Rome gathering information. She understood that whoever emerged victorious in the coming power struggle would determine Egypt's fate. Then she returned to Alexandria.

Caesar's assassination threw much of the Mediterranean into chaos. However, Cleopatra had, to a degree, prepared for the storm. She still had the throne, her son, and Egypt's wealth. What she lacked, however, was the patronage of Rome's master. The next great Roman to enter her life would be Mark Antony, and with him came new opportunities and troubles.

# Chapter 5 –
# Mark Antony and the End

### Cleopatra's Return to Egypt

One month after Caesar's assassination in March 44 BCE, Cleopatra returned to Alexandria with her son Caesarion. The journey back must have been filled with uncertainty. Caesar was dead. Rome was descending into chaos. And Cleopatra had just spent months in the heart of the Roman Republic, openly living as Caesar's mistress, trying unsuccessfully to have their son recognized as his heir. Now she had to return to Egypt and figure out how to survive what came next.

Her first priority was consolidating power at home. During her absence in Rome, Egypt had been overseen by her younger brother and co-ruler, Ptolemy XIV, along with advisors loyal to Cleopatra. But Cleopatra had learned her lesson from the disasters with Ptolemy XIII and his advisors. She wasn't going to let another ambitious brother or his counselors threaten her throne.

Shortly after her return, Ptolemy XIV died under what ancient sources call "mysterious circumstances." He was about fifteen years old. No ancient writer directly accuses Cleopatra of poisoning him, but the timing was awfully convenient, and few modern historians doubt she was responsible. She immediately made the three-year-old Caesarion her new co-ruler, giving him the throne name Ptolemy XV Caesar. Cleopatra was now the undisputed ruler of Egypt, with complete control over her kingdom.

She could see the chaos spreading through the Roman world, and she didn't want a repeat of the Alexandrian War happening while Rome tore itself apart. Her goal was to stabilize Egypt, maintain economic production, and position herself to influence whichever Roman faction eventually won. With Egypt's vast wealth and grain exports, she had the resources to back a winner when the time came to choose.

For now, she would wait and watch from Alexandria while Rome burned.

## Rome's Power Struggle

Caesar had died without a clear succession plan, creating a power vacuum that threatened to tear the Roman Republic apart. Multiple factions emerged, each claiming to be Caesar's true heir or defender of the republic. The assassins—Brutus, Cassius, and their allies—controlled armies in the East. Caesar's supporters rallied around different leaders. It was the kind of chaos that could easily spill into Egypt if Cleopatra wasn't careful.

By the end of 43 BCE, three men had emerged as the dominant powers: Mark Antony, Caesar's longtime friend and consul; Octavian, Caesar's adopted son and designated heir; and Lepidus, a capable general and statesman. They formed what is known as the Second Triumvirate. This power-sharing agreement would allow the men to rule Rome together and avenge Caesar's death.

Of course, these weren't the only players. Cassius, one of Caesar's assassins, built up considerable power in Syria and posed an ongoing threat. Some later accounts suggest he or his supporters approached Cleopatra for aid. She reportedly declined, citing Egypt's internal instability (economic troubles and uncertain Nile floods). Instead, she is said to have quietly backed a loyalist of Caesar (Dolabella), sending support to him in hopes of aligning with the eventual victor. Unfortunately for her, those efforts didn't lead to much. The reinforcements sent under Egypt's backing were intercepted, and her own governor in Cyprus is alleged to have defected to Cassius's side.

In October 42 BCE, the showdown came at the Battle of Philippi in Greece, where the forces of Brutus and Cassius confronted the armies of Antony and Octavian. The Triumvirate won decisively. Both conspirators committed suicide rather than face capture. Caesar had, in effect, been avenged.

After the victory, Octavian, who had recently recovered from illness during the campaign, returned to Rome to consolidate control over the west. Antony, the more experienced general, remained in the East. He toured Greece and Asia Minor, reorganized the eastern provinces, and began preparations for future campaigns. Among his first moves was to summon Cleopatra. Their union would shape the fate of both Egypt and Rome.

### Who Was Mark Antony?

Marcus Antonius (better known as Mark Antony) was born around 83 BCE into a prominent but financially troubled Roman family. He was distantly related to Caesar through his mother's side. His early years were marked by a reputation for reckless behavior, including gambling debts, heavy drinking, and affairs. It was the kind of hedonism that scandalized Rome's conservative elite but made him popular with soldiers and common Romans.

A denarius depicting Mark Antony.[54]

However, Antony wasn't just a playboy. He was also a brilliant military commander and a charismatic politician. He'd cut his teeth in the military under Aulus Gabinius (yes, the same Gabinius who had restored Ptolemy XII to the Egyptian throne), serving in campaigns in Judea and Egypt. He later joined Caesar's staff and became one of his most trusted commanders, serving with distinction in the conquest of Gaul and during the civil war against Pompey.

Antony had probably encountered Cleopatra briefly during her time in Rome with Caesar, but there's no evidence they had any significant interaction. At that time, Antony was married to a politically active, ambitious woman named Fulvia. She would later lead a rebellion on his behalf. He was known for his oratory skills and his ability to work a crowd. His funeral speech after Caesar's assassination had turned public opinion against the conspirators so effectively that they'd been driven from Rome by an angry mob.

Physically, Antony cut an impressive figure. Ancient sources describe him as tall and strong, with a style that reportedly evoked Hercules. He apparently liked to wear his toga draped like the hero's lion skin. He cultivated a connection to Dionysus (the Greek Bacchus), the god of wine and revelry, which fit his personality perfectly. He was passionate, impulsive, loyal to his friends, and dangerous to his enemies.

He was also everything Caesar had not been. Mark Antony was emotional where Caesar was calculating, impulsive where Caesar was strategic, and oriented toward pleasure where Caesar had been oriented toward power. These differences would matter greatly in the years to come.

### The Summons to Tarsus

In 41 BCE, Antony sent messages to Cleopatra demanding she come to Tarsus in Cilicia (southern Turkey) to answer charges. He claimed she had supported Cassius in the recent civil war by providing aid to Caesar's murderers. This was likely exaggerated. Her governor in Cyprus had defected and aided Cassius, but that wasn't necessarily Cleopatra's doing. Her actual support appears to have gone to the Caesarian faction.

The real reason for the summons was likely strategic. Antony needed money and resources for his planned Parthian campaign. Egypt was the wealthiest kingdom in the region, and Cleopatra controlled that wealth. He wanted to assess her loyalty and secure her support. He also wanted to remind her that Rome—specifically, he—held power over Egypt's fate.

Cleopatra didn't rush to comply, though. She received several summons, both from Antony and from his friends, but she delayed. Some sources suggest she was annoyed by the tone of his messages. Others suggest she was being strategic, making him wait while she prepared her entrance. Either way, when she finally decided to come, she made sure it would be memorable.

## The Meeting on the Cydnus

Plutarch, writing about a century later, describes the scene in vivid detail that has captivated imaginations ever since. Cleopatra sailed up the River Cydnus (now known as the Berdan River) toward Tarsus in a barge fit for a goddess. The stern was gilded, the sails were made of purple silk, and silver oars kept time to the music of flutes, pipes, and lutes. She reclined beneath a canopy of gold cloth, dressed and posed as Venus (Aphrodite). Beautiful attendants dressed as sea nymphs and the Graces stood at the rudders and ropes. The air was filled with incredible perfumes and burning incense.

It was theater, and it was brilliant. Cleopatra had done her research. Antony styled himself as the new Dionysus, the god of wine and ecstasy. Cleopatra presented herself as Aphrodite, the goddess of love and beauty. She was appealing to his vanity and his love of Greek culture. And it worked.

Antony invited her to dinner. She declined and invited him to dine with her instead, immediately establishing who held the upper hand. When Antony arrived at her ship, he found a luxurious feast. The entire vessel was decorated with thousands of lamps arranged in geometric patterns. The food and wine were exquisite. The entertainment was spectacular.

Ancient sources preserve a story about their second dinner. Antony boasted that he could provide the finest banquet in the world. Cleopatra bet him she could spend ten million sesterces (an enormous sum) on a single meal. The next night, she served a fine but not exceptional banquet. Antony mocked her, saying she had lost the bet. At the end of the meal, Cleopatra called for a cup of vinegar. She removed one of her enormous pearl earrings—pearls worth millions—dropped it in the vinegar, waited for it to dissolve, and drank it. Before she could dissolve the second pearl, the judge declared her the winner.

Whether this actually happened or is a later embellishment doesn't really matter. What matters is that it captured how contemporaries and later Roman authors saw their relationship. Cleopatra was an exotic, wealthy, powerful queen who could astonish even Rome's most worldly general.

Antony was smitten. He postponed his Parthian campaign and returned with her to Alexandria.

### The Inimitable Livers

Back in Alexandria, Cleopatra and Antony created what they called the "Society of the Inimitable Livers." It was essentially a private club devoted to luxury, pleasure, and living life to its fullest. They hosted elaborate banquets, gambling parties, hunting expeditions, and drinking contests. According to ancient sources, they even roamed the streets at night in disguise, playing pranks on citizens. It was hedonistic, it was excessive, and it was exactly the kind of thing Antony relished.

But it wasn't all pleasure. Cleopatra was also working to secure Antony's support, demonstrate Egypt's wealth and value as an ally, and position herself for whatever came next in Rome's shifting power struggles. She understood that Antony's alliance was crucial for Egypt's survival. Rome was the dominant power in the Mediterranean, and only a strong Roman patron could preserve Egypt's autonomy.

In 41 BCE, during this period in Alexandria, Cleopatra made sure to eliminate a lingering threat.

### The Execution of Arsinoe

Arsinoe IV had been living in exile at the Temple of Artemis in Ephesus since Caesar had paraded her in his triumph in 46 BCE. The temple was a sanctuary. Ancient tradition held that anyone seeking asylum there was under the goddess's protection. For five years, Arsinoe had lived there under that protection, although she remained a potential rival to Cleopatra's throne.

She was dangerous because she was legitimate. As another daughter of Ptolemy XII, she had as much claim to Egypt's throne as Cleopatra did. She had already been proclaimed queen once during the Alexandrian War. As long as she lived, she could be a rallying point for anyone who wanted to challenge Cleopatra. If Cleopatra died, Arsinoe might try to claim the throne. If Cleopatra's enemies wanted a puppet ruler for Egypt, Arsinoe was made for the role.

Cleopatra asked Antony to deal with it, and Antony complied. He sent orders to Ephesus to execute Arsinoe.

The assassination was shocking since it violated the sacred sanctuary. Soldiers entered the Temple of Artemis—one of the Seven Wonders of the Ancient World and one of the most sacred sites in the ancient world— and dragged Arsinoe out. They killed her on the steps of the temple, likely in late 41 BCE. She was in her early twenties.

The killing outraged many. Violating the temple sanctuary was considered sacrilege. It also showed the lengths to which Cleopatra and Antony would go to eliminate threats. It damaged Cleopatra's reputation; even those who understood the political necessity found the method distasteful. But from Cleopatra's perspective, it was worth it. Arsinoe was gone. There were no more rival Ptolemies (except her young son Caesarion, who posed no threat). The throne was secure.

This was the darker side of Cleopatra's rule. She had likely poisoned Ptolemy XIV. Arsinoe was assassinated in a sacred temple. These aren't the actions of a romantic heroine of legend. They were the actions of a ruthless ruler doing what she believed necessary to survive in a brutal political landscape.

The Roman Republic in green and Ptolemaic Egypt in yellow.[55]

## A Romance Interrupted

Antony and Cleopatra's idyllic winter in Alexandria couldn't last. In early 40 BCE, news reached them that the situation in Italy had deteriorated. Antony's wife, Fulvia, and his brother, Lucius, had been campaigning on his behalf against Octavian, and tensions had exploded into open conflict. They had raised an army and rebelled against Octavian's authority in what became known as the Perusine War.

The Parthians had also invaded Roman territory in Syria, taking advantage of Antony's absence and the chaos in Rome. Antony had to leave Egypt. He sailed for Greece and then to Italy.

By the time he reached Brundisium (modern Brindisi, Italy) in the summer of 40 BCE, the situation had changed dramatically. Octavian's forces had crushed the rebellion. Fulvia was dead. Ancient sources say she died of illness, though the timing was awfully convenient. Whether her death was natural or not, it removed a major complication from Antony's life.

At Brundisium, Antony and Octavian nearly went to war with each other. Antony's soldiers refused to let his ships into the harbor. Both sides assembled armies. Civil war seemed imminent. However, cooler heads prevailed. Neither side was ready for all-out conflict. Instead, they negotiated.

The Treaty of Brundisium redivided the Roman world. Octavian would control the west (Italy, Gaul, and Spain). Antony would control the East (Greece, Asia Minor, Syria, and Egypt). Lepidus, who had been increasingly sidelined, got North Africa. To seal the alliance, Antony—now conveniently a widower—married Octavian's sister, Octavia.

Octavia was everything a Roman wife was supposed to be. She was virtuous, dignified, politically astute, and loyal to her family. The marriage was a political arrangement, but by all accounts, Antony treated her with respect and even affection. For three years, they lived together in Athens. She bore him two daughters, Antonia Major and Antonia Minor (the latter would be the mother of Emperor Claudius).

But Antony never forgot Cleopatra. And Egypt's wealth would prove essential for his ambitions in the East.

### Return to the East

For three years (40–37 BCE), Antony governed the eastern provinces with Octavia as his wife, but his mind was on Parthia. The Parthian Empire (roughly modern-day Iran and Iraq) controlled lucrative eastern trade routes and had long challenged Roman power in the East. Back in 53 BCE, Crassus, the third member of Caesar's First Triumvirate, had been killed leading an army against Parthia, and his legionary standards had been captured—a humiliation that still stung Roman pride.

A successful Parthian campaign could transform Antony's fortunes. It would bring glory, wealth from conquests, and the kind of military prestige that could rival Octavian's growing influence in Rome. It might even allow Antony to avenge Crassus's defeat and reclaim the lost standards. However, launching such a campaign would require massive resources, including soldiers, supplies, money, and logistical support.

This meant Antony needed Cleopatra.

## The Meeting at Antioch

In 37 BCE, Antony summoned Cleopatra to meet him at Antioch in Syria. This time, there was no pretense of legal charges. He needed her support for the Parthian campaign, and he was willing to pay for it.

Cleopatra came, and she came with demands. She'd spent three years ruling Egypt, watching Antony's marriage to Octavia and waiting for her opportunity. Now she had leverage, and she intended to use it. Her goal had always been to restore Egypt's former glory. She wanted to recover the territories that earlier Ptolemies had lost to Rome and other powers.

The resulting agreement was unprecedented. In exchange for Egypt's financial support and grain supplies for his army, Antony granted Cleopatra rights over substantial territories, such as parts of Phoenicia (coastal Lebanon), Coele-Syria, Cyprus, and parts of Cilicia (southern Turkey). These were Roman-controlled regions, not Antony's personal property to distribute. No Roman leader had ever extended such authority to a foreign ruler in this way.

The deal angered local rulers whose territories were affected, especially Herod of Judea, who already had a bitter rivalry with Cleopatra and now lost some coastal cities to her influence. It also provided ammunition for Octavian's propaganda machine back in Rome: Antony was giving away Roman conquests to his foreign lover.

But for Cleopatra, it was a triumph. With these territorial grants, Egypt's power and wealth increased dramatically. The eastern Mediterranean seacoast gave her access to valuable timber (Egypt had no trees suitable for shipbuilding), ports, and trade routes. It was the closest she had come to restoring the Ptolemaic Empire's former extent, even if her authority over these regions was more political than administrative.

Antony also formally recognized the twins Cleopatra had borne—Alexander Helios and Cleopatra Selene, now about six years old—as his children. He had apparently known about them since their birth in 40 BCE, but formal recognition was politically significant. It complicated his situation with Octavia and his Roman family, but it showed his commitment to Cleopatra and their partnership.

Cleopatra became pregnant again. Their third child, Ptolemy Philadelphus, would be born later that year.

### The Parthian Disaster

The Parthian campaign of 36 BCE was a catastrophe from start to finish.

Antony assembled a massive army. Ancient sources suggest 16 Roman legions plus auxiliary troops from client kingdoms, possibly totaling over 100,000 men. It was one of the largest armies Rome had ever fielded in the East. The logistics alone were staggering. Antony had to supply tens of thousands of soldiers with food, water, and equipment through hostile territory.

The campaign started poorly. Antony divided his forces, sending his baggage train, which included all the siege equipment, by a different route to speed his advance. This turned out to be a fatal mistake. The Parthian cavalry attacked and destroyed the baggage train, capturing or killing the guards and destroying the siege engines. Without siege equipment, Antony couldn't take fortified cities.

He pressed on anyway, besieging Phraaspa, the capital of Media Atropatene (a Parthian ally). The siege dragged on through the autumn. The Parthian cavalry constantly harassed his supply lines. His Armenian allies, led by King Artavasdes, eventually withdrew their support. Winter was approaching, and his soldiers were running out of food.

Finally, Antony had to admit defeat. He ordered a retreat. It turned into a nightmare. The Parthians pursued his army, constantly attacking. The terrain was harsh, and supplies ran low. Soldiers died from combat, disease, exposure, and starvation. Ancient sources claim he lost over twenty thousand men—possibly as much as a quarter of his army—during the retreat.

He limped back to Syria in the winter of 36/35 BCE, having accomplished nothing. He had won no territory. He took back no standards. He only suffered massive losses and a severely damaged reputation.

Throughout the ordeal and its aftermath, Cleopatra provided crucial support. She sent supplies, money, and clothing for his troops. When he reached the Syrian coast, she was waiting for him with resources to help rebuild his shattered army. Her support might have been what saved his campaign from being even worse, and it certainly increased his dependence on her.

## The Propaganda War

While Antony struggled in Parthia, Octavian had been busy in Rome consolidating his power and building a narrative about his rival. The propaganda campaign against Antony and Cleopatra only intensified after the Parthian disaster.

Octavian portrayed Antony as a man who had abandoned Roman values for Eastern decadence. He had married a foreign queen (never mind that Cleopatra was Greek, not Egyptian). He had given Roman territories to a foreign power. He had also abandoned his virtuous Roman wife for a foreign seductress. Antony was even rumored to be planning to move the capital of Rome to Alexandria and rule as a monarch in the East.

Some of this was exaggeration, and some was outright fabrication. However, some had just enough truth to be effective. Antony really had given territories to Cleopatra's children. He really did spend most of his time in the East. He really had set aside Octavia for Cleopatra. After the Parthian disaster, he looked weak and un-Roman.

Octavia, to her credit, tried to help. In 35 BCE, she traveled east with supplies, money, and fresh troops for Antony in a public display of wifely devotion that would reflect well on him in Rome. But Antony didn't let her reach him. He sent messengers telling her to turn back. Some sources suggest he did this at Cleopatra's urging, not wanting his Egyptian queen and his Roman wife in the same city. Octavia returned to Rome rebuffed, but she refused to leave Antony's house. She maintained the appearance of a loyal wife even as her brother used her rejection as propaganda.

## The Donations of Alexandria

In 34 BCE, Antony staged one of the most controversial acts of his career. He'd managed a minor victory in Armenia against the king who'd betrayed him. He captured King Artavasdes and decided to celebrate with a triumph. But instead of holding it in Rome, as tradition dictated, he held it in Alexandria.

The ceremony was a spectacle. Antony rode through Alexandria in a chariot, with the Armenian king in golden chains walking behind him. It was a deliberately Roman ceremony performed in an Egyptian city. Cleopatra watched from a golden throne, presented in the guise of the goddess Isis. The message was clear: Antony wanted to display his power in the East, even if this did not necessarily mean he saw Alexandria as his capital.

Then came the Donations of Alexandria. In a grand public ceremony, Antony crowned Cleopatra "Queen of Kings" and Caesarion "King of Kings. " He also publicly emphasized Caesarion's parentage, which implicitly challenged Octavian's claim as Caesar's legitimate heir. He distributed territories to Cleopatra's children as well. Alexander Helios received Armenia, Media, and Parthia (the last being aspirational rather than conquered territory). Cleopatra Selene received Cyrenaica and Crete, and Ptolemy Philadelphus received Syria and Cilicia.

These were Roman client territories or spheres of Roman influence. Antony had no legal authority to give them away, especially to the children of a foreign queen. It was an attempt to build a Hellenistic-style dynastic order in the East, with Cleopatra and her children at its center.

The reaction in Rome was explosive. Octavian had exactly the ammunition he needed. To Roman eyes, this was not just an alliance with a foreign monarch; it was a dangerous overreach. Antony appeared to be elevating a foreign dynasty and undermining Roman authority. The Senate didn't declare war yet, but the groundwork was being laid.

In 32 BCE, Antony formally divorced Octavia. He sent her notice to leave his house with their children. It was an insult to Octavia, an insult to Octavian, and a political gift to his rival. Octavian responded by reading what he claimed was Antony's will (how he obtained it remains uncertain—he probably extracted it from the Vestal Virgins, though whether every detail was genuine is debated). The will allegedly stated that Antony wished to be buried in Alexandria with Cleopatra rather than in Rome with his ancestors.

That did it. The Senate declared war. They didn't technically declare war on Antony. War was declared on Cleopatra. That was because Octavian couldn't officially declare war on a fellow Roman, so he framed it as a war against a foreign queen who had seduced and corrupted a Roman general. It was a political fiction. Everyone understood this was a struggle between Octavian and Antony, but the fiction allowed Octavian to pose himself as the defender of Rome against an external threat rather than as a participant in yet another civil war.

The stage was set for the final confrontation.

## The Battle of Actium

In 31 BCE, the forces of Octavian faced off against the combined forces of Antony and Cleopatra in what would be the decisive battle of the Roman civil wars.

Antony and Cleopatra had established their base at Actium, on the western coast of Greece near the entrance to the Ambracian Gulf. It was a defensible position with access to the sea. They had assembled a substantial fleet, perhaps five hundred ships, including Cleopatra's Egyptian squadron. They also fielded an army of maybe sixty thousand to seventy thousand men. On paper, they were formidable.

But there were problems from the start. Octavian's general, Marcus Agrippa, was one of the finest naval commanders in Roman history. He established a blockade that cut off Antony's supply lines and captured several key coastal positions. Soldiers started deserting. Disease spread through the crowded camps. Morale deteriorated. And Antony's officers didn't trust Cleopatra. They saw her as a foreign queen who had led Antony away from Rome and Roman values.

The officers urged Antony to send Cleopatra back to Egypt and fight a land battle, where Roman legions traditionally excelled. However, Antony refused. Cleopatra had provided much of the fleet and significant financing. Her presence was politically important; this was their joint cause and their joint future. Besides, she controlled the war chest, and Antony needed her resources.

On September 2$^{nd}$, 31 BCE, the naval battle began. The details are murky, and ancient sources conflict with each other, but the broad strokes are clear. Agrippa's fleet was more maneuverable. His ships used a new weapon called the harpax, a grappling device fired from a catapult that could lock onto enemy ships and pull them close for boarding. Antony's larger warships, designed for ramming, were at a disadvantage.

At some point during the battle—sources disagree on exactly when—Cleopatra's squadron of about sixty ships broke through the enemy line and sailed away, heading south toward Egypt. Antony, seeing this, abandoned his flagship and transferred to a smaller, faster ship to follow her. His fleet, seeing their commander flee, lost heart. Many ships surrendered. Others tried to escape. It was a rout.

Ancient sources debate Cleopatra's motivations and whether Antony's actions were planned or impulsive. Some claim it was a prearranged escape plan. Cleopatra was supposed to break through with the war chest, and Antony would follow to preserve their resources for continued resistance. Others claim Cleopatra panicked and fled, and Antony impetuously abandoned his men to chase after her. Still others suggest it was a tactical retreat that simply failed.

What's clear is that it looked terrible. A Roman general had abandoned his troops in the middle of battle to follow a foreign queen. Whether or not it was planned, whether or not there were good reasons, the optics were disastrous. Antony's remaining forces—both the fleet and the army camped on shore—soon surrendered to Octavian.

## The Endgame

Antony and Cleopatra returned to Alexandria to find their world collapsing. Most of Antony's eastern allies quickly made peace with Octavian. There would be no coalition to resist him. They spent the winter of 31/30 BCE in a strange mixture of denial and preparation.

Ancient sources describe lavish parties and the creation of a new society called the "Partners in Death"—a grim echo of their earlier "Society of the Inimitable Livers." However, they were also desperately trying to find a way out. Cleopatra sent envoys to Octavian with gifts, trying to negotiate. She offered to abdicate in favor of her children if Octavian would let them rule Egypt as Roman clients. She even reportedly offered him vast sums of money.

Octavian's responses were calculated to divide them. He sent cold, noncommittal replies to Antony while sending more encouraging but vague messages to Cleopatra, suggesting she might save herself if she abandoned Antony. It was psychological warfare. He was trying to make each of them doubt the other's loyalty.

Cleopatra also made practical preparations. She had ships dragged overland to the Red Sea, apparently planning an escape to Arabia or even India if Alexandria fell. However, the plan failed when local Arab tribes, possibly acting independently or at Octavian's behest, burned the ships. She fortified her mausoleum—a tomb she had been building for herself—and moved Egypt's treasury there.

She also began collecting poisons. Different poisons kill in different ways. Some cause convulsions, screaming, and agony. Others were slower and involved hours of suffering. Cleopatra wanted something quick, painless, and dignified. According to ancient sources, she tested various poisons on condemned prisoners, observing the effects with clinical detachment. Which poisons caused pain? Which worked fastest? Which left the body looking peaceful, as if merely asleep? She was essentially conducting lethal experiments, and the condemned prisoners were her unwilling test subjects.

In the summer of 30 BCE, Octavian's forces arrived. He approached from both the west (across North Africa) and the east (through Syria). Egypt's former territories, the ones Antony had given Cleopatra's children, quickly submitted to Octavian. There would be no resistance from them.

Antony managed to win one small cavalry skirmish outside Alexandria, which briefly raised his spirits. However, when the decisive moment came, his remaining forces defected to Octavian without a fight. His fleet rowed out to engage Octavian's ships and then immediately raised their oars in salute and joined Octavian's side. His cavalry did the same. His infantry melted away. In a single day, Antony's army ceased to exist.

Antony retreated to Alexandria. Ancient sources describe him as distraught, ranting that Cleopatra had betrayed him. Whether he actually threatened her or this was simply his despair talking, Cleopatra retreated to her fortified mausoleum with her two handmaidens, Iras and Charmion, and had the doors sealed.

According to ancient sources, someone told Antony that Cleopatra was dead at some point after his army collapsed. Whether this was a mistake, a lie, or part of Cleopatra's own plan is unclear. Believing he had nothing left to live for, Antony attempted to commit suicide in the traditional Roman fashion. He ordered his servant Eros to kill him. When Eros refused and killed himself instead, Antony fell on his own sword.

But he botched it. The wound was fatal but not immediately so. He lay bleeding, calling for someone to finish him. Then word came that Cleopatra was alive, barricaded in her mausoleum. Antony asked to be carried there.

The mausoleum's doors were sealed, as Cleopatra feared Octavian's soldiers would break in if she opened them. So, Antony was hoisted up through a window with ropes. Plutarch describes it as undignified. The dying general was hauled up the side of a building while Cleopatra and her two handmaidens pulled on the ropes. He died in her arms. He was about fifty-three years old.

## Cleopatra's Final Days

Cleopatra surrendered to Octavian after Antony's death, but she had no intention of being paraded through Rome in chains as her sister Arsinoe had been. Ancient sources say Octavian sent one of his officers, Cornelius Dolabella, to negotiate with her, and Dolabella, perhaps charmed by her or perhaps pitying her, warned her that Octavian planned to send her to Rome within days.

She asked permission to visit Antony's tomb and pour libations. Octavian agreed. She went with her two faithful handmaidens, Iras and Charmion, dressed in mourning. She made offerings at Antony's tomb, knowing it would be her last visit to him.

Then she returned to her chambers and requested a final meal. Ancient sources say a basket of figs arrived, brought by a peasant. Hidden in the figs was an asp, a small, venomous snake. Cleopatra wrote a letter to Octavian, asking to be buried with Antony, and had it sent to him.

By the time Octavian's guards had burst into her chambers, it was over. They found Cleopatra dead on her golden couch, dressed in her royal regalia. Iras lay dead at her feet. Charmion was dying, still trying to adjust the crown on her mistress's head. When the guards asked what had happened, Charmion supposedly said, "It is well done, and fitting for a princess descended of so many royal kings," before she too died.

The snake supposedly bit Cleopatra on the arm or breast. Modern historians debate whether it was really a snake. Asp venom isn't always quickly fatal, and Cleopatra had supposedly tested various poisons to find the best method. It might have been poison from another source, with the asp story added later for dramatic effect. What matters is that Cleopatra chose her death. She chose to die as queen of Egypt rather than live as Octavian's captive.

She was thirty-nine years old. It was August 12$^{th}$, 30 BCE.

Octavian, according to sources, was angry that she had denied him his triumph. However, he granted her wish. She was buried with Antony in her mausoleum. The location of their tomb remains unknown to this day.

### The Aftermath

With Cleopatra's death, the Ptolemaic dynasty ended after nearly three centuries. Egypt, which had maintained nominal independence as a Roman client kingdom, became a Roman province. It was essentially Augustus's personal property. No senator would be allowed to visit without the emperor's permission.

Octavian executed Caesarion shortly after. The young man was about seventeen. The official reason was that he posed a threat as a potential rival (as Caesar's alleged son), but really, Octavian couldn't afford any possible challengers. Ancient sources preserve the blunt advice he received: "Too many Caesars is not good." Cleopatra's three children with

Antony—Alexander Helios, Cleopatra Selene, and Ptolemy Philadelphus—were spared and sent to Rome to be raised by Octavia, Antony's widow. She raised them alongside her own children with surprising kindness and dignity.

Cleopatra Selene eventually married King Juba II of Mauretania and became a queen in her own right. The historical record falls silent when it comes to her two brothers. We don't know what became of them. Most historians assume they died young, possibly from illness. It is also possible they were eliminated quietly before they could pose any political threat.

The era of the Hellenistic kingdoms was over. Rome would rule the Mediterranean unchallenged for centuries. Octavian, who would soon take the name Augustus, became the first Roman emperor. The Roman Republic was dead. The Roman Empire had begun.

# Chapter 6 – Legacy

## Queen of the Nile: Cleopatra's Reign

Cleopatra was much more than her relationships. Though her passionate affairs with Julius Caesar and Mark Antony have made her famous, her reign shows that she was also a shrewd politician and diplomat who managed to stabilize the troubled state of Egypt at the start of her rule. While it is debated how much long-term wealth she generated, her economic reforms and cultural patronage strengthened her kingdom's position, and it was partly due to Egypt's resources and strategic value that Octavian found Egypt so desirable as he campaigned through the Mediterranean.

Far from being merely a seductress, Cleopatra was an accomplished monarch who worked tirelessly to maintain Egypt's independence and prosperity in the face of Roman expansionism. However, this view was clouded by the successful propaganda campaign waged against her.

### Egypt at the Start

Cleopatra had the benefit of co-ruling with her father, Ptolemy XII, at the beginning of her reign. Before she ascended to the throne as the sole ruler, she was already involved in administrative and political work. She had a strong understanding of the financial state Egypt was in. Cleopatra had witnessed her father's exile and his dependence on Roman support to reclaim his throne, and she would have known of the debt that had to be paid to the mercenary soldiers he used.

Cleopatra would also have been aware that her father was more of a hedonistic king than a practical one. She would have noticed that he didn't take an active hand in the administrative duties of the kingdom. Historians have found evidence that Cleopatra was a much more hands-on ruler, thanks to her known interventions in official decrees. This hands-on attitude might have come from her education or her observations while in exile with her father. While we cannot be completely sure of her motivations, it is clear that Cleopatra was deeply affected by the state of the kingdom, as she worked to secure a powerful position for Egypt in relation to the expanding Roman Republic.

In 51 BCE, Egypt was in a precarious financial position due to the substantial debts incurred by Ptolemy XII. In his struggle to retain the throne, he gave gifts and bribes to various Roman officials to buy their allegiance and keep them from annexing Egypt. These political interventions were costly, and Ptolemy XII was burdened with massive debts when he returned to the throne. To pay his creditors, he was forced to devalue the Egyptian currency and impose heavy taxes. The debts were so great that even when Cleopatra came to the throne and won the Alexandrian War, Caesar still demanded that she repay the remaining debts of her father.

### Environmental Factors in Egypt

Ptolemy's debts were not the only factor that destabilized Egypt at the start of Cleopatra's reign. In 46 and 44 BCE, at least one major volcanic eruption likely changed the global climate enough to affect precipitation along the Nile. According to recent research, volcanic activity around that time might have weakened the monsoon winds, which were crucial for precipitation in eastern Africa that fed the Nile. This weakening of the monsoon systems has been linked to prolonged dry spells that kept the Nile from flooding. The annual flooding of the Nile was so crucial to Egyptian agriculture that it formed the basis for the Egyptian calendar. Without the Nile's flood, harvest yields were smaller, and famine swept throughout the kingdom. This, in turn, weakened the population of Egypt and disrupted trade patterns throughout the Mediterranean. It led to economic instability in Egypt, which relied on its agricultural exports, especially grain, to keep its economy going. It also caused significant social unrest as the government began to rely more heavily on taxation for revenue.

### Administration and Government

By the time Cleopatra came to power, the administration of the Egyptian government was functional but strained. The upper levels of government had been staffed by Ptolemaic Greeks, but as Alexandria struggled through civil war after civil war, many key officials died or were assassinated, destabilizing certain parts of the government. The strict Ptolemaic administration could not operate at its normal efficiency since officials were replaced and struggled to maintain stability while the country was in crisis.

Agricultural output and trade were affected not only by environmental factors but also by political instability. The country could not function properly if it were constantly at war, and from 55 to 47 BCE, Egypt was embroiled in a series of civil wars and conflicts between claimants to the throne. Egypt possessed valuable resources, including grain and minerals, that were valuable to the Romans and gave Egypt a lot of economic leverage throughout the Mediterranean. But without a proper administration, secure government, and effective trade strategies in place, these resources could not be fully utilized. When Cleopatra finally secured the throne, she had the unenviable task of stabilizing the chaos in the administration and implementing strict reforms to return Egypt to the economic prosperity it was capable of achieving.

### Cleopatra's Vision for a New Egypt

The first few years of Cleopatra's reign were spent fighting her younger brother for control of Alexandria. When this was over, she set about consolidating her rule. A major aspect of this was reforming the economy and administration of Egypt. As we have seen throughout this book, Cleopatra's goal was to maintain Egypt's independence while securing Rome's protection. It was a delicate balance that required Egypt to be valuable enough to Rome that they would not annex it but strong enough that it did not become completely dependent on Roman loans. She swiftly implemented a series of administrative reforms to revitalize Egypt's economy, along with a policy of cultural diplomacy to maintain her popularity in Egypt.

### Economic Reforms

The first and most significant were the monetary reforms she put in place. During her father's reign, Cleopatra saw him debase (devalue) the Egyptian currency to pay his debts to Rome. Cleopatra changed the nature of bronze coins in circulation. She modified them so that the value of each coin was determined by Cleopatra's decree rather than the intrinsic value or weight of the metal in the coin. This was done to help align the value of Egyptian coinage more closely with the Roman denarius, the standard coin used throughout the Hellenistic world. This meant that no matter how much actual bronze was used to make one Ptolemaic bronze coin, it would still be valued at whatever Cleopatra decided it was worth. This was similar to the modern form of currency exchange.

Though this seemed to have stabilized the Egyptian economy to a certain extent, there was still some debasement of the Ptolemaic currency throughout her reign. By the end of her rule, her silver coins were at about 40 percent purity (40 percent of the coin was made up of the metal of its nominal value) compared to a Roman denarius at around 95 to 98 percent purity.

Cleopatra also strengthened the economy by maintaining price controls, upholding state monopolies on certain goods (textiles and papyrus, in particular), and enforcing laws to keep peasant farmers in their villages during the crucial planting and harvesting seasons. This stabilized Egypt's agricultural output and ensured that government officials would be able to accurately collect taxes based on the farmers' output. These measures were put into place after years of famine, during which Cleopatra took direct action by ordering the royal granaries to distribute food to the peasants. Reforms such as these helped prevent the population from revolting against Cleopatra and also strengthened her image as a benevolent and active ruler. This was in stark contrast to her father, who was seen as self-indulgent and ineffective.

## Cultural Diplomacy

Throughout her life, Cleopatra was known to be an intelligent politician, skilled in the art of diplomacy. She reportedly spoke several languages and was the first Ptolemaic pharaoh known to speak Egyptian, which likely helped endear her to the population she ruled. A significant part of her legacy is her cultural awareness and her efforts to preserve Egyptian religion and cultural practices. As a pharaoh, she chose Isis as her divine counterpart, the goddess who represented motherhood and protection; this was as much a public relations choice as a personal one. Cleopatra wanted to be seen as the mother of her people because it would help solidify her power and earn her reverence within the kingdom.

She also aimed to elevate the status of Egyptian religion to enhance Egypt's prestige throughout the Mediterranean. During her reign, she supported the construction and restoration of temples honoring both Egyptian and Greek deities, appealing to both aspects of her diverse population. She is believed to have contributed to the Dendera Temple Complex in Upper Egypt, where reliefs depict her and her son, Caesarion, presenting offerings to the gods Hathor and Horus. She might also have supported construction at the Hathor-Isis Temple, where inscriptions appear in both ancient Greek and Demotic Egyptian, again including images of herself and Caesarion worshiping Egyptian gods. The most significant of these efforts was likely the Caesareum, a temple near the seafront of Alexandria, later dedicated to the worship of Julius Caesar. The entrance was later flanked by two giant granite obelisks, which came to be known as Cleopatra's Needles. She also ordered repairs to major structures in Alexandria that had been damaged during the Alexandrian War. Including her son in temple reliefs and honoring Caesar helped to reinforce and strengthen the legitimacy of her rule, her connection to Rome, and the cultural duality of the Ptolemaic state.

A hallmark of Ptolemaic rule had been artistic and cultural patronage, as evidenced by monuments built by previous kings, like the Lighthouse and the Great Library of Alexandria. By supporting public works and commissioning sculptures, such as depictions of Hathor and Caesarion, Cleopatra upheld the Ptolemaic tradition of encouraging the arts and blending cultures to create a unique identity. Under her reign, Alexandria remained a center of intellectual and artistic activity. While concrete evidence of her direct patronage is limited, she was known to engage with elite society and reportedly participated in private social circles such as the "Inimitable Livers." All of this enhanced her image as an enlightened ruler—that was, until her association with Mark Antony. The lavishness of their court gave her enemies the material they needed to turn public opinion against her.

### Political Legacy

Cleopatra's most significant political accomplishment was maintaining Egypt's independence and wealth in the face of Roman encroachment. For twenty years, she skillfully navigated the complex political landscape of the Mediterranean during an era marked by back-to-back civil wars and dramatic power plays. She leveraged Egypt's resources and formed strategic alliances to secure her position as pharaoh.

Her diplomatic skills were most evident during her time with Caesar. Though their relationship was romanticized, at its core, it was a political alliance built on mutual benefit. Egypt provided Rome with crucial grain shipments, and Caesar's legions provided military support. Cleopatra even found strategic benefit in her passionate romance with Mark Antony. Though their union ended tragically, she briefly regained control of some eastern Mediterranean territories during their time together.

Cleopatra also gives us one of the earliest examples of public relations in history. She tailored her presentations to different audiences, knowing when to make dramatic entrances for maximum effect, as seen in her meetings with Caesar and Antony. She used gift-giving to demonstrate Egypt's wealth and influence to foreign powers, yet spoke Egyptian to communicate directly with her subjects. She developed a well-informed political strategy using trusted advisors and intelligence networks. While later historians would use these tactics as examples of her seductive behavior, from a modern perspective, it is clear that Cleopatra was a sophisticated political operator.

Her reign ultimately ended with Egypt's incorporation into the Roman Republic (although it would very soon become the Roman Empire), but her political shrewdness left a lasting legacy. She showed that a woman could rule a major power in the ancient world as effectively as her male peers. It has taken history a long time to unwind the propaganda set down by her enemies, but historians continue to shed new light on her reign. For instance, environmental upheaval once blamed on poor judgment is now understood to have resulted from volcanic activity that disrupted the Nile's flooding.

### Legacy of a Legendary Queen

Cleopatra's legacy has been a subject of fascination, controversy, speculation, and reinterpretation since the moment she died. We know very little about her early life. Most of what we know is speculation based on what we understand of the Alexandrian elite and Ptolemaic royalty during the Hellenistic period. Her story has been twisted and untwisted by historians from ancient times to the modern day, always through the lens of various historical, political, and cultural forces. Whether you think of her as a seductress or a political genius, you cannot deny that the mystery surrounding Cleopatra has endured for over two thousand years, making her one of (if not the most) famous women in all of history.

### Early Depictions of Cleopatra: Roman Propaganda

In the immediate aftermath of Cleopatra's death, her image was greatly skewed by Octavian's propaganda campaign. Octavian sought to discredit Cleopatra to justify his actions and ensure that the Antony-Cleopatra faction would no longer threaten Rome. He portrayed her as a dangerous foreign queen who had seduced both Caesar and Mark Antony and corrupted them, turning them against their Roman values. His narrative painted Cleopatra as a threat to Roman stability, emphasizing her extravagance, the hedonistic nature of her relationship with Mark Antony, her (alleged) manipulation of the men she had relationships with, and the exoticism of her Egyptian heritage. Roman writers of the time echoed themes consistent with Octavian's propaganda narrative. They portrayed her as a "femme fatale" who was a threat to Rome's dominance. In this way, Octavian managed to justify the annexation of Egypt without destroying his own character. Octavian appeared to offer clemency and pity toward his fellow countrymen, and in her death, Cleopatra became the villain of her own story.

### Cleopatra's Story Begins to Evolve

The tide did not shift until the 1ˢᵗ century CE when Plutarch began to write his *Parallel Lives*. Meant to be a philosophical exploration and a way to provide moral and ethical instruction, Plutarch reexamined the lives of famous historical figures from the ancient world. He attempted to choose those figures whose lives paralleled one another and those from whom his audience could learn. Cleopatra was not a central figure in his book—she appeared in the volumes that explored Julius Caesar and Mark Antony's lives—but he provided a more nuanced portrayal of Cleopatra than those who had come before him.

Though Plutarch offers a somewhat more neutral portrayal of Cleopatra's intelligence and political skill, his account remains influenced by the gender and cultural stereotypes of his era. But still, he acknowledged her intelligence, wit, and diplomatic abilities. He was one of the first to recognize that Cleopatra was a polyglot. Plutarch presented her as a complex political figure rather than a one-dimensional villain, though he still emphasized her use of charm and personal appeal to influence powerful Roman men.

His portrayal of Cleopatra and Antony as a tragic love story went on to inspire many other works of literature and art. It is from Plutarch that we get many of the stories that are famous today, like the story about Cleopatra sneaking into Caesar's quarters in a bed sack and the decadent image of Cleopatra, dressed as Aphrodite, sailing up the Cydnus to encounter Mark Antony. These stories, while iconic, should be understood as literary anecdotes rather than confirmed historical facts.

With Plutarch's account, historians and artists now had a more balanced perspective to draw from instead of the purely negative Roman propaganda. The balance between these interpretations shifted over time as societal morals, customs, and new discoveries shaped how writers looked at Cleopatra's story. For example, during the Middle Ages, a period of intense moral and religious piety, Cleopatra's life was often moralized and used as a cautionary tale about the dangers of lust and indulgence and the fleeting nature of worldly power. She was frequently depicted as a fallen queen, with her downfall attributed to her immorality, such as in Giovanni Boccaccio's *De Claris Mulieribus* (Latin: *Concerning Famous Women*). During the Renaissance, historians again began to reevaluate Cleopatra's legacy. They drew from Plutarch's portrayal and his description of Cleopatra as a witty and intelligent woman, and they began to portray her in a more sympathetic light that emphasized her passion, nobility, and political ability. This pendulum would swing back and forth during the Enlightenment and Romantic periods, reaching a peak in the Orientalism of the 19th century, which once again focused on Cleopatra as an exotic and sexual figure.

A woodcut illustration of Cleopatra and Antony from De Claris Mulieribus. The first scene is a banquet, while the second shows the two's deaths. [56]

## Modern-Day Views of Cleopatra

To this day, Cleopatra continues to be a popular figure from antiquity, but modern scholars have changed their focus when examining her life. In recent decades, they have made efforts to reassess her historical legacy, challenging the long-held assumptions, stereotypes, and biases that have colored the popular perception of Cleopatra. In modern scholarship, Cleopatra's political acumen and her administrative and economic reforms have gained more prominence. The focus is now on Cleopatra as a capable ruler who navigated complex political relationships as she tried to defy Roman expansion. Feminist scholars have also reexamined Cleopatra's story. They were the ones to argue that the negative portrayal that has followed Cleopatra throughout history stems from sexist attitudes toward female leaders, pointing out that her ambition was often recast as ruthlessness. Meanwhile, these traits were admired in her male contemporaries, like Julius Caesar.

## Racial Interpretations of Cleopatra

Debates about Cleopatra's ethnicity have gained prominence in recent years, with scholars arguing for a reexamination of how she is painted and portrayed and advocating for a more nuanced understanding of her Macedonian Greek heritage and how that interacted with Egyptian culture. Most recently, a documentary that depicts Cleopatra as Black has stirred up the controversy again, with some emphasizing that the modern understanding of "race" is a concept dating from the 18th century and that Cleopatra's life existed beyond that concept. In fact, Cleopatra was of Macedonian Greek heritage, and in the interest of consolidating power, the Ptolemies likely maintained that Greek heritage during their three hundred years of rule. However, there were gaps in the Ptolemaic dynasty tree that could have been filled by indigenous Egyptians, Romans, or other people from the Mediterranean and Middle East. The important thing to note is that the differences we see in these ethnicities today did not exist within the same context during Cleopatra's lifetime.

Historian Rebecca Futo Kennedy, writing in *Time Magazine*, makes an important point. We keep having the same argument about Cleopatra's race over and over instead of trying to understand how people in the ancient world actually thought about identity. Ancient artists depicted Cleopatra differently depending on whom they were creating the image for. They made her more Greek-looking for Greek audiences and more Egyptian-looking for Egyptian ones. This wasn't deceptive or contradictory. It reflected the reality that identity in the ancient Mediterranean was more fluid and context-dependent than our modern categories allow. By insisting on a single, definitive answer to "what race was Cleopatra," we are imposing 21st-century ideas onto a world that did not think in those terms.

Regardless of the color of her skin, Cleopatra showed that she deeply identified with her Egyptian heritage. She is the only member of the Ptolemaic dynasty known to have spoken the Egyptian language, and in much of her iconography, she associated herself with Egyptian gods and goddesses. In surviving artifacts like coins and busts, she is depicted as having curly hair and an aquiline nose, though the specific characteristics of her features are lost to history. The territory she once protected and fought for is now considered part of the Arab world, a change that happened gradually, beginning with the Arab Muslim conquest of Egypt in 641 CE, almost seven hundred years after she died. The primary language in the region is now Egyptian Arabic, which replaced Coptic (the latest stage of the ancient Egyptian language) by the 12th century. Even the idea of an "Arab world" is a modern concept, one that emerged in the mid-20th century.

In surviving busts and paintings from the 1st century CE, depictions of Cleopatra emphasize her Greek heritage. In one mural, she is painted as having pale, olive-toned skin and darker hair. This could be considered as accurate an account as we have of Cleopatra's skin color, but it is important to note that at this time, her Egyptian "otherness" would have been set aside in favor of a more "Greek" appearance.

A mural of Cleopatra from the 1st century CE. [57]

The fact is, there is no definite answer to what was Cleopatra's "race" or skin color because her life has been clouded by bias from the beginning of its recorded history. In Rome, Cleopatra depicted herself as more Greek, while in Egypt, she was more Egyptian. The way we view her within the context of history swings back and forth between an exotic seductress and a shrewd politician, and there is no doubt the visual representations of Cleopatra were also colored by these shifting perceptions of her.

## Cleopatra in the Art World: The Eternal Muse

If we were to list all of the paintings, sculptures, frescoes, and murals that have depicted Cleopatra and her life, this book would never end. She has been painted by artists throughout history and sculpted by those in her time and beyond, each honing in on a different aspect of her life. During her lifetime, Caesar is reported to have dedicated a bronze statue, possibly covered in gold, to Cleopatra and had it installed in the Temple of Venus Genetrix in Rome. Later, scenes from her life would be painted over and over again by artists from the Renaissance right up to the famous surrealist artist Salvador Dalí.

## The Berlin Cleopatra

The earliest known depiction of Cleopatra and the one considered by some scholars to be the most accurate is the Berlin Cleopatra. The marble bust is dated to the mid-1$^{st}$ century BCE and is currently housed at the Altes Museum in Berlin, hence its name. The bust was likely sculpted around the time Cleopatra was in Rome, though its exact origin is uncertain, and its identification as Cleopatra is based on stylistic features and comparisons with coinage.

Its style and expression are, in their own ways, a nod to the two sides of her heritage. Her hair is

Berlin Cleopatra. [58]

styled in a signature "melon" hairstyle, with one knot at the neck and delicate curls protruding from the forehead, but she is also wearing the royal diadem of the Ptolemaic kings. Her face is sculpted in a serious manner, with a closed mouth and neutral expression, which is similar to other Greco-Roman busts sculpted around that time. Based on remnants left on the marble, scholars believe it may once have been covered in gold and was sculpted in two separate parts that were brought together.

Authentic, unromanticized depictions of Cleopatra are rare, making this bust extremely important for historians and scholars as a potential reference point for evaluating the accuracy of other paintings, sculptures, and frescoes featuring Cleopatra. It also provides them with insights into how the queen might have been perceived (retaining her Ptolemaic Egyptian characteristics while nodding to her Greek ancestry). The Berlin Cleopatra was unearthed at an ancient Roman villa along the Via Appia near Rome, and it was identified as a portrait of the queen in 1930. It has been on display at the Altes Museum in Berlin since 2010, where it sits beside the so-called Green Caesar.

### Dante's *Inferno*

For many centuries after Cleopatra's death, she largely disappeared from visual art in Europe. While ancient Romans had depicted her in coins and possibly in frescoes or sculptures, the centuries after Rome's fall saw Cleopatra fade from artistic view. Christianity brought different priorities to art, like saints, biblical scenes, and religious stories. A pagan ruler associated with passion and luxury did not easily fit.

When Cleopatra did appear in medieval culture, it was more often in literature, and she wasn't portrayed kindly. One of the most famous and influential medieval depictions appears in Dante Alighieri's *Divine Comedy*, specifically the Inferno section, completed around 1314. Dante's epic poem takes readers on a journey through Hell, Purgatory, and Paradise. Each section of Hell is reserved for different categories of sinners, with punishments designed to fit the crime.

Cleopatra appears in Circle Two of Hell—the Circle of Lust. This circle is for people who let their desires overpower their reason, who are controlled by passion rather than being in control of it. She is in distinguished company: Dido, the queen of Carthage, who killed herself over Aeneas; Helen of Troy, whose beauty started the Trojan War; and Semiramis, the legendary Assyrian queen. Their sexuality led to their damnation.

The punishment Dante came up with for the lustful is both poetic and brutal. The souls are caught in a violent, eternal windstorm. Just like they were swept away by passion in life and couldn't control their desires, they're now swept away by winds forever, unable to control where they go. They can't talk to each other, can't rest, can't find any peace—just tossed around by forces beyond their control.

Dante's choice to put Cleopatra here is telling. He doesn't place her in the circles for fraud, treachery, or violence—sins you might associate with a ruler who had her siblings killed and who aligned herself with powerful Roman leaders for political gain. Instead, he focuses on her sexuality and her relationships with Caesar and Antony. In Dante's view, Cleopatra's defining sin was lust. She was a woman who let passion rule her, who was swept away by desire, and who couldn't control herself.

This reflects how medieval Christian culture often viewed female sexuality as morally dangerous and in need of strict control. Cleopatra became a symbol of what happened when women gave in to their desires—not just sexual desire but also ambition, power, and worldly pleasures. The Roman Catholic Church emphasized chastity, especially for women, and saw sexual passion as a distraction from spiritual devotion. Cleopatra, with her famous love affairs and her life filled with luxury and spectacle, represented many of the temptations medieval morality warned against.

### Boccaccio's *Concerning Famous Women*

A few decades after Dante, another hugely influential text appeared: Giovanni Boccaccio's *Concerning Famous Women*, written between 1361 and 1362. This was one of the first collections of biographies focused exclusively on women, covering 106 women from Eve to Queen Joanna I of Naples. On the surface, it sounds progressive: an entire book about famous women at a time when women were rarely written about as historical figures. However, Boccaccio's purposes weren't exactly feminist. He used these biographical sketches primarily for moral instruction, and many of the women he included served as negative examples, warnings about the dangers of vice.

Cleopatra gets a prominent spot in *Concerning Famous Women*. Boccaccio presents her as an example of moral corruption. He acknowledges her intelligence and political skill, but he frames these qualities as dangerous because they were combined with her sexuality and ambition. In Boccaccio's telling, Cleopatra used her beauty and charm to seduce noble Roman men, corrupting them and leading them away from their duty to Rome. She represented luxury, indulgence, Eastern decadence, and the dangers of women wielding power.

Boccaccio describes Cleopatra as a fallen queen, and he attributes her downfall largely to her own character flaws. In his version, it wasn't Roman politics or military defeat that destroyed her; it was her own immorality. The moral of the story, for Boccaccio's medieval readers, was crystal clear:

this is what happens when women step outside their proper place, when they seek power and pleasure, and when they refuse to be modest and chaste.

What's particularly interesting is how Boccaccio handles Cleopatra's intelligence. He doesn't deny it—the historical record was too clear. But he reframes it as dangerous. In his view, a clever woman is more dangerous than a foolish one because she can do more damage. Cleopatra's wit and political skill became weapons she used for immoral purposes. Where a male ruler might be praised for his intelligence and strategic thinking, Cleopatra's qualities are presented as evidence of her corrupting influence.

*Concerning Famous Women* was enormously popular. It was translated into multiple languages and widely read by educated Europeans for centuries. Boccaccio's portrayal of Cleopatra shaped how she would be understood for generations. Even writers who later took more sympathetic views of her had to respond to Boccaccio's influential negative portrait. His framing of her as a dangerous, lustful, ambitious woman who brought down great men became one of the most enduring interpretations.

## Chaucer's *The Legend of Good Women*

Not every medieval writer took such a dim view of Cleopatra. Geoffrey Chaucer, writing his *Legend of Good Women* around 1386, offered a surprisingly sympathetic portrait that stood in stark contrast to Dante and Boccaccio. The poem was a collection of stories about women from classical literature and history, framed as a penance the narrator had to perform after writing negatively about women in his earlier works. The result is a fascinating document that presents famous women in a much more positive light than was typical for the period.

In Chaucer's version, Cleopatra's relationship with Antony isn't a tale of lust and corruption. It's a story of tragic romantic devotion. While Chaucer does not explicitly invoke the conventions of courtly love, his portrayal of Cleopatra emphasizes loyalty and sacrifice over seduction and manipulation. Cleopatra becomes a devoted lover, and Antony is a noble figure bound to her by love.

Chaucer essentially shifts Antony from one of Rome's most powerful men to the role of a tragic lover bound to Cleopatra, and he elevates her from a lustful figure to a martyr of love—someone who died for devotion and whose commitment was so absolute that she chose death rather than life without him. In Chaucer's telling, Cleopatra builds the tomb where she and Antony would be buried, fills it with serpents, and throws herself in after Antony's death, choosing to die among the snakes rather than live without him.

Modern scholars debate whether Chaucer's poem is sincere or satirical. Some read it as a genuine attempt to rehabilitate famous women who had been treated harshly by male writers. Others see it as a playful critique of literary conventions, using heightened language to parody the genre. The ambiguity is part of what makes it so interesting. But whether Chaucer meant it seriously or ironically, he created a version of Cleopatra that was very different from what his contemporaries were writing.

## The Abreujamen Manuscript

Literature dominated medieval depictions of Cleopatra; visual representations were very rare. One remarkable exception appears in a 14th-century manuscript created at the papal court in Avignon, known as the *Abreujamen de las estorias.* This illuminated manuscript contains an image of Cleopatra that is unique and reveals medieval attitudes toward race, religion, and the enemies of Christianity.

In the *Abreujamen* illumination, Cleopatra is dressed as a European noblewoman, wearing the fashions of 14th-century aristocracy. However, the artist deliberately emphasized certain physical features, like her dark brown skin, conspicuously white teeth, and a rounded nose. This likely wasn't based on historical knowledge of what Cleopatra actually looked like.

The illuminator used these same racialized characteristics throughout the manuscript to depict other figures the medieval Christian world considered enemies. The entire Ptolemaic lineage is shown this way. So are ancient Persian kings and 12th-century Muslim leaders like Saladin. The artist appears to have linked Christianity's perceived enemies across more than a thousand years of history through shared physical characteristics that marked them as "Other," as outside the Christian community.

In medieval manuscripts, dark skin was used to mark enemies of Christianity. Cleopatra's inclusion here is particularly telling because she lived centuries before Christianity even existed and had no connection to the Crusades. But as queen of Egypt—the land of the pharaohs who enslaved the Israelites, where the Holy Family fled from Herod, and by the medieval period, a Muslim land—she could be lumped in with

Christianity's enemies. In the medieval mind, these different "Egypts" all blurred together.

The *Abreujamen* manuscript is one of the very few known images in which Cleopatra is shown as anything other than a White woman. But we must remember this depiction was not an attempt at historical realism or a recognition of African ancestry. It was about using physical appearance as a visual for religious and political hostility. The artist wasn't trying to depict what Cleopatra might have looked like; he was trying to mark her as an enemy of Christianity.

### The Boucicaut Master

The early 15^th century marked the beginning of a transition. The Renaissance was starting to emerge in Italy and spread across Europe, bringing renewed interest in classical antiquity. Artists and scholars began studying ancient texts more carefully, and figures from Greek and Roman history became popular subjects. Around 1409, an artist known as the Boucicaut Master created an illumination of the tomb of Cleopatra VII and Mark Antony for a version of a work by Giovanni Boccaccio. It was one of the earliest visual representations of Cleopatra in many centuries.

The Boucicaut Master was an illuminator working in the early 1400s. He was probably French or Flemish. His name comes from a prayer book (a "book of hours") commissioned by Jean II Le Meingre, Marshal Boucicaut. Before the printing press, books were copied by hand, and wealthy patrons commissioned richly decorated manuscripts. Skilled illuminators like the Boucicaut Master were among the leading artists of their day.

The Boucicaut Master's illumination shows Cleopatra and Antony lying together in a Gothic-style tomb, with a snake near Cleopatra's chest and a sword through Antony's chest. Unlike earlier medieval works that used Cleopatra mainly as a moral lesson, this image treats her and Antony as historical figures in an actual story that involves love, tragedy, and death.

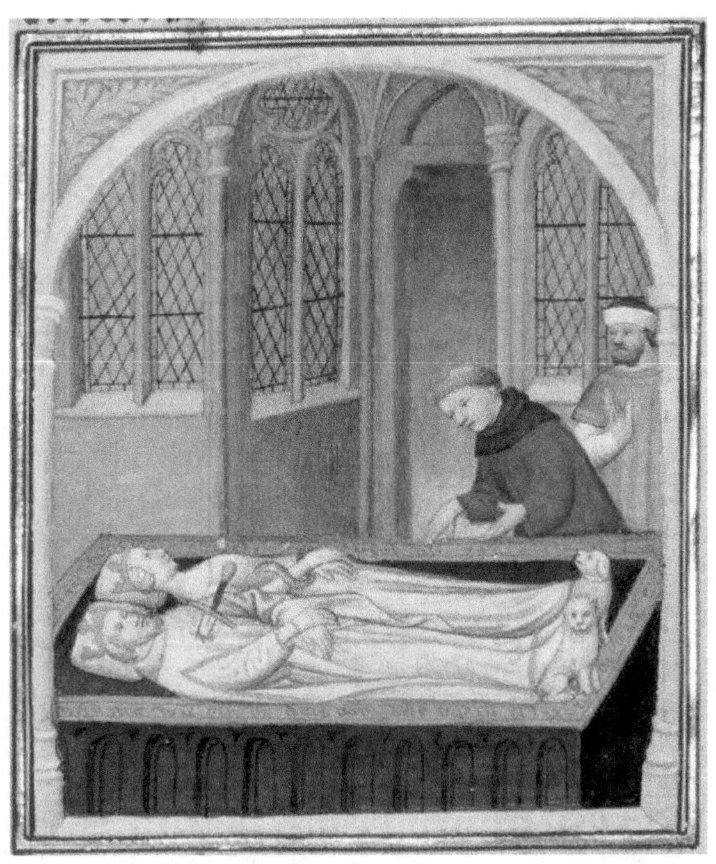

The Tomb of Cleopatra and Mark Antony. [59]

This shift was important. Medieval moralists like Dante and Boccaccio had been interested in Cleopatra primarily as an example or a warning. The specific details of her life mattered less than the moral lessons her story could teach. But the Boucicaut Master's illumination suggests a different approach, one more interested in the narrative and dramatic aspects of her life. This reflects the early Renaissance fascination with classical history, not just as a source of moral instruction but as something worth depicting for its own sake.

Because manuscripts were expensive, this kind of imagery would have been seen only by wealthy people who could commission such works. The fact that these patrons wanted images of Cleopatra suggests her story was becoming fashionable again among the aristocracy and educated classes. The medieval moralized version hadn't disappeared, but it was being joined by a growing interest in the drama and romance of classical antiquity.

## Giampietrino's *Death of Cleopatra*

By the early 1500s, the Renaissance fascination with classical subjects was in full swing, and Cleopatra had become an acceptable—even desirable—subject for artists. Around 1515, the Italian painter Giampietrino created his *Death of Cleopatra,* a work that shows both the opportunities and the problems of how Renaissance artists approached her story.

Giampietrino was a follower of Leonardo da Vinci and worked in Milan. His painting shows Cleopatra at the moment of her death, but the way he depicts this moment is revealing. In the painting, Cleopatra is completely nude, reclining with her body on display. A snake—unmistakably phallic—bites her exposed breast. The viewer's eye is drawn not to her face or expression but to her body and the snake at her breast.

Death of Cleopatra by Giampietrino. [60]

This isn't a painting about Cleopatra's political defeat or her choice to die rather than be captured. It isn't about her dignity or defiance. It's an erotic image that connects female nudity, sexuality, and death together. The scene that should be about agency—Cleopatra choosing her own death rather than being paraded through Rome—becomes a voyeuristic spectacle. The woman who spent twenty-one years ruling Egypt, spoke multiple languages, and negotiated with Rome's most powerful men is reduced to a naked body for viewers to look at.

This approach established a pattern that would dominate Cleopatra's visual representation for centuries. The Renaissance brought her back into visual art after centuries of medieval moral warnings, but the paintings often cared more about displaying the female body than exploring who Cleopatra actually was or what her death meant. Art historians have noted that by the 17th century, patrons had the flexibility to commission works that pushed toward their own desires. If you wanted erotic art, asking for a painting of Cleopatra's death was perfectly respectable.

Artists also depicted Cleopatra according to European beauty standards. She has remarkably pale skin, often blonde or light brown hair, and delicate features that bear no resemblance to her actual Macedonian Greek heritage. Her death scene was consistently sexualized, and her story was told through a male gaze far more interested in spectacle and eroticism than in understanding the woman herself. Cleopatra would often be depicted reclining, often nude or semi-nude, with the snake as both a murder weapon and a phallic symbol. Her expression was either ecstatic or peaceful; it never showed pain or the actual horror of death by poison. These images told viewers that even in death, Cleopatra's primary function was to be beautiful and sexually available to the viewer's gaze. The Renaissance might have brought her back into art, but it reduced her to a single sexualized moment.

### Jean Mignon's Cleopatra

In the mid-1500s, French artist Jean Mignon created an etching of Cleopatra's death that took a different approach from painters like Giampietrino. Where Giampietrino focused narrowly on Cleopatra's body, Mignon opted for an ornate, richly detailed scene. His etching is decorated with many elements, including a bedchamber, ornamental garlands, cherubs or putti, and a decorative frame that shows the story as part of a broader, symbol-laden composition.

Mignon belonged to the School of Fontainebleau, a group of artists at the French royal court known for elaborate and decorative works. These artists often treated classical and mythological themes with a sense of pageantry and lavish detail, which was in contrast to some Italian Renaissance works that emphasized more focused, dramatic moments.

Cleopatra Bitten by an Asp by Jean Mignon. [61]

In Mignon's etching, Cleopatra's death is shown as a dramatic, staged event, not just a private or erotic moment. The bed, the ornamental setting, the surrounding decorative elements, and the overall theatrical framing treat her death as a story steeped in luxury, symbolism, and spectacle. This treatment reinforces the idea of Cleopatra as excessive and indulgent, with her final moment surrounded by the trappings of luxury and material excess. The etching visualizes what older tales described in words. Unlike medieval texts that warned in abstract moral terms, Mignon showed that excess visually.

Mignon's work stands somewhere between medieval moralizing traditions and the Renaissance's revived fascination with classical stories. The etching does not seek to explore Cleopatra's politics or personality but to evoke a powerful story.

### *Cleopatra with the Asp* - Guido Reni (c. 1628)

After disappearing from mainstream visual art for over a thousand years during the Middle Ages, Cleopatra returned in the early Renaissance, though often in problematic ways that sexualized her death. By the Baroque period, artists were creating more sophisticated interpretations that drew inspiration from Plutarch's *Parallel Lives*.

One of the most famous Baroque interpretations came from the Italian artist Guido Reni. The Renaissance had sparked renewed interest in figures and stories from classical antiquity, and Baroque artists took this further. The figure of Cleopatra was now regal and intellectual while still passionate and tragic—all elements that can be found in Reni's painting. The painting is infused with emotional intensity from the technique of chiaroscuro, which was used by many Baroque painters to convey drama and emotion and to guide the viewer's eye. The painting enhances Cleopatra's sense of loneliness as she meets her fate. Her body takes over the canvas, and the asp is a stark contrast to her skin. The painting manages to romanticize Cleopatra's tragic end without resorting to classic depictions of luxury and excess. It stands in stark contrast to Jean Mignon's etching from the 1500s.

Cleopatra with the Asp by Guido Reni. [62]

## *Cleopatra* - John William Waterhouse (1888)

In the mid-1800s, the Western world experienced a renewed fascination with ancient cultures, but this time, they honed in on one period of classical antiquity. As more and more Europeans went on archaeological excavations in Egypt, the obsession with the ancient civilization grew. Fueled by discoveries like the Rosetta Stone, the continent was soon swept up in Egyptomania and began to incorporate Egyptian themes into Victorian-era art, literature, and decor.

John William Waterhouse, the pre-Raphaelite painter known for his romantic depictions of tragic heroines like Ophelia and the Lady of Shalott, added Cleopatra to his list of subjects, making her one of the few historical figures to receive his romantic treatment. The painting shows Waterhouse's signature style, blending elements of pre-Raphaelite and academic painting with a historical figure in a pose that emphasizes her intelligence, power, and sensuality.

Cleopatra by John William Waterhouse. [63]

Waterhouse paints Cleopatra sitting in her cushioned throne, her hand draped over a lion's head armrest. Her face is contemplative, yet her clothing is soft and shows the curves of her body beneath it. It tells the viewer that Waterhouse viewed Cleopatra as more than a tragic or sexual subject. The golden hues in Cleopatra's jewelry and surroundings are enough for the audience to get a sense of luxury and opulence, but her eyes remain the focal point, conveying a mix of intelligence and determination and engaging the viewer directly.

As a part of Waterhouse's catalog, Cleopatra stands out as a tragic figure who still has agency. Unlike Ophelia or the Lady of Shalott, she isn't staring up into the sky, pleading with someone. This is a very personal portrait, though it is not typical in Waterhouse's broader body of work. It is fitting for an age when women's roles were starting to be reexamined and when Britain was being ruled by its own complicated and tragic figure, Queen Victoria.

For a long time, scholars didn't know what happened to this painting. It was somewhat unusual in Waterhouse's body of work, as he didn't usually paint such intimate, close-up portraits, and they thought for a long time that it might have been destroyed. The painting resurfaced in the early 2000s in the collection of a man in Colorado, who claimed to have acquired it when he bought a business and its contents back in the 1960s. The painting was put up for auction and was estimated to sell at £500,000, but it did not reach its reserve price and remained unsold.

### *Cleopatra Before Caesar* - Jean-Léon Gérôme (1866)

About two decades prior to Waterhouse's intensely emotional painting, Jean-Léon Gérôme produced a scene that shows Cleopatra in almost the opposite light. Gérôme's painting is practically a scene out of a film. In this work, Cleopatra's vulnerability comes from her exposure, with Gérôme using her light-colored body and clothing in contrast with the rich reds surrounding her to convey to the audience the potentially dangerous situation Cleopatra found herself in. Gérôme's painting brings to life a part of Cleopatra's myth that had rarely been shown in art—the moment she smuggled herself into Caesar's private chambers. This painting helped popularize that myth and contributed to making it feel like a historical fact. George Bernard Shaw drew on the "carpet" story, which appears in 18th-century translations of Plutarch, as inspiration for his play *Caesar and Cleopatra*, and the carpet myth carried over into film once Cleopatra's story crossed onto the silver screen.

Cleopatra Before Caesar by Jean-Léon Gérôme. [64]

While Gérôme's and Waterhouse's paintings come from the same period in history and are both influenced by the Egyptomania of the time, Waterhouse's depiction of Cleopatra is more intimate and subtly emphasizes Cleopatra's intellect and political acumen. Gérôme's, on the other hand, is more focused on Cleopatra's sensuality and the dramatic elements of her story. He shows us the Cleopatra who was committed to spectacle and indulgence, from the elaborately detailed Persian carpet to the fact that her breasts are partially visible in her loose dress.

Each of these paintings shows us how the different elements of Cleopatra's life story have been emphasized at different points in time. Whether it is a cautionary tale, as with Jean Mignon's etching, or a renewed focus on Cleopatra as a powerful female figure, Cleopatra has been a muse throughout history and a vessel for artists to explore modern ideas.

### Cleopatra on Stage and Screen

It would take longer for Cleopatra to be reimagined for the stage. Painters could use her as an allegory for good and evil or for the dangers of indulgence versus chastity, but as dramatic as her story was, it would take a few hundred years before it was widely adapted for the stage. Once Shakespeare broke the seal on dramatizing the events of Cleopatra's life, audiences and dramatists alike could not get enough. The first was an almost cautionary tale of tragedy and the inevitability of fate. Later on, George Bernard Shaw would use Cleopatra as he did other historical figures: as a vessel for exploring his own politics and philosophy, though he would use Cleopatra's shrewd political ability to examine gender politics and the relationships between men and women. When Cleopatra finally appeared on the silver screen, artists and directors were finally able to truly convey the luxurious riches of her time.

Cleopatra was as much a pop culture figure as she was a historical one. This wasn't anything new. The British and French had glamorized her life in the 19th century as they excavated the riches of the ancient Egyptian world. In the 20th century, it was Hollywood's turn to do the same. From the beginning, Cleopatra was synonymous with excess and wealth, and in a way, her story finally came of age as the modern world turned to examine Cleopatra as a human rather than a goddess.

*Antony and Cleopatra* and *Caesar and Cleopatra*

The two major works about Cleopatra's life, ironically, focus on the two major relationships she had. Shakespeare's *Antony and Cleopatra* and George Bernard Shaw's *Caesar and Cleopatra* dramatize two significant periods in Cleopatra's life, but they differ considerably in their approach and thematic focus. For starters, the two playwrights didn't necessarily use or treat the source material in the same way. Shakespeare's main source would have been Plutarch's *Parallel Lives*. While Shaw might have used the same source, it would have been a different translation (likely the Langhorne translation, which was among the first to describe Cleopatra's arrival in a carpet rather than a bedding sack). The one Shakespeare used was probably Thomas North's translation, which was rendered from Greek into French before being translated into English. In both cases, parts of Cleopatra's story were lost or embellished for dramatic effect.

Shakespeare's play explores the themes of passion, power, and conflict, while Shaw's presents a more focused view of the political and intellectual mentorship between Caesar and Cleopatra. Shakespeare's play treats Cleopatra and Antony as one of history's great tragic romances, reinforcing the image of Cleopatra as a seductive queen. The play also follows the same basic narrative that Octavian promoted and that medieval writers used: Cleopatra's relationship with Antony is a cautionary tale about passion and downfall.

As far as tragedies go, Shakespeare's is more straightforward. We see two characters fall in love, fall to their hubris, and then fall on themselves. The image of Cleopatra as a seductress and the emphasis on the luxury of her life would have been more entertaining for audiences as well, and Shakespeare was known to be a playwright who wrote for the masses rather than for philosophical inquiry. A play about hubris was entertaining if you fell in love with the characters and empathized with their downfall. Shaw, on the other hand, was a more philosophical and political writer. It makes sense that he wrote a play about Cleopatra's more political relationship since, as a writer, Shaw often used the characters in his plays as a mouthpiece for his own ideas.

Shaw's play was less historically accurate, but it digs into power and politics in a way Shakespeare's doesn't. Shakespeare's play stuck closer to Plutarch's version of events, but he made them dramatic by covering a huge geographical area and a long timespan, using shorter scenes and poetic language to pull the audience into a story that was about more than just politics. Shaw did the opposite. He kept the setting focused on a shorter period and fewer characters so he could bend the facts to fit his themes about power and politics. He used more straightforward language that his audience could easily understand, with humor mixed in to make it digestible. Neither play is a biography. Both writers changed Cleopatra's life to fit their dramatic purposes, and both relied on Plutarch's account, which was told from the perspective of the men around her. We don't get Cleopatra's view of her relationships with Caesar and Antony because Plutarch only wrote about her as a side character in their stories.

The two plays made a huge impact on how Cleopatra has been portrayed ever since, though. They have been reinterpreted over and over throughout the 20th and 21st centuries. Shakespeare's work presents an older, more emotionally complicated Cleopatra in a sweeping historical drama, while Shaw's play shows her as a young woman learning politics. Together, they let us explore why Cleopatra's story has remained so fascinating and the different ways her life can be turned into drama. Without these plays, we might not have gotten the most famous depictions of Cleopatra on film, and she might not have become the pop culture icon she is today.

### Cleopatra on Film

If there are two things that make films about Cleopatra stand out, they are the budget and the cultural impact. Once directors and actresses began to translate Cleopatra's story to the silver screen, her impact became much greater than ever before. True, she had been the subject of art for centuries, but this new interpretation came with an emotional element that had been missing. Until the 20th century, Cleopatra was seen through an artist's eyes, and her story was told as if it were a myth or an allegory. Through the cinematic portrayals of the 20th century, we gained a new understanding of Cleopatra through the actresses who played her, giving us a more nuanced look at her emotions and determination. With that came the grandeur of Hollywood and ancient Egypt, two places where you couldn't get enough of gold, silk, and a good story.

### Cleopatra in the Silent Age

The first depiction of Cleopatra on screen was actually in 1899, when the film pioneer Georges Méliès made *Robbing Cleopatra's Tomb*, a short horror film in which a character named Cleopatra appears as a ghost or resurrected mummy. In 1912, American actress Helen Gardner produced and starred in a silent film titled *Cleopatra*, one of the earliest feature-length films in the United States. Gardner's Cleopatra was portrayed as a strong and calculating femme fatale, and the film was notable for its elaborate costumes and sets, many of which Gardner designed herself.

## HELEN GARDNER AS "CLEOPATRA"

Helen Gardner in Cleopatra. [65]

In 1917, Theda Bara appeared in a silent film that was a combination of the adaptations by Shakespeare and the French playwrights Émile Moreau and Victorien Sardou. This film was partially lost, but some film stills remain depicting Bara as Cleopatra. She wears costumes clearly influenced by the Victorian Orientalist view of the queen. This is the first in a long line of Cleopatra adaptations that pushed the boundaries of budget and excess, with a budget of up to $500,000 (equivalent to about $12 million today). The production built copies of the Great Pyramid and the Great Sphinx of Giza, contracted a fleet of ships in the Balboa Peninsula, and had over fifteen thousand extras and two thousand horses. For the silent film era, this was one of the most expensive films ever made.

Theda Bara as Cleopatra. [66]

Because we don't have much of the film, it is difficult to make an analysis of how Theda Bara portrayed Cleopatra. However, in the 1930s, Hollywood brought Cleopatra back to the screen. One notable interpretation from that era was Claudette Colbert's portrayal in Cecil B. DeMille's *Cleopatra* (1934), a film not directly based on any single historical source but still shows the classic scenes of Cleopatra's life, namely her first encounter with Caesar. Colbert portrayed a seductive and cunning version of Cleopatra, an interpretation fitting for the glamour and excess of 1930s Hollywood. The film is memorable for its sensual sets and atmosphere, fitting right in with other DeMille movies.

## Famous Actresses and a Famous Name

The next two women to play Cleopatra were already famous, strong, and complicated women themselves, and each gave a performance that was both influential and culturally impactful. Vivien Leigh and Elizabeth Taylor were two actresses who, although they were from different generations, were known to be beautiful, complex women who gave iconic performances. Leigh, with the iconic role of Scarlett O'Hara under her belt, partnered with Claude Rains, who played Caesar, in a film adapted from the George Bernard

Vivian Leigh as Cleopatra. [67]

Shaw play. Leigh's performance differs from other, more glamorous portrayals of Cleopatra, as she offers a more nuanced portrayal of the character. Leigh's Cleopatra isn't fully formed; she transforms before the audience's eyes from an ambitious but naive young woman to a formidable leader and a queen. Before this point, people usually focused on Cleopatra as a fully formed queen, one who seemed to roll out of the carpet as a political genius. In this portrayal, the audience watches as Caesar molds Cleopatra's instincts, leaving them wondering who is manipulating whom.

In Elizabeth Taylor's epic film, we see a very different Cleopatra. Taylor presents Cleopatra as a powerful, seductive, and politically astute queen. She does not offer the same vulnerability; instead, she shows the audience Cleopatra's charm, intelligence, and allure. The most impactful part of this performance, however, might have been the allure of what was going on behind the scenes. The film was among the most expensive films ever made up to that point, with a production cost that ultimately reached about thirty million dollars (with some reports estimating total expenditures, including reshoots and overruns, at around forty-four million dollars). The cost overruns nearly bankrupted the studio. Taylor and her co-star Richard Burton's intense on-screen chemistry spilled over onto set, and the pair became embroiled in a widely publicized affair that would remain one of the most-talked-about relationships in the history of Hollywood. After the film was released, the decadent sets, lavish costumes, and Taylor's Cleopatra became iconic, contributing significantly to the film's cultural legacy.

Elizabeth Taylor as Cleopatra. [68]

The women who played Cleopatra on screen embodied the fascinating complexities of her character in an age when feminism and evolving cultural attitudes began to influence how history's figures were reimagined for modern audiences.

# Conclusion

We began this journey in the shadow of the great Ptolemaic pharaohs—Ptolemy I Soter, who built a kingdom from the ashes of Alexander the Great's empire, and Ptolemy II Philadelphus, who made Alexandria the intellectual crown jewel of the ancient world. We watched as that dynasty slowly crumbled through civil wars, weakened by debt and Roman encroachment, until it produced one final remarkable ruler: Cleopatra VII Thea Philopator.

She was born into a kingdom in crisis, exiled as a teenager, and forced to fight her own siblings for the throne. She allied with Julius Caesar and watched him die. She rebuilt her kingdom's prosperity through shrewd economic reforms while famine ravaged the land. She gambled everything on Mark Antony and lost. And when she knew the end had come, she chose to die on her own terms rather than be paraded through Rome in chains.

Cleopatra's life bridged the twilight of the Hellenistic era and the dawn of the Roman Empire. For twenty-one years, she kept Egypt independent through her intelligence, diplomacy, and sheer determination. She was the only Ptolemaic ruler who bothered to learn Egyptian and could speak to her subjects without a translator. She was an educated woman in a world that often didn't value female intellect. She practiced what we would now call public relations, tailoring her image to different audiences and making dramatic entrances when they would have maximum effect. She understood instinctively that politics is performance.

Her relationships with Julius Caesar and Mark Antony have overshadowed everything else about her for two thousand years. The truth is more complex than the narratives. These relationships were fundamentally political. They were strategic alliances between a queen fighting for her kingdom's survival and Roman strongmen who needed Egypt's wealth. But they were also genuine. Caesar and Antony weren't mindless puppets. They were two of the most brilliant, ambitious men of their age, and they chose Cleopatra as their partner for reasons that went beyond cold calculation. She matched them intellectually, understood their ambitions, and shared their vision of what the Mediterranean world could become.

Sometimes her calculations failed. Her commitment to Mark Antony in the 30s BCE, when Octavian was clearly winning Rome's final civil war, marked the beginning of her downfall. The Battle of Actium in 31 BCE sealed her fate. She had worked her entire adult life to secure Egypt's independence, to protect her children's inheritance, and to prove that a Hellenistic kingdom could survive in Rome's shadow. In the end, she realized she had bet on the wrong man and miscalculated Rome's internal politics. There was nothing left to do but orchestrate one final dramatic scene—dying on her golden couch in royal regalia, the asp hidden in a basket of figs, poison coursing through her veins as Roman soldiers battered at the mausoleum doors.

Beneath all the myth and propaganda, there was a real woman. She grew up in a palace where siblings were rivals, and murder was policy. She received the finest education available in the ancient world. She was exiled at twenty-one and had to build an army to reclaim her throne. She smuggled herself into Julius Caesar's presence (perhaps in a sack) because she understood that fortune favors the bold. She gave birth to four children. She made brilliant decisions and catastrophic miscalculations. She was fully human. Cleopatra was neither the monster her Roman enemies painted nor the perfect feminist icon modern admirers might wish her to be.

Modern historians have worked hard to separate fact from fiction. We now understand how Octavian's smear campaign shaped the ancient sources, how Plutarch's focus on great men relegated Cleopatra to a supporting role, and how each era's biases influenced its portrait of her. This book has tried to give a more nuanced picture—a queen who was genuinely brilliant but also ruthless, politically astute but also sometimes wrong, genuinely in love but also calculating, devoted to Egypt's independence but also willing to kill her siblings to secure power. She was a leader trying to save her kingdom in an age when kingdoms like hers were being overtaken by Rome.

The Ptolemaic dynasty ended with Cleopatra. After her death, Egypt became just another Roman province. The Great Library eventually burned down or fell into disrepair. The Mouseion declined. The Roman Empire would last another five centuries in the west, another thousand years in the east, but it would be a different kind of empire. It was more brutal, more efficient, and less interested in the cultural synthesis that had made Alexandria so remarkable.

Over two millennia, Cleopatra has been transformed from a historical figure into a myth, becoming a mirror in which each civilization sees its own values reflected back. Medieval Christians saw her as a cautionary tale about sin. Renaissance artists reimagined her as a tragic romantic figure. Victorians saw her as an example of exotic Eastern decadence. Modern feminists see her as a powerful woman destroyed by male propaganda. Each interpretation tells us as much about the interpreters as it does about Cleopatra herself.

This is her true legacy—not her dramatic life or tragic death but her ability to make us think. For over two thousand years, people have argued about her character, her choices, her loves, and her ambitions. Was she a victim of Roman imperialism or an ambitious player in Mediterranean power politics? Was she a brilliant ruler or someone whose charisma exceeded her judgment? Did she genuinely love Caesar and Antony, or were they useful allies? These questions have no simple answers, and that's precisely why Cleopatra endures when so many other historical figures have faded into footnotes.

Here was a woman who refused to be conquered, even when conquest was inevitable. She played the game as well as it could be played. She lost, but she made sure that her loss would be remembered as something magnificent. She understood that how we are remembered matters as much as how we lived. She was right.

# Here's another book by Enthralling History that you might like

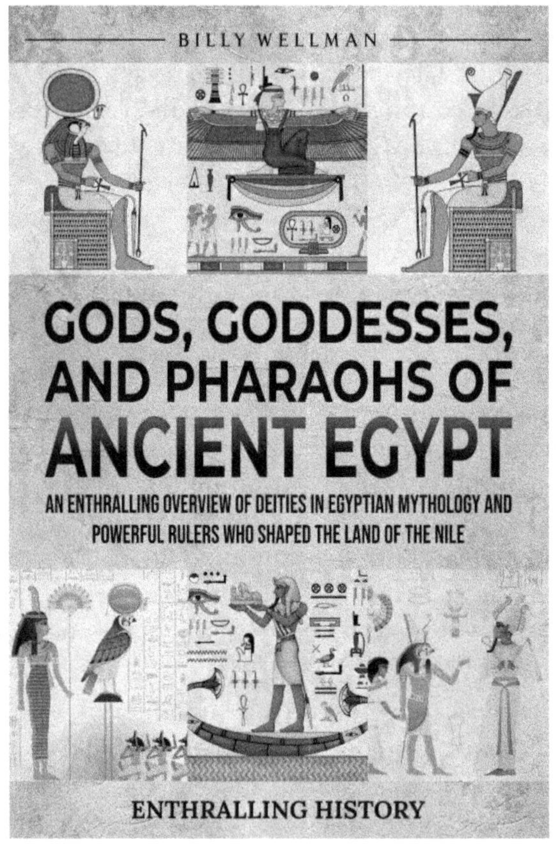

# Free limited time bonus

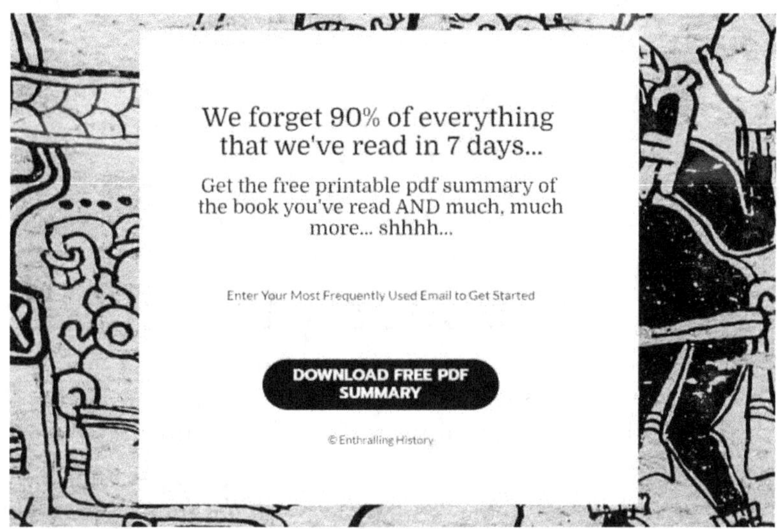



Stop for a moment. We have a free bonus set up for you. The problem is this: we forget 90% of everything that we read after 7 days. Crazy fact, right? Here's the solution: we've created a printable, 1-page pdf summary for this book that you're reading now. All you have to do to get your free pdf summary is to go to the following website:

**https://livetolearn.lpages.co/enthrallinghistory/**

## Or, Scan the QR code!

Once you do, it will be intuitive. Enjoy, and thank you!

# Bibliography

**Part 1: The Ptolemaic Kingdom**

Africanus, Sextus Julius. "The king lists of Africanus." Pharoah.se. Accessed November 27, 2024. https://pharaoh.se/africanus-king-list.

Arrian. "Alexander the Great." In *The Anabasis and the Indica*. Translated by Martin Hammond. Oxford University Press, 2013.

Bennett, Bob and Mike Roberts. *The Wars of Alexander's Successors, 323–281 BC Volume 1: Commanders and Campaigns*. Pen & Sword Military, 2013.

Bennett, Bob and Mike Roberts. *The Wars of Alexander's Successors 323–281 BC Volume 2: Battles and Tactics*. Pen & Sword Military, 2009.

Bevan, E. R. *The House of Ptolemy*. Methuen Publishing, 1927. https://penelope.uchicago.edu/Thayer/E/Gazetteer/Places/Africa/Egypt/_Texts/BEVHOP/6*.html.

Buraselis, Kostas. "Ptolemaic Grain, Seaways and Power." In *The Ptolemies, the Sea and the Nile: Studies in Waterborne Power*, edited by Kostas Buraselis, Mary Stefanou, and Dorothy J. Thompson. Cambridge University Press, 2013.

Clayman, Dee L. *Berenice II and the Golden Age of Ptolemaic Egypt (Women in Antiquity)*. Oxford University Press, 2014.

De la Bedoyere, Guy. *The Fall of Egypt and the Rise of Rome: A History of the Ptolemies*. Yale University Press, 2024.

Dillon, John, and Lloyd P. Gerson. *Neoplatonic Philosophy: Introductory Readings*. Hackett Publishing Company, 2004.

Diodorus, Siculus. *Library of History*. Translated by C. Bradford Welles. Harvard University Press, 1963.

Eusebius. *The Egyptian Chronicle*. Translated by Robert Bedrosian. Accessed November 27, 2024. http://www.attalus.org/armenian/euseb.html.

Fisher-Bovet, Christelle. *Army and Society in Ptolemaic Egypt (Armies of the Ancient World)*. Cambridge University Press, 2014.

Flavius, Josephus. *The Antiquities of the Jews*. Translated by William Whiston. Project Gutenberg eBook, October 1, 2001. https://www.gutenberg.org/cache/epub/2848/pg2848-images.html.

Grainger, John D. *The Ptolemies, Rise of a Dynasty: Ptolemaic Egypt 330–246 BC*. Pen & Sword Books, 2022.

Hauben, Hans. "Review of 'Army and Society in Ptolemaic Egypt: From Invasion to Integration' by Christelle Fischer-Bovet," *The Bulletin of the American Society of Papyrologists* 53 (2016): 395–409. http://www.jstor.org/stable/44968458.

Herodotus, *The Histories*. Translated by George Rawlinson. Dutton & Co, 1862. http://classics.mit.edu/Herodotus/history.html.

Hölbl, Günther. *A History of the Ptolemaic Empire*. Translated by Tina Saavedra. Routledge, 2000.

Homer. *The Odyssey*. Translated by Samuel Butler. Internet Classics Archive. Accessed November 27, 2024. http://classics.mit.edu/Homer/odyssey.html.

Johstono, Paul A. *The Army of Ptolemaic Egypt 323-204 BC: An Institutional and Operational History*. Pen & Sword Military, 2020.

Justinus. *Epitome of Pompeius Trogus' Philippic Histories*. Translated by J. S. Watson, 1853. https://www.attalus.org/translate/justin4.html#26.1.

Manning, J. G. *Land and Power in Ptolemaic Egypt*. Cambridge University Press, 2007.

Manning, J. G., F. Ludlow, A.R. Stine, W. Boos, M. Sigl, and J. R. Marlon. "Volcanic Suppression of Nile Summer Flooding Triggers Revolt and Constrains Interstate Conflict in Ancient Egypt." *Nature Communications* 8, no. 900 (2017). https://doi.org/10.1038/s41467-017-00957-y.

Marr J. S., and C. H. Calisher. "Alexander the Great and West Nile Virus Encephalitis." *Emerging Infectious Diseases*, 9, no. 12 (December 2003):1599-603. https://doi.org10.3201/eid0912.030288 . PMID: 14725285; PMCID: PMC3034319.

Matyszak, Philip. *Greece Against Rome: The Fall of the Hellenistic Kingdoms 250-31 BC*. Pen & Sword Military, 2020.

Plutarch. "Moralia." *Isis and Osiris*. Loeb Classical Library, 1936. https://penelope.uchicago.edu/Thayer/e/roman/texts/plutarch/moralia/isis_and_o siris*/b.html.

Plutarch. *Plutarch's Lives*. Translated by Bernadotte Perrin. Harvard University Press, 1920. https://www.perseus.tufts.edu/hopper/text?doc=Perseus%3Atext%3A2008.01.000 7%3Achapter%3D61.

Plutarch. *The Life of Alexander the Great.* Translated by John Dryden. Modern Library Paperback Edition, 2004.

Polyaenus. *Stratagems: Book Seven.* Translated by R. Shepherd, 1793. http://www.attalus.org/translate/polyaenus7.html.

Polybius, *The Histories.* Book V. Loeb Classical Library Edition, 1923. https://penelope.uchicago.edu/Thayer/E/Roman/Texts/Polybius/5*.html.

Siani-Davies, Mary. "Ptolemy XII Auletes and the Romans." *Historia: Zeitschrift Für Alte Geschichte* 46, no. 3 (1997): 306–40. http://www.jstor.org/stable/4436474.

*The Complete Tanakh: The Jewish Bible with a Modern English Translation and Rashi's Commentary.* Accessed November 27, 2024. https://www.chabad.org/library/bible_cdo/aid/63255/jewish/The-Bible-with-Rashi.htm.

*The Letter of Aristeas to Philocrates.* Translated by R. H. Charles, 1913. https://www.attalus.org/translate/aristeas1.html.

Theocritus. *The Project Gutenberg eBook of Theocritus.* Accessed November 27, 2024. https://www.gutenberg.org/files/11533/11533-h/11533-h.htm#IDYLL_XIV.

Von Reden, S. *Money in Ptolemaic Egypt.* Cambridge University Press, 2010.

Worthington, Ian. *By the Spear: Philip II, Alexander the Great, and the Rise and Fall of the Macedonian Empire (Ancient Warfare and Civilization).* Oxford University Press, 2016.

Zielinski, Sarah. "After 2,000 Years, Ptolemy's War Elephants are Revealed." *Science News: Archaeology,* January 21, 2014. https://www.sciencenews.org/blog/wild-things/after-2000-years-ptolemys-war-elephants-are-revealed.

**Part 2: Cleopatra**

"Antony against Parthia." Roman History 31 BC - AD 117, 12 Sept. 2017, https://ancientromanhistory31-14.com/an-end-of-the-republic/triumvirs/acts-of-the-triumvirs/antony-against-parthia/.

"Antony, Octavian, Cleopatra." Www.vroma.org, www.vroma.org/vromans/bmcmanus/antony.html.

BBC. BBC - History - Cleopatra. 2014, www.bbc.co.uk/history/historic_figures/cleopatra.shtml.

"Behind the Throne: Exploring the Life and Reign of Queen Cleopatra of Egypt." Www.memphistours.com, www.memphistours.com/Egypt/Egypt-Wikis/Egypt-History/wiki/queen-cleopatra-of-egypt.

Bianchi, Bob. "Cleopatra the Great: Last Power of the Ptolemaic Dynasty." ARCE, 2023, arce.org/resource/cleopatra-great-last-power-ptolemaic-dynasty/.

Bileta, Vedran. "The Battle of Actium: The Death of Ptolemaic Egypt." TheCollector, 2 Oct. 2021, www.thecollector.com/battle-of-actium/.

Blakemore, Erin. "Who Was Cleopatra?" National Geographic, 28 Apr. 2023, www.nationalgeographic.com/history/article/cleopatra-egypt-pharaoh-life-history.

Bowen, Shannon. "PR Prose: Cleopatra: The Queen of Public Relations? - College of Information and Communications | University of South Carolina." Sc.edu, 6 May 2016, https://sc.edu/study/colleges_schools/cic/journalism_and_mass_communications/news/2016/pr_prose_cleopatra_queen_of_pr.php.

Bowen, Shannon A. "Finding Strategic Communication & Diverse Leadership in the Ancient World: The Case of Queen Cleopatra VII, the Last Pharaoh of Egypt." Cogent Arts & Humanities, vol. 3, no. 1, 18 Mar. 2016, www.tandfonline.com/doi/full/10.1080/23311983.2016.1154704, https://doi.org/10.1080/23311983.2016.1154704.

Bressan, David. "How a Climate-Changing Volcano Helped the Roman Conquest of Egypt." Forbes, 2 Sept. 2019, www.forbes.com/sites/davidbressan/2017/10/18/demise-of-ancient-egypt-linked-to-a-climate-changing-volcano/. Accessed 6 Sept. 2024.

Britannica. "Cleopatra's Achievements." Encyclopedia Britannica, 23 Sept. 2020, www.britannica.com/summary/Cleopatras-Achievements.

British Museum. "Explore the Rosetta Stone." The British Museum, www.britishmuseum.org/collection/egypt/explore-rosetta-stone.

Brooke, Thomas. "The Siblings of Cleopatra, a Family like No Other...." Historical Novels and Epic Fantasy, 7 Oct. 2015, https://thomasmdbrooke.com/2015/10/07/the-siblings-of-cleopatra-a-family-like-no-other/

Christiansen, Keith. "Cleopatra, the Ultimate Femme Fatale." The Metropolitan Museum of Art, 18 Feb. 2017, www.metmuseum.org/articles/cleopatra-guido-cagnacci.

"Cleopatra." BBC, 2 Dec. 2010, www.bbc.co.uk/programmes/b00w7clj.

"Cleopatra and Mark Antony's Decadent Love Affair." History, 13 Feb. 2019, www.nationalgeographic.com/history/history-magazine/article/antony-and-cleopatra.

"Cleopatra the Beauty - Unknown." Google Arts & Culture, https://artsandculture.google.com/asset/cleopatra-the-beauty-unknown/bQEBFTu0tOisaw?hl=en.%20%E2%80%9CCleopatra%3A%20Rome%20and%20Egypt%2C%2069%E2%80%9330%20BC%20OCR%20Teachers%E2%80%99%20Guide.%E2%80%9D%20Warwick.ac.uk%2C%20warwick.ac.uk%2Ffac%2Farts%2Fclassics%2Fwarwickclassicsnetwork%2Fstoa%2Fanchist%2Fgcse%2Fcleopatra%2Fteachersguide%2F

"Cleopatra: What Is the Real Legacy of the Last Pharaoh?" HistoryExtra, www.historyextra.com/period/ancient-egypt/cleopatra-legacy-last-pharaoh-ptolemaic-dynasty/.

"Cleopatra's Impact on Rome: Politics, Culture, and Fashion." AncientScholar, 30 July 2024, ancientscholar.org/cleopatras-impact-on-rome-politics-culture-and-fashion/. Accessed 6 Sept. 2024.

"Cleopatra's Death." Uchicago.edu, 2019, https://penelope.uchicago.edu/~grout/encyclopaedia_romana/miscellanea/cleopatra/rixens.html.

Cohen, Alina. "How Millennia of Cleopatra Portrayals Reveal Evolving Perceptions of Sex, Women, and Race." Artsy, 6 May 2018, www.artsy.net/article/artsy-editorial-millennia-cleopatra-portrayals-reveal-evolving-perceptions-sex-women-race.

Cook, M. Climate Contributed to the Fall of Egyptian Dynasty | Real Archaeology. 29 Oct. 2017, pages.vassar.edu/realarchaeology/2017/10/29/climate-contributed-to-the-fall-of-egyptian-dynasty/.

Dowson, Thomas. "Green Caesar & Cleopatra in the Altes Museum, Berlin." Archaeology Travel, 27 Mar. 2023, https://archaeology-travel.com/artefacts/green-caesar-cleopatra/.

Fichter, Kero. "Constructing Racism in Western Art – Hans Makart and the Case of Cleopatra." DailyArt Magazine, 29 Apr. 2024, www.dailyartmagazine.com/the-case-of-cleopatra-constructing-racism-in-western-art/. Accessed 6 Sept. 2024.

Gouck, Michael. "Victorian Egyptomania: Why Was England so Obsessed with Egypt?" TheCollector, 22 Aug. 2022, www.thecollector.com/victorian-egyptomania/.

Haughton, Brian. "Cleopatra & Antony." World History Encyclopedia, 10 Jan. 2011, www.worldhistory.org/article/197/cleopatra--antony/.

---. "Cleopatra & Antony." World History Encyclopedia, 10 Jan. 2011, www.worldhistory.org/article/197/cleopatra--antony/.

health, William Wan National correspondent covering, et al. "Ancient Egypt's Rulers Mishandled Climate Disasters. Then the People Revolted." Washington Post, 17 Oct. 2017, www.washingtonpost.com/news/energy-environment/wp/2017/10/17/climate-change-sparked-revolts-in-ancient-egypt-study-says/.

Hill, Marsha. "Egypt in the Ptolemaic Period." Metmuseum.org, 2019, www.metmuseum.org/toah/hd/ptol/hd_ptol.htm.

Hillard, T. W. "The Nile Cruise of Cleopatra and Caesar." The Classical Quarterly, vol. 52, no. 2, Dec. 2002, pp. 549–554, https://doi.org/10.1093/cq/52.2.549. Accessed 22 May 2019.

History Extra. "Cleopatra, Julius Caesar and Mark Antony: How the Last Pharaoh's Love Affairs Shaped Ancient Egypt's Fate." HistoryExtra, 21 Aug. 2020, www.historyextra.com/period/ancient-egypt/cleopatra-love-affairs-julius-caesar-mark-antony/. Accessed 22 May 2019.

Holmes, Robert C. L. "Caesar under Siege: What Happened during the Alexandrine War 48-47BC?" TheCollector, 15 Nov. 2020, www.thecollector.com/julius-caesar-siege-of-alexandria-war/.

https://www.facebook.com/thoughtcodotcom. "Cleopatra's Family Tree Has Few Branches." ThoughtCo, 2019, www.thoughtco.com/queen-cleopatras-family-tree-4083409.

Huang, Shuoheng. Cleopatra's Autonomy as Ruler of Ptolemy Egypt and the Examination of the Roman Influence over Egypt. Shenzhen College of International Education.

"Julius Caesar, Cleopatra and the Alexandrian War | UNRV.com." Www.unrv.com, www.unrv.com/julius-caesar/cleopatra-alexandrian-war.php.

Kennedy, Maev, et al. "Victorian Masterpiece Turns up in Rocky Mountain Log Cabin." The Guardian, 31 May 2003, www.theguardian.com/uk/2003/may/31/arts.world.

Lary, Morris H. "Julius Caesar and Cleopatra: The Ancient World's Power Couple | History Cooperative." History Cooperative, 16 Aug. 2023, https://historycooperative.org/julius-caesar-and-cleopatra/

Little, Becky. "Cleopatra's Complicated Inner Circle: Siblings, Successors and Lovers." HISTORY, 13 July 2023, www.history.com/news/cleopatras-complicated-inner-circle-siblings-successors-and-lovers.

Mark, Joshua. "Cleopatra VII." World History Encyclopedia, 30 Oct. 2018, www.worldhistory.org/Cleopatra_VII/.

Mark, Joshua J. "Battle of Actium." World History Encyclopedia, 18 Nov. 2019, www.worldhistory.org/Battle_of_Actium/.

Marshall, Cynthia. "A Modern Perspective: Antony and Cleopatra | Folger Shakespeare Library." Www.folger.edu, www.folger.edu/explore/shakespeares-works/antony-and-cleopatra/antony-and-cleopatra-a-modern-perspective/.

McEvoy, Colin. "As a Ruler, Cleopatra Was as Charismatic as She Was Ruthless." Biography, 10 May 2023, www.biography.com/royalty/a43842745/was-cleopatra-a-good-ruler.

Milligan, Mark. "The Early Life of Cleopatra." HeritageDaily - Archaeology News, 24 Dec. 2021, www.heritagedaily.com/2021/12/the-early-life-of-cleopatra/142343.

Muhs, Brian. "The Ptolemaic Period (332–30 BCE)." The Ancient Egyptian Economy: 3000–30 BCE. Cambridge: Cambridge University Press, 2016. 211–252. Print.

"Mural of Cleopatra and Caesarion as Venus and Cupid." World History Encyclopedia, www.worldhistory.org/image/8287/mural-of-cleopatra-and-caesarion-as-venus-and-cupi/.

Nestruck, Kelly. "A Shaw Thing in Stratford-Upon-Ontario." The Guardian, The Guardian, 11 Sept. 2008, www.theguardian.com/culture/2008/sep/11/shakespeare.theatre.stratford. Accessed 6 Sept. 2024.

Owen Jarus. "Cleopatra: Facts & Biography." Live Science, Live Science, 13 Mar. 2014, www.livescience.com/44071-cleopatra-biography.html.

Penner, Jay. "Historical Accuracy of the Movie Scene of Cleopatra's Entry into Rome." Jaypenner.com, https://jaypenner.com/blog/the-cleopatra-procession-scene-historical-accuracy-and-realism.

Powers, Hermenia. "Cleopatra's Legacy in Art: Famous Pharaoh and Femme Fatale | Art UK." Artuk.org, 26 Mar. 2020, https://artuk.org/discover/stories/cleopatras-legacy-in-art-famous-pharaoh-and-femme-fatale.

"Ptolemaic Kingdom of Egypt | History Timeline." History Timelines, 2019, https://historytimelines.co/timeline/ptolemaic-kingdom-of-egypt. Accessed 6 Sept. 2024.

"Ptolemy XIII Theos Philopator | Macedonian King of Egypt." Encyclopedia Britannica, www.britannica.com/biography/Ptolemy-XIII-Theos-Philopator.

Robertson, Nan. "Claudette Colbert, 80 and Busy." New York Times, 16 Apr. 1984, pp. C-15, www.nytimes.com/1984/04/16/movies/claudette-colbert-80-and-busy.html. Accessed 6 Sept. 2024.

Saggu, Mehakpreet. "Cleopatra's Champagne." The Varsity, 4 Sept. 2023, https://thevarsity.ca/2023/09/04/cleopatras-champagne/. Accessed 6 Sept. 2024.

Schiff, Stacy. "Rehabilitating Cleopatra." Smithsonian, Smithsonian.com, Dec. 2010, www.smithsonianmag.com/history/rehabilitating-cleopatra-70613486/.

Shakespeare Birthplace Trust. "Antony and Cleopatra." Shakespeare Birthplace Trust, 2016, www.shakespeare.org.uk/explore-shakespeare/shakespedia/shakespeares-plays/antony-and-cleopatra/.

Sifuentes, Jesse. "The Propaganda of Octavian and Mark Antony's Civil War." World History Encyclopedia, 20 Nov. 2019, www.worldhistory.org/article/1474/the-propaganda-of-octavian-and-mark-antonys-civil/.

Stanley Mayer Burstein. The Reign of Cleopatra. Norman Univ. Of Oklahoma Press, 2007.

Strauss, Barry. "Cleopatra and Caesar." Barry Strauss, 5 July 2023,
https://barrystrauss.com/cleopatra-and-caesar/.

---. "The Battle That Saddled Cleopatra with an Undeserved Bad Rep." The
Daily Beast, 30 Mar. 2022, www.thedailybeast.com/the-battle-that-saddled-
cleopatra-with-an-undeserved-bad-rep.

Strootman, Rolf. ANE Today – Cleopatra's Languages - American Society of
Overseas Research (ASOR). 6 Feb. 2024,
www.asor.org/anetoday/2024/02/cleopatras-languages.

Syed, Armani. "What the Debate over Cleopatra's "Race" Gets Wrong." Time,
20 Apr. 2023, https://time.com/6273435/cleopatra-race-debate-netflix/.

Thayer, Bill. "LacusCurtius • a Gateway to Ancient Rome."
Penelope.uchicago.edu,
http://penelope.uchicago.edu/Thayer/E/Roman/home.html

Translation source of : Plutarch, "Parallel Lives" and Dio Cassius "Roman
History."

Thayer, Bill, and B.L Ullman. Cleopatra's Pearls. Bill Thayer University of
Chicago, Feb. 1957,
https://penelope.uchicago.edu/Thayer/E/Journals/CJ/52/5/Cleopatras_Pearls*.ht
ml. Accessed 5 Sept. 2024.

The Editors of Encyclopedia Britannica. "Ptolemy XII Auletes | Macedonian
King of Egypt." Encyclopedia Britannica, 15 Oct. 2009,
www.britannica.com/biography/Ptolemy-XII-Auletes.

"The Global Egyptian Museum | Buchis." Globalegyptianmuseum.org, 2024,
www.globalegyptianmuseum.org/glossary.aspx?id=98. Accessed 6 Sept. 2024.

Voight, Heather. "Cleopatra's Education." Heather on History, Heather on
History, 6 Feb. 2011, https://heathervoight.com/2011/02/06/cleopatras-
education/.

Wasson, Donald. "Caesar as Dictator: His Impact on the City of Rome." World
History Encyclopedia, 18 Jan. 2012, www.worldhistory.org/article/112/caesar-as-
dictator-his-impact-on-the-city-of-rome/.

---. "Ptolemaic Dynasty." World History Encyclopedia, 29 Sept. 2016,
www.worldhistory.org/Ptolemaic_Dynasty/.

Watkins, Thayer. "The Timeline of the Life of Cleopatra." Sjsu.edu, 2020,
www.sjsu.edu/faculty/watkins/cleopatra.htm.

Welch, Craig. "How Volcanoes Caused Violent Uprisings in Cleopatra's Egypt."
Science, 17 Oct. 2017, www.nationalgeographic.com/science/article/volcanoes-
Nile-flood-climate-Egypt.

"When Cleo Met Julius ... By Rolling Herself up in a Carpet." Google Arts &
Culture, https://artsandculture.google.com/story/when-cleo-met-julius-by-rolling-

herself-up-in-a-carpet-altes-museum-staatliche-museen-zu-berlin/4QWxJNrY6GEQJQ?hl=en.

"When Cleopatra Visited Ancient Rome with Julius Caesar, All Hell Broke Loose." History Skills, www.historyskills.com/classroom/ancient-history/cleopatra-in-rome/.

# Image Sources

1    Zoomed in, labels added. Source: Joe Roe, CC BY-SA 4.0
<https://creativecommons.org/licenses/by-sa/4.0>, via Wikimedia Commons:
https://commons.wikimedia.org/wiki/File:Middle_East_topographic_map.png

2    Gunawan Kartapranata, CC BY-SA 3.0 <https://creativecommons.org/licenses/by-sa/3.0>, via Wikimedia Commons:
https://commons.wikimedia.org/wiki/File:Bastet.svg

3    https://commons.wikimedia.org/wiki/File:Cambyses_II_capturing_Psamtik_III.png

4    https://commons.wikimedia.org/wiki/File:Makedonische_phalanx.png

5    https://commons.wikimedia.org/wiki/File:Meister_der_Alexanderschlacht_003.jpg

6    https://commons.wikimedia.org/wiki/File:Alexander_and_Bucephalus_-_Battle_of_Issus_mosaic_-_Museo_Archeologico_Nazionale_-_Naples_BW.jpg

7    https://commons.wikimedia.org/wiki/File:Ptolemy_I_Soter_Louvre_Ma849.jpg

8    Stella, CC BY-SA 4.0 <https://creativecommons.org/licenses/by-sa/4.0>, via Wikimedia Commons:
https://commons.wikimedia.org/wiki/File:Ptolemy_I_as_Pharaoh_of_Egypt.jpg

9    Photo zoomed in, labels highlighted. Source: Jeff Dahl, CC BY-SA 4.0
<https://creativecommons.org/licenses/by-sa/4.0>, via Wikimedia Commons:
https://commons.wikimedia.org/wiki/File:Ancient_Egypt_map-en.svg

10 Gnauth, Adolf, CC BY-SA 2.5 <https://creativecommons.org/licenses/by-sa/2.5>, via
Wikimedia Commons:
https://commons.wikimedia.org/wiki/File:Ancient_Alexandria_(1878)_-_TIMEA.jpg

11 drawing by Kaidor, English text by Ashaio, CC BY-SA 3.0
<https://creativecommons.org/licenses/by-sa/3.0>, via Wikimedia Commons:
https://commons.wikimedia.org/wiki/File:Ptolemaic_Alexandria_-_en.svg

12 Віщун, CC BY-SA 4.0 <https://creativecommons.org/licenses/by-sa/4.0>, via Wikimedia Commons https://commons.wikimedia.org/wiki/File:Pharos_of_Alexandria,_reconstruction_2021.jpg

13 Epiphanesnikophoros, CC BY-SA 4.0 <https://creativecommons.org/licenses/by-sa/4.0>, via Wikimedia Commons: https://commons.wikimedia.org/wiki/File:Ptolemaic_Kingdom_Ptolemy_I_Soter.jpg

14 Massimo Finizio, CC BY-SA 2.0 via Wikimedia Commons: https://commons.wikimedia.org/wiki/File:Seleuco_I_Nicatore.JPG

15 Scan by NYPL, CC BY-SA 4.0 <https://creativecommons.org/licenses/by-sa/4.0>, via Wikimedia Commons: https://commons.wikimedia.org/wiki/File:Ptolemy_(II)_Philadelphos.jpg

16 Sailko, CC BY-SA 3.0 <https://creativecommons.org/licenses/by-sa/3.0>, via Wikimedia Commons: https://commons.wikimedia.org/wiki/File:Cammeo_gonzaga_con_doppio_ritratto_di_tolomeo_II_e_arsinoe_II,_III_sec._ac._(alessandria),_da_hermitage.jpg

17 Miguel Hermoso Cuesta, CC BY-SA 3.0 <https://creativecommons.org/licenses/by-sa/3.0>, via Wikimedia Commons: https://commons.wikimedia.org/wiki/File:Ptolomeo_III.JPG

18 [1], CC BY-SA 4.0 <https://creativecommons.org/licenses/by-sa/4.0>, via Wikimedia Commons: https://commons.wikimedia.org/wiki/File:Ptolemaius_III_Euergetes_a_Berenice_II-Propylon_Khonsu_Tempes.png

19 Sailko, CC BY 3.0 <https://creativecommons.org/licenses/by/3.0>, via Wikimedia Commons: https://commons.wikimedia.org/wiki/File:Egitto_tolemaico,_berenice_II,_octodracma_di_efeso,_246-222_ac_ca.JPG

20 Classical Numismatic Group, Inc. http://www.cngcoins.com, CC BY-SA 3.0 <http://creativecommons.org/licenses/by-sa/3.0/>, via Wikimedia Commons: https://commons.wikimedia.org/wiki/File:Silver_tetradrachm,_Ptolemy_IV_Philopator,_221-205_BC.jpg

21 Nicolaes Witsen, Public domain, via Wikimedia Commons: https://commons.wikimedia.org/wiki/File:Thalamegos_Nicolaes_Witsen_1671.jpg

22 ArchaiOptix, CC BY-SA 4.0 <https://creativecommons.org/licenses/by-sa/4.0>, via Wikimedia Commons: https://commons.wikimedia.org/wiki/File:Egypt_-_king_Ptolemaios_V_-_204-203_BC_-_gold_oktadrachm_-_bust_of_Ptolemaios_V_-_cornucopiae_-_Berlin_MK_AM_18203067.jpg

23 https://commons.wikimedia.org/wiki/File:Rosetta_Stone_BW.jpeg

24 Metropolitan Museum of Art, CC0, via Wikimedia Commons: https://commons.wikimedia.org/wiki/File:Faience_Sistrum_Inscribed_with_the_Name_of_Ptolemy_I_MET_DP246588.jpg

25 Photo zoomed in. Hedwig Storch, CC BY-SA 3.0
    <https://creativecommons.org/licenses/by-sa/3.0>, via Wikimedia Commons:
    https://commons.wikimedia.org/wiki/File:Kom_Ombo,_Sobek_0319.JPG

26 https://commons.wikimedia.org/wiki/File:Bust_Serapis_Chiaramonti.jpg

27 https://commons.wikimedia.org/wiki/File:Maler_der_Grabkammer_
    des_Sennudem_001.jpg

28 Igor Merit Santos, CC BY-SA 4.0 <https://creativecommons.org/licenses/by-sa/4.0>,
    via Wikimedia Commons:
    https://commons.wikimedia.org/wiki/File:The_Great_Library_
    of_Alexandria,_O._Von_Corven,_19th_century.jpg

29 Yair Haklai, CC BY-SA 4.0 <https://creativecommons.org/licenses/by-sa/4.0>, via
    Wikimedia Commons: https://commons.wikimedia.org/wiki/File:Bust
    _of_Demetrius_Phalereus_at_Kunsthistorisches_Museum.jpg

30 https://commons.wikimedia.org/wiki/File:Ptolem%C3%A4er-_Ptolemaios_III._-
    _M%C3%BCnzkabinett,_Berlin_-_5531438.jpg

31 Ptolemaic Kingdom III-II century BC - ru.svg: Kaidor (talk · contribs)derivative work:
    rowanwindwhistler (talk)derivative work: Amphipolis, CC BY-SA 4.0
    <https://creativecommons.org/licenses/by-sa/4.0>, via Wikimedia Commons:
    https://commons.wikimedia.org/wiki/File:Ptolemaic_Kingdom_III-II_century_BC_-
    _en.svg

32 https://commons.wikimedia.org/wiki/File:The_Ptolemy_Philophator%27s_
    %22forty%22_ship,_from_Man_upon_the_sea_-
    _or,_a_history_of_maritime_adventure,_exploration,_and_
    discovery,_from_the_earliest_ages_to_the_present_time_(1858)_(14596783329).jpg

33 Photo zoomed in. https://commons.wikimedia.org/wiki/File:Egyptian_harvest.jpg

34 Sailko, CC BY 3.0 <https://creativecommons.org/licenses/by/3.0>, via Wikimedia
    Commons:
    https://commons.wikimedia.org/wiki/File:Applique_in_faience_per_tempietti_in_legn
    o,_periodo_tolemaico,_falco_01.JPG

35 Photo zoomed in.
    https://commons.wikimedia.org/wiki/File:NileMosaicOfPalestrinaSoldiers.jpg#file:

36 Khruner, CC BY-SA 4.0 <https://creativecommons.org/licenses/by-sa/4.0>, via
    Wikimedia Commons:
    https://commons.wikimedia.org/wiki/File:Machimoi_by_Khruner.jpg

37 https://commons.wikimedia.org/wiki/File:Ballista_bw.png

38 Photo zoomed in. https://commons.wikimedia.org/wiki/File:Egypt_and_the
    _S%C3%BBd%C3%A2n;_handbook_for_travellers_(1914)_(14783598172).jpg

39 https://commons.wikimedia.org/wiki/File:Peltast.jpg

40 https://commons.wikimedia.org/wiki/File:Eleazars_exploit.jpg#file

41 https://commons.wikimedia.org/wiki/File:Ring_with_engraved_portrait_of_
    Ptolemy_VI_Philometor_(3rd%E2%80%932nd_century_BCE)_-_2009.jpg

42 Scan by NYPL, CC BY-SA 4.0 <https://creativecommons.org/licenses/by-sa/4.0>, via Wikimedia Commons: https://commons.wikimedia.org/wiki/File:Ptolemy _Philometor_and_Cleopatra_II.jpg

43 American Numismatic Society, CC0, via Wikimedia Commons: https://commons.wikimedia.org/wiki/File:Ptolemy_VIII.jpg

44 https://commons.wikimedia.org/wiki/File:Ptolemy_IX._Soter_II_-_tetradrachma.jpg

45 Scan by NYPL, CC BY-SA 4.0 <https://creativecommons.org/licenses/by-sa/4.0>, via Wikimedia Commons: https://commons.wikimedia.org/wiki/File:Berenice_III.jpg

46 Scan by NYPL, CC BY-SA 4.0 <https://creativecommons.org/licenses/by-sa/4.0>, via Wikimedia Commons: https://commons.wikimedia.org/wiki/File:Ptolemy_XII_Dionisos.jpg

47 Photo zoomed in. https://commons.wikimedia.org/wiki/File:Venus_and_Cupid_from _the_House_of_Marcus_Fabius_Rufus_at_Pompeii,_most_likely_a_depiction_of_Cl eopatra_VII_(2).jpg

48 https://commons.wikimedia.org/wiki/File:Castro_Battle_of_Actium.jpg

49 cmglee, David Monniaux, jimht at shaw dot ca, CC BY-SA 4.0 <https://creativecommons.org/licenses/by-sa/4.0>, via Wikimedia Commons: https://commons.wikimedia.org/wiki/File:Eratosthenes_measure_of_Earth_circumfer ence.svg

50 Photo zoomed in. ZDF/Terra X/Gruppe 5/ Susanne Utzt, Cristina Trebbi/ Jens Boeck, Dieter Stürmer / Fabian Wienke / Sebastian Martinez/ xkopp, polloq, CC BY 4.0 <https://creativecommons.org/licenses/by/4.0>, via Wikimedia Commons: https://commons.wikimedia.org/wiki/File:Archimedes%27-Lever.png

51 https://commons.wikimedia.org/wiki/File:PhiloThevet.jpg

52 https://commons.wikimedia.org/wiki/File:Ptolemy_XII_Auletes_Louvre_ Ma3449.jpg

53 https://commons.wikimedia.org/wiki/File:Retrato_de_Julio_C%C3%A 9sar_(26724093101).jpg

54 Byzantium565, CC BY-SA 4.0 <https://creativecommons.org/licenses/by-sa/4.0>, via Wikimedia Commons, https://commons.wikimedia.org/wiki/File:Octavian_ and_Antony_denarius_(obverse).jpg

55 Alvaro qc by the original work of User:Husar de la Princesa, CC BY 2.5 <https://creativecommons.org/licenses/by/2.5>, via Wikimedia Commons, https://commons.wikimedia.org/wiki/File:Roman_Republic_in_40bC.svg

56 https://commons.wikimedia.org/wiki/File:Woodcut_illustration_of_ Cleopatra_and_Mark_Antony_-_Penn_Provenance_Project.jpg

57 https://commons.wikimedia.org/wiki/File:Posthumous_painted_ portrait_of_Cleopatra_VII_of_Egypt,_from_Herculaneum,_Italy.jpg

58 https://commons.wikimedia.org/wiki/File:Kleopatra-VII.-Altes-Museum-Berlin1.jpg

59  https://commons.wikimedia.org/wiki/File:Tomb_of_Cleopatra_and_
    Mark_Antony,_illuminated_manuscript_of_Boccaccio,_miniature_by_the_Boucicaut
    _master,_1409_AD_(cropped).jpg

60  https://commons.wikimedia.org/wiki/File:Giampietrino_Death_of_Cleopatra.jpg

61  https://commons.wikimedia.org/wiki/File:Cleopatra_Bitten_By_an_Asp_
    MET_DP855160.jpg

62  https://commons.wikimedia.org/wiki/File:Guido_Reni_(Bologna_1575-
    Bologna_1642)_-_Cleopatra_with_the_Asp_-_RCIN_405338_-_Royal_Collection.jpg

63  https://commons.wikimedia.org/wiki/File:Cleopatra_-_John_William_Waterhouse.jpg

64  https://commons.wikimedia.org/wiki/File:Cleopatra_and_Caesar_by_Jean-Leon-
    Gerome.jpg

65  https://commons.wikimedia.org/wiki/File:Helen_Gardner_as_Cleopatra.jpg

66  https://commons.wikimedia.org/wiki/File:ThedaBara-Cleopatra.jpg

67  https://commons.wikimedia.org/wiki/File:Vivien_Leigh_-_Cleopatra.jpg

68  https://commons.wikimedia.org/wiki/File:Elizabeth_Taylor_Cleopatra_1963.JPG

www.ingramcontent.com/pod-product-compliance
Lightning Source LLC
Chambersburg PA
CBHW071544120726
48009CB00002B/77